ⓒ 國際商品買賣契約法

著　者　鄧越今
發行人　劉振強
著作財
產權人　三民書局股份有限公司
印刷所　三民書局股份有限公司
　　　　復興店／臺北市復興北路三八六號五樓
　　　　重慶店／臺北市重慶南路一段六十一號
　　　　郵撥／〇〇〇九九九八一五號

初　版　中華民國七十四年十月
再　版　中華民國八十二年十月

編　號　S 55112

基本定價　壹元捌角

ISBN 957-14-0457-8 (平裝)

國際商品買賣契約法

鄧 越 今 著

學歷：上海光華大學畢業
　　　美國紐約市立大學研究所進修
經歷：臺灣糖業公司業務處經理、顧問
　　　駐伊朗大使館商務專員
　　　中華民國對外貿易發展協會處長
　　　、主任秘書

三 民 書 局 印 行

自　序

　　國際商品買賣，係屬不同國境之商業行為。由於買賣雙方之營業處所，均設在不同社會文化背景與政治經濟體制的國度裏，彼此從事此項超國界之國際貿易，除須考慮到雙方不同之行銷環境與市場特性外，且須注意到國際貿易之一般慣例及公約。因此一個從事國際貿易之從業人員，除應了解其經營產品之專業知識外，並應熟悉國際貿易通常採用之一般交易條件、契約成立要件、以及買賣雙方所應負之責任和義務，俾一旦發生貿易糾紛時知道如何去謀求補救。最重要者，應瞭解國際貿易在一旦發生糾紛時所應採取之處理途徑及有關法律問題。一個從業人員，如能深切體認，考慮週全，必可訂立對自己有利且有保障的契約。

　　國際商品買賣，從賣方之報價到成交、訂約、裝船而至買方之付款、提貨，手續至為繁複。譬如買賣雙方所依據之貿易條件規範如何？貨物風險何時移轉買方？買賣雙方對貨物之付款交貨應負何種責任與義務？一旦發生貿易糾紛時應適用何國法律？由於各國法律及商業習慣有異，對上項問題之有關法律解釋容或不同，其處理方式與裁判，自難期一致。因此一九一九年在巴黎成立之國際商會 (International Chamber of Commerce)，乃從事各項國際貿易條件之規則制訂，首於一九三六年制定「貿易條件之國際解釋規則」(International Rules for the Interpretation of Trade Terms, 簡稱 INCOTERMS)。這是國際間第一個具有國際性之貿易條件的定義解釋。嗣於一九五三及一九八〇年一再修訂，並參酌近年來貨物運輸工具及技術改進之新發展，增訂許多條款。目前已益臻完善，廣為世界各國所普遍採用。其次，值得一提者為該會所訂「信用狀統一慣例」(Uniform Customs and Practice for Documentary Credits)。該慣例訂於一九三三年，其間曾於一九五一、一九六三、一九七四年三度修訂，並於最近一九八三年六月再度修訂，一九八四年十月開始實施。目前已約有 176 國家及地區之銀行接受使用此「信用狀統一慣例」。

關於國際商品買賣方面，最早曾由羅馬統一私法國際研究所 (International Institute for the Unification of Private Law in Rome) 依據德國比較研究學家 Ernst Rabel 之建議，起草兩種國際買賣統一法，經過卅年之準備，終於在一九六四年四月二十五日在海牙舉行之國際會議，成立了「統一國際商品買賣法」(The Uniform Law on International Sale of Goods) 及「統一國際商品買賣契約締結法」(Uniform Law on the Formation of Contracts for the International Sale of Goods)。前者旨在統一國際買賣之實體法，規定買賣雙方之義務及貨物風險之移轉。後者在補充前項實體法。這兩種公約，業經英、比、西德、意、荷、甘比亞及聖瑪利諾等國批准，英國首先在一九六七年制訂「國際買賣統一法案」，於一九七二年實施。可惜美國蘇聯未予採納，參加國家中批准者亦少，亞、非及拉丁美洲發展中國家更不用談了。聯合國國際貿易法規委員會為致力國際貿易法規定之統一，曾於一九七九年根據上項兩種公約起草「國際商品買賣公約」(聯合國中譯原文稱「國際貨物銷售合同公約」)，於一九八〇年四月提交聯合國在維也納舉行之會議通過，並規定自第十個國家向聯合國以書面提出批准、接受、核准或加入該公約國家起十二個月後第一天生效。此為國際組織致力於統一國際買賣之最週密而完善的公約，可望為世界各國所廣泛接受與批准採用。

　　本書之編撰，卽以上述國際商會所訂「貿易條件之國際解釋規則」及「信用狀統一慣例」以及聯合國「一九八〇年國際商品買賣公約」為依據，並列舉英、美法律及有關法院判例或學者論著，以資闡明，用供參攷。仍希讀者多研讀各國專家著述，以及書刊所載英、美等國仲裁或法院判例，俾在洽訂國際貿易契約或處理貿易糾紛時，不致有所疏忽而遭損失。

　　著者曾從事國際貿易多年，嗣後在貿易推廣機構工作，深知業者對國際貿易契約之認識，極為迫切需要，爰於退休餘暇，整理舊稿，編撰此書。由於撰輯之時間匆促，對資料之蒐集，難免疏漏之處，尚望學者專家，不吝賜教，以匡不逮。本書出版前，曾承外貿協會武副董事長冠雄先生諸多指正，特此誌謝。

　　　　　　　　　　　　　　　　　鄧越今　謹誌
　　　　　　　　　　　　　　　民國七十四年四月于臺北

國際商品買賣契約法
目　　次

自序

第一章　國際商品買賣之定義

第二章　契約成立之要件

第五章　國際商品買賣契約之主要條款

第六章　國際商品買賣契約之標準化

第一章 國際商品買賣之定義

1-1 何謂商品

　　本書所稱商品，英文名為 Goods，依照 Webster's New World Dictionary of the American Language 及 Concise Oxford Dictionary 之解釋，係指可移動之財產 (movable property) 或商品 (merchandise)，亦可譯為貨物。這裏所稱商品，即係指在簽訂買賣契約時可以「確定」及「移動」的東西，包括製造、開採及生產之工業品、礦產、動植物及生長中之農作物。也可說是市場上可以買賣到的農工礦產品。

　　買賣契約中的標的物，在訂約時即已為賣方所有者，稱為存貨 (existing goods) 或現貨，須待將來生產、製造或取得者為期貨 (future goods)，故前者是可以認定的 (identified) 特定商品 (specified goods)，後者則有時不太確定 (unascertained)，譬如農民指定將明年收成之某種農作物訂售給某商人，其收成之品質及數量，均無法預先確定，自不能與質量明確之現貨比擬❶。

---

❶ P. S. Atiyah: *The Sale of Goods*, ch. 5, pp. 31-34.

1-2　國際商品買賣之特性

1-2-1　交易型態

從交易型態言，國際商品買賣係一種國際貿易，有別於國內貿易。一般說來，具有下列各種特點：

(1)買賣雙方均在不同國境內設立營業處所，從事超越國境之貿易。

(2)商品必須委託承運人使用一種或多種之運輸工具，從賣方之國土運往買方國境內之目的地交貨。由賣方向承運人取得運輸單據後向買方或買方之委託銀行收款。該運輸單據之移轉，即象徵貨物產權之轉移 (Transfer of bill of lading symbolizes the transfer of property)。

(3)交易條件必須依照國際貿易之一般交易條件的統一解釋規則辦理。——目前國際商品買賣之交易條件，多採用國際商會歷經多次修正之「貿易條件之國際解釋規則」(International Rules for the Interpretation of Trade Terms)。

(4)訂約後，雙方均同意受有關國際公約、習慣法、國際判例、國際間特定貿易之慣例、以及當事人彼此間確立之習慣做法所約束。如在一般原則的情況下不能解決時，應按國際私法規定適用的法律來處理❷。

1-2-2　交易方式

從交易方式，約可分爲下列三種型態：

(1)自由貿易 (free trade)——西方國家大率採用此一制度，即買賣

---

❷ *United Nations Convention on Contracts for the International Sale of Goods.* ch. II, art. 7&9.

雙方在不同的國家或地區裏，可向對方自由選擇及買賣所需之商品。

⑵互惠貿易（bilateral trade）——兩國間在互惠之條件下，訂立雙方所需進出口之商品、金額及優惠關稅稅率。

⑶相對貿易（counter trade）——又可分爲相對採購（counter purchase）及補償貿易（compensation trade）兩種，東歐社會主義集團國家多採用之。前者情形，西方國家在出售機器設備至該集團國家時，買方均附有採購等值產品或原料之條件；後者最顯明的例子，爲西方國家在銷輸機器設備及技術至這些國家時，須向其購回所售機器設備生產之產品，以抵償其應付之分期付款。所謂相對採購，最近產油國家因油價下跌，外滙短缺，亦有採用此種方式進口物資者。

1-2-3　商品之市場特性

從國際行銷環境言，國際市場至爲複雜，在不同的國度裏，不論地理環境、人口特徵、文化模式、所得水準、工業發展程度以及政治法律制度等，均有其不同之特質；從消費型態言，由於各國消費者之所得水準不同，加上其社會習俗與文化特質，乃有不同之消費偏好與習慣。凡此種種，均足以影響產品之購買種類、購買方式、產品式樣、品質標準與包裝方式等。因此在產品之製應方面，必須力求差別化，以適應各個市場之特性。

第二章 契約成立之要件

2-1 契約成立之必要條件

2-1-1 要約與承諾 (Offer & Acceptance)

雙方當事人之要約與承諾, 爲構成具有約束力的契約 (binding contract) 之最重要條件。本書將於下節再詳細論述之。

2-1-2 簽訂契約之資格 (Contractual Capacity)

雙方當事人在法律上必須具有簽訂契約的資格。依據契約法, 未成年人無能力對其行爲負責; 具有心理缺憾 (mental deficiency) 的人, 亦無足够之判斷能力去處理法律事務, 故一個醉漢 (intoxicated person) 在神智不清下簽訂契約, 其法律效力自受影響。在商業社會裏, 具有簽訂契約資格者爲合法登記之貿易商, 爲在法令限制內享有權利及負擔義務能力的法人 (legal entity)❶。

---

❶ Frances E. Zellers & Gail H. Foreman: *Practical Business Law*, ch. 4.

Ronald A. Anderson & Walter A. Kumpf: *Business Law*, part II, ch. 7.

2-1-3　對待給付（**Consideration**）

　　對待給付係指一方當事人要求另一當事人在接受其約定（promise）時給付相對之代價（price）。約定人（promisor）通常僅在收到另一當事人之相對給付後其約定始生約束力。故對待給付一詞，可解釋為約定人要求另一當事人之相對承諾（counterpromise），因此這也是構成有效契約之必要條件之一❷。譬如賣方以特定數量價格之商品向買方報價，約定買方如在某特定期間內開立卽期付款之信用狀，則立卽裝船。此項約定，係以買方在特定期間開立信用狀為其交易之必要條件，如買方接受其條件，則買方之開立信用狀與賣方之履行交貨約定，乃構成相對承諾。由於賣方之履行其交付商品之約定，乃構成買方承諾給付等值價款之義務。此項對待給付，無形中構成雙方為履行其約定之契約上的法律義務（legal obligation）❸。

2-1-4　合法（**Legality**）

　　任何契約之訂立，必須保證不違法及不違背或危害國家之公共政策（public policy），否則無效。譬如與人訂約仿製冒牌洋酒、製造冒牌假藥或以不正當之手段獨佔市場，危害消費大眾利益，均屬危害國家公共政策之不法行為，其所訂契約均屬無效❹。

---

❷　Anderson & Kumpf: *Business Law*, ch. 9, p. 147.

❸　M. P. Furmston: *Cheshire & Fifoot's Law of Contract*, part II, ch. 2.

❹　Anderson & Kumpf: *Business Law*, part II, ch. 10.

2-2　要約與承諾

2-2-1　要　約

2-2-1-1　要約之必要條件

有效的要約（valid offer）必須符合三個條件，即(1)要約人（offeror）必須具有訂立契約的意向（contractual intention），(2)所提的條件必須是明確的（definiteness & certainty of terms），(3)要約必須送達被要約人（offeree）❺。玆分述如次：

1.必須具有訂立契約的意向——要約人對被要約人提出要約，必須誠信（good faith），並表明是項約定具有法律上執行的效力。譬如某甲購一新轎車，駕駛後幾度發生車禍，並送修車廠修理。某日甲送修時，對修車廠店主說：我願將該車以二分錢賣給你，店主當即接受。這分明是甲某多次車禍後之戲言，絕無以二分錢賣車之眞正意向（real intent）❻。

一般人常誤會廠商所送通函（circulars）或型錄所附價目表（price lists）爲賣方要約。其實，這祗能視作賣方願與買方照所列條件商談的邀約（intention to negotiate），因爲一個商人無法對接到通函或型錄之所有買方提出訂立強制契約作無限度供應的意圖。我國民法第一五四條亦有「價目表之寄送，不視爲要約」之規定。又依買方要求所寄之報價是否可視爲要約或要約之邀請，應以雙方意向表示之事實爲準。如彼此

---

❺ Zellers & Foreman: *Practical Business Law*, ch. 4.
　　Anderson & Kumpf: *Business Law*, ch. 5. pp. 89-95.

❻ Zellers & Foreman: *Practical Business Law*, ch. 4, p. 52.

尚無往來或商談，亦無貿易習慣之約束，祇提供指示價格（price indication），可視爲商談之邀約，但應在報價單加予說明，以免買方誤會❼。美國統一商法（Uniform Commercial Code）第2-206條(1)款關于要約及定貨單（order）有下列規定：

除非文字或情況另有明白之規定，(a)一個要求建立契約之要約，在任何合理方式、或任何媒體之情況下（in any manner and by any medium reasonable in the circumstances），得視爲承諾之邀約（inviting acceptance）；(b)一個要求立卽或最近裝運之買貨定單或其他要約（an order or other offer to buy goods for prompt or current shipment），得視爲邀約立卽承諾裝運或立卽或最近裝運貨物。

2.要約條件必須明確——要約之條件必須明確、清楚，才可構成有效之要約。如所提之要約條件不甚明確(indefinite)、模糊不淸（vague）或缺乏必要之規定條款（lacking of an essential provision），則無從引發對方接受訂立契約的意向，且往往會引起對方的誤會。譬如 Willimanson 擁有不同尺寸及價格之帆船二艘，向 Brown 洽售說：「我擬以450鎊之價格將我的帆船賣給你」，但未明確指定兩者中究竟洽售那一艘帆船？這分明是一種「不明確」的要約❽。

3.要約必須送達被要約人（offeree）——依照聯合國國際商品買賣公約第十五條規定，要約必須在送達被要約人時生效。由郵政寄送之信件要約，被要約人必須在有效期間收到該要約方才有效；如信件遺失，要約無效，因祇有被要約人纔能接受要約。

要約係一方當事人對另一方之特定人（specific person）提出，別人不得代庖，亦無權接受。如 Gonzales 向 Henderson 發價（offer）

---

❼　Anderson & Kumpf: *Business Law*, ch. 5, p. 90.

❽　Zellers & Foreman: *Practical Business Law*, ch. 4, p. 60.

洽售某種產品，Sheehan 適在旁表示他可以接受。此項承諾（acceptance）不能成立，因 Gonzales 係向 Henderson 提出要約，Sheehan 無權接受，Gonzales 亦無必要受其約束❾。依照聯合國國際商品買賣公約第十四條規定:

(1)向一個或一個以上之特定人（specific persons）提出訂立契約的建議，如果十分確定（definite），且表明要約人（offeror）在接到承諾時即願承受約束的意旨（intention），即構成要約。如一個建議，指明商品，並明白或默示地規定數量、價格或決定數量價格之條款，即爲十分明確之建議。

(2)凡非明白指明向一個或一個以上之特定人提出建議，應視爲要約之邀請（invitation to make offer）。

國際貿易比較複雜，故一般要約包括下列幾個要件:

1.商品規格、說明及數量

2.價格及付款條件

3.交貨條件——包括裝運日期、交貨地點、運輸方式、包裝及保險等。

要約如出自賣方，一般稱爲賣方要約（selling offer）或發價；如出自買方，則稱爲買方要約（buying offer）或出價（bidding），出價者亦稱出價人（bidder）。

2-2-1-2 普通要約與固定要約

商業上所謂要約，可分爲普通要約（ordinary offer）及固定要約（firm offer）兩種，前者在對方未接受前得隨時撤銷（revocable），後者在要約有效期間不得撤銷（irrevocable），但有個例外，即「撤回通知」必須在要約送達被要約人之前或同時抵達。因此，聯合國之國際商

❾ Zellers & Foreman: *Practical Business Law* ch. 4, p. 60.

品買賣公約有下列兩條規定:

第十五條: (1)要約于送達被要約人時生效。(2)一項要約, 卽使係不可撤銷的, 亦得撤回, 但此撤回通知必須在要約送達被要約人之前或同時抵達（指固定要約）。

第十六條: (1)在未訂立契約前, 要約得予撤銷, 如此項撤銷通知于被要約人發出承諾通知之前送達被要約人（指普通要約）。(2)但在下列情況下, 要約不得撤銷:

  a. 要約寫明接受要約期限或以其他方式表示要約爲不可撤銷者; 或

  b. 被要約人有理由信賴該要約爲不可撤銷, 並已對該要約信賴行事者。

美國之統一商法（Uniform Commercial Code）Sect. 2-205 關於固定要約亦有下列規定:

商人爲買賣商品簽發無「對待給付」之書面要約, 可依照條件保證在指定時間內固定有效, 不予撤銷; 如無合理時間（a reasonable time）之規定者, 其不可撤銷之有效期限, 無論在任何情況下最多不得超過三個月。

2-2-1-3 要約之終止

1. 要約人撤銷要約

普通要約得在對方未接受前之有效期內隨時撤銷, 但必須適當通知被要約人, 並以收到通知爲準。一個書面之撤銷通知, 送達被要約人之住址、營業處所或其代理, 應可認定其業已收到; 反是, 如被要約人在未收到撤銷通知前業已發出電報或郵寄函件表示承諾, 或業已依照要約人之指示以行爲表示承諾（或支付貨款）者, 則已構成有效契約, 要約人之撤銷無效。茲舉 Byrne v. Van Tienhoven 一案以說明要約撤銷

之通知在被要約人發出承諾電報後抵達之案例如下:

　　被告 Cardiff 于十月一日在英國發函給紐約之原告，要約洽售1000
　　箱白鐵皮。十月八日被告復再函原告取消該要約。十月十一日原告
　　電復被告接受其報價，並于十月十五日寄函確認。被告之撤銷通知
　　函件于十月二十日抵達原告。

　　英國法官 Lindley 判決: 郵寄之要約撤銷函件，係在十月二十日到
　　達被要約人，故要約應繼續有效至二十日收到撤銷通知時，而原告
　　在此期間業已發出承諾，其承諾應屬有效❿。

2. *被要約人拒絕接受要約*

　　依照聯合國商品買賣公約第十七條規定: 一項要約，即使是不可撤
銷的，于拒絕通知送達要約人時終止。故要約一旦爲被要約人拒絕，雖
原要約期限尚未到達，該要約卽因拒絕而告終止，被要約人不得於拒絕
後再行接受。譬如 Mr. Browning 于五月二十一日向 Mr. Harding 洽
售一本書籍，訂明售價美金 5 元，但爲 Harding 拒絕接受。五月二十
五日 Harding 變更主意，擬照價購買。從法律觀點言，Browning 之要
約已不復存在，除非 Harding 願意重新要約 (renew the offer)，否
則已無要約可供 Harding 接受⓫。

3. *被要約人還價*

　　被要約人在接受時變更或增加條件，叫做還價 (counter-offer)。
還價之先決條件必須推翻原要約，故還價不但終止原要約，且在提出
新要求而構成新要約 (new offer)，使被要約人轉變爲要約人。譬如
某甲向某乙洽售舊汽車一輛，報價 1000 美元，乙某還價750美元。如
此，原要約卽告終止。 我國民法第一六〇條對 要約擴張、 限制或變更

❿　Furmston: *Cheshire & Fifoot's Law of Contract*, pp. 50-51.
⓫　Zellers & Foreman: *Practical Business Law*, ch. 4, p. 63.

為承諾者，亦視為拒絕要約而另訂新要約。我國立法要旨，殆與英美法同。

4.要約有效期消失

要約均訂有承諾之有效期限，被要約人必須在限期內接受，如有效期限已過仍未接受，則要約即告終止。譬如 Mr. Houston 向 Mrs. Mason 洽售割草機，訂明售價美金15元，並給她10天期限考慮是否接受。10天已滿，未見 Mrs. Mason 回復，其要約自然失效⑫。要約如未指定期限，則在合理時間消逝後 (lapse of a reasonable amount of time) 要約即告終了。所謂合理時間，應以個別案情而異，但首須考慮標的物之性質、市場情況、季節性及供需狀況。易腐或價格波動性大之商品，其合理時間必較一般商品為短。譬如某商向水菓商洽售一整車香蕉，訂價每磅一角，但未訂明承諾時間。此項易腐水菓，其合理之有效時間絕不可能長達六個月⑬。我國民法第一五七條規定：「非對話為要約者，依通常情形可期待承諾之達到時期內，相對人不為承諾時，其要約失其拘束力」。又同法第一五八條規定：「要約定有承諾期限者，非于其期限內承諾，失其拘束力」。可見中外之立法精神大致相同。

5.要約之標的物毀滅

要約之標的物如在被要約人接受前即已毀滅，該要約即告終了，無須通知對方。譬如 Mr. Landowner 于二月三日向 Western Lumber Co. 要約洽售其林場之林木，不幸該林場于二月四日失火，林木全部焚毀，而該公司却於二月六日發出承諾通知。事實上，要約之標的物早於承諾前兩天業已焚毀，不復存在⑭。

---

⑫ Zellers & Foreman: *Practical Business Law*, ch. 4, p.62.

⑬ Zellers & Foreman: *Practical Business Law*, ch. 4, p. 62.

⑭ Zellers & Foreman: *Practical Business Law*, ch. 4, p. 63.

6. 法律之干預

要約之標的物，在要約時原屬合法之銷售商品，但在要約或承諾後，可能政府立法禁止出售而變成非法商品。此項法律干預，乃促使要約無效。如農藥商某甲向農民某乙洽售某種特定之殺蟲劑一批，某乙于接受後，政府發現該農藥對人體有害，突公佈停止銷售及使用，該商品之出售乃變成違法，要約自屬無效❺。

2-2-2　承　諾

2-2-2-1　承諾之性質

1. 承諾之方式

承諾之表達，並無一定之文字格式或特別之表明方式，只要以口頭聲明、書面或行為以表達其完全接受要約人之條件卽可。聯合國國際商品買賣公約第十八條關于承諾方式亦有下列規定：

(1)被要約人以聲明（statement）或其他行為表示同意接受要約，卽構成承諾（acceptance）。

(2)接受要約之承諾通知，于收到時生效。如表示承諾之通知不在規定時間內到達，或無時間規定而不在合理時間內到達，均屬無效，但須適當考慮交易情況與要約人所用通訊工具之迅捷程度。

譬如 Brown 對 Gray 說：「我願以75美元之價格將一車南瓜賣給你」，Gray 當卽當面表示：「我接受購買，這裏是75美元價款，我的工人立卽前來卸貨」。此係口頭要約及行為表示承諾之最好例子❻。又如一個出口商回復買方說：「你所寄五月二十七日定單，業已通知分店依

---

❺　Zellers & Foreman: *Practical Business Law*, ch. 4, p. 63.

❻　Zellers & Foreman: *Practical Business Law*, ch. 4, p. 64.

照立卽裝貨」。這也是以行為表示承諾之又一事例 ⓘ。

依照我國民法第一五六條規定:「對話為要約者,非立時承諾,卽失其拘束力」。聯合國商品買賣公約第十八條第(2)款亦規定:「除情況特殊者外,對口頭要約必須立卽接受」。同條第(3)款並規定:「依照要約指示或當事人間確立之習慣做法或慣例,被要約人得以行為表示承諾時生效,無須向要約人發出通知,如發送貨物或支付貨款之有關行為是。惟此項承諾之行為表示,必須在要約規定之時間內方為有效」。

2.承諾之要件

被要約人必須完全同意 (assent) 要約之條件,始可構成承諾;否則,如改變或限制任何條件或實質上在增加新條件,則表示不同意,並不接受其要約 ⓘ。 我國民法第一六〇條卽規定:「將要約擴張、限制或變更而為承諾者,視為拒絕原要約 而為新要約」。因此, 聯合國國際商品買賣公約第十九條第(1)款亦有下列規定:

對要約表示接受,但載有添加、限制或其他變更 (additions, limitations or other modifications) 之回復, 卽為拒絕要約,並構成還價 (counter-offer)。

3.添加不同條件而實質上不變更原要約亦可構成承諾

聯合國國際商品買賣公約第十九條第(2)(3)款關于要約之本質有極明確之解釋如下:

如添加或不同條款涉及商品之價格、品質、數量、交貨地點以及對另一方之責任與 解決爭端範圍,均視為實質上變 更要約條件。 反是, 承諾通知雖載有添加或 不同條件, 但此項添加或 不同條件在「實質上」並不變更原要約條件時,除非要約人在不過分遲延的情

ⓘ Anderson & Kumpf: *Business Law*, ch. 6, p. 103.

ⓘ Anderson & Kumpf: *Business Law*, ch. 6, p. 103.

況下以口頭或書面通知反對，仍構成承諾。

事實上，美國統一商法 Sect. 2-207 第(1)款早已有是項規定，玆摘錄如下：

在合理時間內發送一項表示確定及季節性之承諾或書面確認，倘此項承諾雖含有添加或不同條件、而「實質上」並未變更所同意之要約條件的本質時，仍構成承諾；但承諾在明白表示對方必須同意其實質上不同之添加條件時，是當別論。

4. 緘默不表示承諾

如非先有約定，在多數情況下，被要約人對要約表示緘默及不作為，不得視為承諾 (In most case, the silence of the offeree and his failure to act in response to an offer cannot be regarded as an acceptance)⓳。因此，聯合國國際商品買賣公約第十八條第(1)款規定：「緘默或不行為 (silence or inactivity) 本身並不等於承諾」。玆舉英國 Felthouse v. Bindley 一案例說明如下：

原告 Paul Felthouse 于二月二日函告其侄 John，願出價30鎊15先令向其購買飼養之馬，並言明如未聞表示其他意見，則該馬應照價歸其所有。其侄未予回復，但通知正在為其進行拍賣存貨之被告 Bindley（拍賣商）將該馬保留不賣，可是該被告一時粗心，已將該馬於二月二十五日拍賣給第三者，因此原告 Felthouse 乃控告被告强占 (conversion)。

英國高等民事裁判所裁示，在二月二十五日前，John 並未接受其叔父 Felthouse 之要約，因此原告實無資格告人强占⓴。

⓳ Anderson & Kumpf: *Business Law*, ch. 6, p. 105.
⓴ Furmston: *Cheshire & Fifoot's Law of Contract*, p. 41.

這在說明要約人不得以被要約人之緘默認爲係表示承諾，亦無理由以最後通牒方式强迫被要約人回復。玆再舉一個慣性銷售 (inertia selling) 的例子，以供參攷。普通商人慣性將未經商得同意之商品 (unsolicited goods) 發送給消費者，並附函說明在 10 天內如不退貨，則表示接受購買。依照英國之習慣法 (Common Law) 規定，消費者如不接受，無義務爲其退貨。不退貨並不表示接受，自無須付款 ❷。

5. 承諾必須由被要約人提出

要約係由要約人直接向特定之被要約人提出，故承諾必須由被要約人自行提出，第三者提出無效。被要約人如爲公司，則公司任何授權之代表人均可代表公司接受。玆舉一案例以說明之：

Shuford 公司向 State Machinery Co. 報價洽售特定之機器一部，Nutmeg State Machinery Corp. 聞悉，立卽通知 Shuford 接受承購。Shuford 不予受理，亦不交貨，Nutmeg Corp. 乃控告 Shuford 違約。

法院判決，認爲 Shuford 係向 State Machinery Co. 報價，祇該公司可以接受，與 Nutmeg 並無契約關係，第三者不能接受要約 (Nutmeg State Machinery v. Shuford—129 Conn. 659, 30A. 2d 911) ❷。

6. 遲到之承諾

所謂遲到之承諾 (late acceptance)，係指逾期送達之承諾。聯合國國際商品買賣公約第二十一條對此項遲到承諾有下列明確之規定：

(1)要約人對遲到之承諾，如立卽以口頭或書面通知被要約人可以接受，則仍具承諾之效力。

---

❷ Furmston: *Cheshire & Fifoot's Law of Contract*, pp. 41-43.

❷ Anderson & Kumpf: *Business Law*, ch. 6, p. 105.

(2)如信件或書面之遲到承諾，係在一向傳遞正常，估計可及時送達要約人之情況下發寄者，則該逾期承諾之接受仍具效力，除非要約人毫不遲延地以口頭或書面通知被要約人此一要約已經失效。

2-2-2-2　承諾之接受時間

聯合國國際商品買賣公約第二十條關于承諾之有效時間，有下列之規定：

(1)要約人在電報或信件內規定之接受時間，從電報交發時刻或信上載明之發信日期起算；如信上未載日期，則從信封上所載日期起算。要約人以電話、電傳或其他快速通訊方法規定之接受時間，從要約送達被要約人時起算。

(2)在計算接受時間時，接受期間內之正式假日或非營業日應計算在內，但如遇接受通知在接受期間之最後一天適係要約人營業處所之正式假日或非營業日而未送達時，其接受期限得順延至下一個營業日。

2-2-2-3　承諾之傳遞方式

從前法界之權威人士認爲：一個要約之承諾傳遞方式，必須與要約同，或承諾必須在要約人實際收到時生效。新近之法院判決趨勢，似乎在支持美國統一商法 Sect. 2-206 之規定，除非文字或情況另有明白指示，只要在任何合理方式及傳遞媒體行使承諾即可，足見在程度上已有若干改進。關于使用信件或電報爲承諾之通知者，如要約規定承諾必須在收到時生效，法律將尊重其意旨；倘無上項規定，凡以信件回復者，在正確投郵（properly mailed）時生效；以電報回復者，于電報送至電報局時生效。依照美國統一商法之一般解釋，所有要約之承諾如訂有「到達期限」之規定，應如約定辦理。其傳遞方式及生效日期，約可分爲下列三種情形：

要約傳遞方式	承諾傳遞方式	生　效　日　期
郵　　　遞 （對承諾之回復方式未規定）	郵　遞 電　報	被要約人有權使用同樣之傳遞媒體，由郵政寄送承諾通知，並於發出時生效（以信封郵戳日期或郵政收據日期爲準），但應于限期內送達爲準。 被要約人得用電報回復，並以電報送達電報局時生效（以收據日期爲準），但應于限期內到達爲準。
電　　　報 （對承諾之回復方式未規定）	電　報 郵　遞	一般希望被要約人同樣用電報回復（其生效日期及限期到達原則同上）如郵政延誤，無法在限期內到達，或郵運遺失，均無效。
電報或郵遞 （訂明承諾之回復方式須用電報，並在限期內抵達）	電　　　報	在要約人之營業處所于限期內收到

　　英國習慣法對於承諾之傳遞方式，尚無特別規定。法院之判例，係以要約性質及提出要約時之個別情況作裁定。

　　依照英國上訴法庭一八七九年對 Household Fire & Carriage Accident Insurance Co. v. Grant 案創立之判例，要約如無特別指示，被要約人以郵遞方式傳遞其承諾通知者，只要信件寫明要約人之營業地址投郵（put into the post），且已蓋郵戳（properly stamped），承諾即已生效[23]。

　　一般規定，承諾通知應於送達要約人時生效，前面聯合國國際商品買賣公約第十八條已有此項規定。又依照聯合國公約規定，要約人對遲

---

[23] Furmston: *Cheshire & Fifoot's Law of Contract*, p. 46.

到之承諾雖仍有酌情接受可能， 但承諾信件如遭遺失， 則就無法補救
了。一個重要交易之承諾通知， 如一旦遲到或遺失， 勢將構成雙方之爭
執。這些問題， 值得大家注意和防範。

2-2-2-4　承諾之撤銷

　　依照聯合國國際商品買賣公約第二十二條規定：「承諾得 予撤回，
惟此項撤回通知， 應於原承諾生效前或同時抵達要約人」。 此係適應目
前日見複雜之國際貿易環境的一個比較進步的規定。

第三章 契約內容

我們應該曉得，一個有效契約的訂立，必須以「明文」確定其所創立之義務範圍，以及其所訂契約之特性與可確定之界限。事實上，契約之真正內容，並不限於書面之契約條文，蓋買賣雙方可能已依據商業上一般「默示」之商事習慣或當地確立之慣例進行契約之商談，或依照該業商事慣例上通常對該業一般契約慣用條款或方式所賦予之意義解釋進行訂約，而契約之明示語文（express language），僅係契約之實質內容，祇在確定雙方當事人應負之責任範圍而已。至契約一旦發生履行上之挫折，受害一方必須採取仲裁或訴訟途徑以解決糾紛時，則契約當事人須受合意選定之國家法律支配；又雙方當事人如係國際有關公約之締約國，則仍須遵照該公約有關規定之約束。交付仲裁或選定之國家管轄法庭處理時，則又須遵照仲裁人或法官從個案情形所涉及之國際公約、國內法及有關貿易慣例及法院判例為依據，作適當之裁斷。因此，契約之明示條款（express terms），可說是契約之實質條款（substantive terms），亦可稱為契約之內在的實質內容；而在履行契約或糾紛發生時應遵守之有關國際公約、契約適用法律、以及當事人表示可以適用之商事習慣或彼此間所確立之慣例與法院判例，則可視為契約之外在的默示條款（implied terms）。我國民法第一五三條對契約成立之原則，亦規定當事人之意思表示不拘為明示或默示，必須互相一致。足證我國民法對契約內容，亦有明示及默示條款之認定。

3-1　明示條款

所謂明示條款（express terms），依據一般規定，可全爲口語或書面文件（wholly by word of mouth or wholly in writing），或部份口語及部份書面文件（or partly by word of mouth and partly in writing）。契約之全由書面表示者，可從文字之書面表達去裁斷，但如係口頭契約（oral contract），則必須由當事人說明事實眞象並據證，故較難處理。依照英國之誓證規則（Parole Evidence Rule），口頭誓證祗能在適當限度內對契約之客觀理論加以說明，但不得增加、變更或牴觸書面契約或文件。

在交易進行中，買賣双方必有一連串之商談。這些意思之表示及陳述（statement），除口頭契約外，往往見諸來往之電報、函件及備忘錄等文件或書面契約中，而此類書面文件，均包括促成契約所應具備之條件（conditions）或保證（warranty）條件，但並非所有意思之表達均可構成契約條款（contractual terms）。譬如在 Routledge v. Mckay 一案，買方有意向機器脚踏車經銷商洽購機車一輛，因詢問該商經銷之機車出廠年份，該商根據登記簿記載，回復係一九四二年份。買方旋向該商簽約訂購，但未提及製造年份。事後發現該車之實際出廠年份爲一九三〇，於是向賣方要求賠償損失。本案英國上訴法庭認爲賣方之說明，僅係陳述之表達（mere representation），並非保證，乃判決買方敗訴❶。又 Bannerman v. White 一案，買方向賣方洽購蛇麻子一批，聲明該批蛇麻子如經硫磺處理則不值得報價。賣方答稱，該貨未經硫磺處

---

❶ Furmston: *Cheshire & Fifoot's Law of Contract*, pp. 117-118.

理，買方乃決定向賣方訂購。第交貨時，發現部份已遭硫磺處理，因卽向賣方取消契約，賣方則向法院訴請買方付款。法官認爲賣方所說「未經硫磺處理」爲整個契約之基本條件（fundamental condition），賣方違背約定，買方自可不付貨款❷。依照英國商品買賣法規定，契約之任何規定如構成條件（condition）時，對方一旦違反該項條件，另一方得取消契約；惟違反保證條款，祇能要求對方賠償損失，而無權拒絕收貨。

前述契約之明示條件，普通可分爲前提條件（condition precedent）、共存條件（condition concurrent）及事後條件（condition subsequent）三種。前述蛇麻子必須「未經硫磺處理」，卽係前提條件之最好的例子。在買賣契約中，往往訂明對方必須在一定期間內履行某項義務，此卽係以「履約時間」（time of performance）爲訂約之基本前提條件；換句話說，一方必須先履行約定之特定義務，始可有權責成對方完成其所應履行之約定義務。譬如契約中訂明買方必須在某特定時間內將信用狀開到賣方始裝船，或賣方必須在某特定期間內交貨買方始付款，如任何一方違反前提條件之約定，則對方得拒絕履行其契約義務，甚或取消契約，訴請賠償損失。一面交錢一面交貨，則係付款與交貨同時共同存在之交易條件。事後條件，爲事態發生後一方當事人規定受害人必須在一定時間內通知處理之條件。譬如保險公司規定，承保之貨物如發生火災，必須在指定之時間內（within a stated period）將損害情形通知保險公司處理，逾時則不予賠償。這卽是事後條件之最好的例子 ❸。在國際貿易中，以前兩者最常見。

---

❷ Furmston: *Cheshire & Fifoot's Law of Contract*, p. 117.

❸ Corley & Robert: *Principles of Business Law*, ch. 4, pp. 247-249.

3-2 默示條款

普通的商業契約，並非一個獨立的商業文書，它是一個商業行為涉及權利義務的文件，其所訂明示條件的含意，可能來自商事習慣，也可能根據成文法，亦可能參引法院判例，以加強表明其合約之意向。

3-2-1 商業習慣採用之默示條款 (Terms Implied by Custom)

一般公認，貿易上之習慣與慣例，雖未列入契約條文，但在習慣上，除非另有協議，多受其約束。在仲裁或法院定案時，亦多參採之。譬如在 Produce Brokers Co. Ltd. v. Olympia Oil & Cake Co.Ltd. 一案，契約之仲裁條款規定，紛爭應交由指定之仲裁人解決，仲裁人乃根據該項貿易之特殊習慣進行裁斷。法官 Sumner 認定其堅持依據貿易習慣之裁斷極為正確，蓋該案糾紛事態之發生，起因習慣問題，而非出自契約或其他原因 ❹。要之，習慣之引用，必須有助於當事人解決問題，不得在任何情況下違反契約宗旨，或與明示條款有所牴觸。

3-2-2 成文法規定之默示條款 (Terms Implied by Statute)

英國海上保險法 (Marine Insurance Act) 之所有條文，即係根據一般長期習用之默示條款演變為成文法之最好的例子。一般貿易慣例 (trade customs) 之納入契約，而契約又長期採用此項慣例，乃逐漸演變成法律術語 (statutory language)。最顯明的例子是英國一八九三年之商品買賣法，它係彙集商品買賣契約歷年發展所認定之習慣條款 (customary terms) 制定的成文法。該法規定，此類默示條款超越當

---

❹ Furmston: *Cheshire & Fifoot's Law of Contract*, pp. 122-123.

事人之意圖而適用於任何商業契約。依據英國商品買賣法，在任何買賣契約中，不拘有無明文規定，商品必須適合買方採購之目的用途，品質且須適合市場銷售 (merchantable quality)。美國統一商法在 Sect. 2-314 及 2-315 亦有同樣之默示保證 (implied warranty) 的規定。這是成文法對商品買賣契約的默示條款，目前已成爲世界公認之商事法則。

3-2-3 法院認定之默示條款 (Terms Implied by the Courts)

英國法院在審判貿易糾紛案件時，經常引用或認定有關默示條款，就當事人訂約意旨，尋求或認定契約中未經明示條款 (an unexpressed terms)，以補救其內在之表達缺失。如契約中之明示條款，訂得極爲清楚而不含糊，則須尊重契約當事人之意旨，依照該規定之清晰條文去處理，法院縱有更適合條款之想法，亦不應採用。譬如在 Sethia Ltd. v. Partabmull Rameshwar 一案，原告倫敦英商於一九四七年向被告印度商人訂購黃麻一批，訂明運往意大利之 Genoa 交貨，双方均了解應由印度政府發給輸出許可證始可裝船。從一九四七年起，印度政府公佈採用出口配額制，出口商得按一九三七～一九四六年輸往各國之實績，選擇其中任何一年爲其輸往各國之配額計算年度，被告因選擇一九四六年爲其輸往意國之出口實績計算年度，但是年該商並無輸意實績，印度政府乃照契約數量批准少於三分之一的配額。原告控告被告違約，被告辯稱：該約應包含 "Subject to Quota" 之默示條款。英國上訴法庭拒絕採用該默示條款，其理由爲：如賣方認爲黃麻之出口，必須 "Subject to Quota"，則係明示條款，應在契約中預先訂明；今未在契約內表明，即表示被告已接受絕對交貨之義務。且原告對被告之出口實績及配額情況並不知悉，自不能承受其後果❺。這個法院判例，在說明默示條款之引

---

❺ Furmston: *Cheshire & Fifoot's Law of Contract*, p. 135.

用，不能浮泛，必須係双方當事人在特定貿易涉及同類交易所廣泛知曉之習慣做法或慣例而經常爲同業遵守者，或此類默示條款業經演變爲成文法而爲業者所普遍遵守者。法官之依據默示條款辦案，必須依照契約條文及當事人之意旨，在契約未經明示或所訂明示條款未見明晰之情況下，尋求合理審判。

第四章 國際商品買賣契約法則

4-1 國際商品之買賣條件

所謂國際商品買賣，係指國際間的貿易商經過貿易途徑提供製造或生產所需與消費者所需之商品，這些商品在訂約時均係可以「確定」及「移動」的東西，但並不包括市面上可以流通的股票、證券、商業票據或金錢等，他如海外工程、技術轉移、專利商標及其他勞務輸出，亦不屬本範圍。

任何國際商品之買賣，必須考慮下列三個問題:

(1)應由誰來安排及支付運費，將商品由一個指定的地方運至另一個地方交付？

(2)如上項商品之交付工作不能完成，應由誰來承擔此項風險？

(3)在運輸過程中，誰來承擔此商品滅失或損害之風險？

這些問題，均涉及商品由賣方轉入買方手中將採用何種運輸方式之問題。至風險之承擔，也自然涉及運輸途中可能發生之費用以及其所應擔當之風險與責任; 換句話說，這些都是買賣雙方對商品運輸所應具之權利義務。因此每一商品之運交方式不同乃生產不同之交易條件 (trade terms)，以確定買賣雙方在不同之條件下所應負之費用及風險與責任。

在不同國境裏之買方或賣方，均不喜歡遵照對方國家之法律或習慣訂約，而願以本國之法律及習慣爲準。其所採用之交易條件，又往往各有不同之解釋而發生無可避免的貿易糾紛。

目前國際間對商品買賣之交易條件，約有下列四種解釋規則:

(1)國際商會之貿易條件國際解釋規則

國際商會于一九三六年開始訂定「貿易條件國際解釋規則」(International Rules for the Interpretation of Trade Terms)，英文簡稱 INCOTERMS 1936，于一九五三年再度修訂，計列貿易條件九種，並採納國際間較爲廣泛通用之解釋範圍。一九六七年復補充 "Delivered at Frontier" 及 "Delivered Duty Paid" 兩種，一九七六年再補充 "FOB Airport" 一種，使適用範圍再予擴大。嗣以貨櫃運輸發達，多種運輸型態之複式運輸 (multi-model transport) 乃應運而生，「戶到戶」(door-to-door) 之交貨方式已爲世界各國所廣泛採用。國際商會爲適應國際貿易發展之需要，乃于一九八〇年增訂 " Free Carrier (named point)"(FRC) 及 "Freight or Carriage and Insurance Paid to (named point of destination)" (CIP) 兩種貿易條件，並修訂 "Freight or Carriage Paid to (named point of destination)" (DCP) 條件，使能擴大適用于一貫作業之複式運輸 ●。合計目前已有14種貿易條件之國際解釋規則，將于下節再行詳晰介紹。

(2)美國之對外貿易定義

美國之對外貿易定義 (American Foreign Trade Definitions) 于1919年制定頒佈，于1941年由美國商會、美國進口商全國委員會及全國對外貿易委員會三個機構組織之聯合委員會加以修訂實施。此係美國之

● International Chamber of Commerce: *Guide to INCOTERMS*, 1980 edition.

貿易條件解釋規則，計分 Ex (point of origin)、FOB、FAS、C&F、CIF 及 Ex Dock 六種，其中 FOB 又分下列六類:

1. FOB (named inland carrier at named inland point of departure)

2. FOB (named inland carrier at named inland point of departure) Freight Paid to (named point of exportation)

3. FOB (named inland carrier at named inland point of departure) Freight Allowed to (named point)

4. FOB (named inland carrier at named point of exportation)

5. FOB Vessel (named port of shipment)

6. FOB (named inland point in country of importation)❷

上項美國貿易定義所列六種修訂之貿易條件，在說明每一定義前，均表明此係賣方報價之條件，並在前言中建議買賣雙方共同接受此項條件時，應在契約內訂明，並列為契約之一部份，方具法律效力。

以上 Ex (point of origin)，係指在美國原在地交貨之條件，包括在工廠、工場、倉庫、礦場或農場 (Ex factory, mill, warehouse, mine or plantation) 等地交貨條件。在 FOB 六類交易條件中，除 FOB Vessel 及 FOB (named inland point in the country of importation) 兩類可供外銷業者採用外，其餘四類則屬內銷條件，買方如係外銷商，仍得自行辦理出口手續。依照其 FOB 條件之評註，業者依該定義交易者，對下列事項應加注意:

(1)內陸運輸方法，諸如卡車、鐵路貨車、駁船、內河貨輪、或飛

---

❷　國際貿易局與司法行政部民事司編譯「國際貿易法規暨慣例彙編」第一册 pp. 640-673—"Revised American Foreign Trade Definitions, 1941."

機，應予明確規定。

(2)在內陸運輸中，如涉及任何轉駁費用，則應事先協議由賣方或買方負擔。

(3)「FOB（指定港口）」條件，因未指明賣方責任終止與買方責任開始之分界點，應避免使用。該條件之使用，對貨物在港口、及在交付或裝上海洋運輸工具之前發生滅失或損害，究竟為賣方或買方責任，易起爭執。為避免誤會，應指定交貨之特定地點時間。

(4)貨物由內陸運輸工具搬運至船邊，如需駁船或卡車，則必發生費用，此項費用究應由賣方或買方負擔，須事先加以訂明。

(5)賣方應將獲得一整車廂載量（carload）、一卡車載量（truckload）或一內河貨輪載量（bargeload）費率所需之最少數量，確實通知買方。

(6)在各類 FOB 條件下，除「FOB（進口國家內指定內陸地點交貨）」條件外，洽取海運艙位及購買海上保險與兵險，均屬買方義務。這些雖屬買方之義務部份，但在頗多交易中，賣方都在替買方洽取海運艙位、代購海上保險、兵險及代辦裝船事項。因此，對洽取艙位及購買海上保險與兵險一事，究應由賣方或買方負責抑由賣方代替買方辦理，雙方必須事先有所了解。

(7)賣方為保護其本身權益，應在契約中規定，買方購買海上保險應包括標準之倉庫到倉庫條款（standard warehouse-to-warehouse clause）❸。

又依據美國定義之 C&F 及 CIF 評註，認為買賣雙方在 C&F 或 CIF 條件下訂立契約時，對下列各點應取得協議：

1.對於雜項費用，如過磅或檢驗等費用，應事先協議究應由何方支

---

❸ 國際貿易局與司法行政部民事司編譯「國際貿易法規暨慣例彙編」第一冊張錦源教授譯「美國對外貿易定義」pp. 656-658.

付。

2. 應衡量在進口港所容許的免費期間內，船舶到達和卸貨時買方提取貨物的能力，事先協議裝運任何一艘船舶的數量。

3. 在 C & F 與 CIF 條件下，雖一般解釋規定領事發票及產地證明書的費用是由買方負擔，並分別計收，但在許多交易中，這些費用已由賣方包括在其貨價中，因此，買賣雙方應事先協議這些費用究為售價的一部分，抑或將另行計收。

4. 如船舶是在貨物實際目的地以外的港口卸貨，則最後目的地所在應確切加以指明。

5. 如海運艙位取得困難，或運送契約不能以確定的運費率訂定時，則買賣契約應規定在約定期間內裝運須以賣方可獲得海運艙位為條件，並應規定自出售時到裝運時之間海運費的變動，歸由買方負擔。

6. 在正常的情形下，賣方有義務先付海運運費。不過在某些場合，是以運費到付的方式裝運，而由賣方在其所提出的發票上扣除該項運費金額。對於這點，必須事先加以協議，以避免因可能影響實際運費的匯率波動所引起的誤會，以及憑信用狀融通時可能發生的利息所引起的誤會。因此，除了賣方事先已與買方特別約定貨物得以運費到付的方式裝運外，賣方通常總是應先付海運運費。

7. 買方應該瞭解，他在接受單證之前無權堅持檢驗貨物。如賣方已盡相當的努力由正常的途徑寄送該項單證，買方不得因遲收單證而拒絕提取貨物。

8. 奉勸買賣雙方，不要將任何與本定義所規定的 CIF 契約義務相牴觸的不確定的條款列入 CIF 契約中。在美國及其他國家的法院，曾多次判決 CIF 契約因列入不確定的條款而告失效。

9. 利息應包括在貨價的計算中，而不應在 CIF 契約中另列利息項目，除非買賣雙方事先已另有協議。然而在那種場合，應使用 CIF and I（原價、保險費、運費、及利息在內）條件。

10. 關於 CIF 交易項下的保險，買賣雙方對於下列各點必須要有確切的協議：

(a)海上保險的性質應加以協議，究竟為 W. A.（水漬險）或為 F. P. A.（平安險），以及任何其他在特定交易中應投保的特別險類，或買方為其個別保障所期望投保的特別險類。在這些特別險類中，買賣雙方應加考慮及協議的是偸竊、挖竊、漏損、破損、潮損、為其他貨物污損，以及對任何特定交易所特有的其他危險。對於偶發的或到付的運費，以及關稅等均應加保險，以彌補單獨海損，以及貨到通關後提貨前所發生的全損。這點極為重要。

(b)賣方有義務盡其通常的注意力及努力，選擇財務情況良好的保險人。但兵險索賠獲致解決的風險仍歸由買方負擔。

(c)在本條件下兵險是由賣方以買方的費用及風險代為購買。賣方應就此點與買方確切協議，尤其是有關費用部分，這點極為重要。貨物投保海上保險與保險最好由同一保險人承保，這樣對於損失原因的認定自不致引起爭論。

(d)賣方應確定其海上保險或兵險，已包括標準的罷工、暴動、及內亂險。

(e)買賣雙方對於保險價值的估算應加以協議，記住：商品在共同海損的分攤中，是根據某些估算的標準計算，而這些估算標準隨各種交易而異，因此最好就敎於有資格的保險經紀人，以期投保足額並避免糾紛 ❹。

---

❹ 國際貿易局與司法行政部民事司編譯「國際貿易法規暨慣例彙編」第一冊 張錦源敎授譯「美國對外貿易定義」pp. 667-671.

根據美國貿易定義分析，其內銷之 Ex (point of origin) 條件，有似 INCOTERMS 之 Ex Works (or Factory) 條件，其餘純粹適用於外銷者，則 FOB Vessel, FOB (named inland point in the country of importation), FAS, C&F, CIF 及 Ex Dock 頗相似 INCOTERMS 之 FOB, Delivered Duty Paid (named place of destination), FAS, C&F, CIF 及 Ex Quay 條件。下節將再作較詳細之比較分析。

(3)國際法學會對 CIF 契約之解釋規則

國際法學會 (International Law Association) 爲提供 CIF 買賣契約一套標準格式與可資應用之一般條件，爰於一九三二年在英國牛津開會，依據一九二八年之「華沙規則」(Warsaw Rules) 加以修訂，故稱「華沙牛津 CIF 契約規則」(Warsaw-Oxford Rules for CIF Contracts)。本規則共二十一條，關于賣方對裝船之責任、日期，提單之交付，商品之保險，品質數量等單證之提供及風險與所有權之轉移，以及買方支付貨款之義務與商品之檢查等，均有詳晰之規定。惟此項解釋規則，迄今已閱五十餘年，由於交通事業之日新月異，若干規定，業難適應，所幸該總則已有聲明，本規則之任何部份，得予變更、修正或插入其他條件；又本規則與契約條件牴觸時，應以契約爲準。希讀者注意及之 ❺。

(4)社會主義國家商品交付之一般條件

此項商品交付之一般條件，係由蘇俄與東歐社會主義集團國家組織之經濟互助協會 (Council For Mutual Economic Assistance) 于一九六八年所訂，旋于一九七六年一月一日再度修訂，計十七章，一一〇

❺ 國際貿易局與司法行政部民事司編譯「國際貿易法規暨慣例彙編」第一冊, pp. 621-639, Warsaw-Oxford Rules for CIF Contracts, 1932.

條。重要條款包括: (1)契約之成立、(2)交付之基礎、(3)交付時間、(4)品質、(5)數量、(6)包裝標示、(7)技術文件、(8)品質證明、(9)保證、(10)裝運指示及交運通知、(11)付款手續、(12)免責、(13)索賠、(14)罰則、(15)仲裁、(16)索賠期間之限制及(17)其他條款。以上均屬交易之一般條件，故稱商品交付之一般條件，英文全名爲 General Conditions of Delivery of Goods between Organizations of the Member-countries of the Council for Mutual Economic Assistance (GCD CMEA 1968)❻。

在國際商業政治環境日趨複雜的今天，最重要的是如何選擇每筆交易之最適當條件，買賣雙方均須尋求選擇一項較爲明確之統一解釋規則，俾彼此之權利義務可在契約中訂明。在契約自由 (freedom of contract) 之原則下，雙方當事人自可自由決定價格、付款交貨方式與風險之負擔。自然，所謂自由原則，並非絕對的，在契約之進行、訂立及履行期間，仍須隨時注意有關政府及國際間之法規、公約及貿易慣例，尤其在晚近對消費者保護法令之日見增加中，雙方當事人必須事前多加了解，俾契約之履行不致發生障礙。

業者在引用上項任何之解釋規則時，最好在契約中予以訂明。爲因應日趨複雜之國際貿易環境，必要時可變更、修訂或增加條件，俾契約益臻完善。國際商會在 "How to use INCOTERMS" 之序文中，卽說明買賣雙方可引用 INCOTERMS 爲其契約之一般基礎，此外並增加或變更有關條件，以適應其個別貿易情況之特殊需要。INCOTERMS 之基本原則在規定賣方之最低義務 (minimum liability)，買方在契約中得增加賣方之義務。譬如買方擬增加賣方之保險責任，可在契約中

---

❻ UNCITRAL 1968 Version—Translation: General Conditions of Delivery of Goods between Organizations of the Member-countries of the Council for Mutual Economic Assistance (GCD CMEA 1968).

訂明 "CIF INCOTERMS with All Risks Insurance"。再者，INCOTERMS 並不足以決定契約雙方之法律關係，一旦違約或涉及商品之所有權問題時，仍得借助法律或其他貿易條件解決之。

　　美國一九四一年修訂之對外貿易定義，亦在其「前言」中說明，這些修訂之定義，除非經過特別立法或法院之判決加予確認，否則不具法律上之地位。因此，建議買賣雙方均同樣接受時，可列為契約之一部份，使該項定義具有法律效力。上述華沙牛津規則，亦有同樣規定。

　　至蘇聯集團國家所採用之商品交付一般條件，在東歐國家向自由民主國家採購時均普遍採用，但這些國家亦有接受 INCOTERMS 為其交易條件者，業者在採用 INCOTERMS 條件與東歐國家交易時，應注意將它列入契約，方可發生法律效力。

4-1-1　國際商會之貿易條件簡介

　　國際商會一九八〇年修訂之十四種貿易條件，除大部份已由國內專家學者全文譯述在此擬僅作要點之介紹外，其餘增訂之 "FOB Airport" (1976)，"Free Carrier(named point)" (FRC-1980) 及修正之 "Freight or Carriage Paid to" (DCP-1980)，因坊間尚不多見，似有加以譯述必要，故特逐條逐譯如下，以供讀者參攷。至"Freight or Carriage and Insurance Paid to" (CIP-1980)，雖係一九八〇年增訂，但其條款大致與 DCP 相同，祇增加「保險」條款而已，故不再逐條詳譯，而僅加扼要介紹如下：

（一）Ex Works

Ex Works 係指在工廠交貨之貿易條件。賣方僅須負責將貨物製好在其廠房（即工場或製造廠）交貨，除非另有約定，無須負責將貨物裝至買方所提供之車輛上。因此買方必須擔負所有費用及風險，從賣方工廠將貨物裝上其準備之車輛運至目的地。——此項交易條件，賣方所負的義務最少。

(二) FOR/FOT (Free on Rail/Free on Truck)

FOR/FOT 係指在火車或貨車上交貨之貿易條件。 賣方必須負責在約定日期或期間內將貨物交送至車廂 （火車之車廂或無蓋貨車）。 如貨物已構成整車廂 wagon-load (carload, truckload) 之運量而適用整車之按量費率時，賣方須在適當時間洽訂適當型式、容量及必要時具有蓬布蓋之車廂，並負擔所有費用將貨物如期裝上。如載量不滿一整車廂或其重量不足以申請使用重量費率者， 則賣方須將貨物如期運至鐵路起運車站交由鐵路局接管裝車 或交由鐵路局 提供之車輛運 交起運站 (dispatching station)。 惟鐵路規章規定須由賣方負責裝貨至車廂者，則不在此限。賣方尚須提供發票及經常所需運輸文件給買方。買方應適時通知賣方交貨時間、地點及付運費。當買方收到賣方所送發票及運輸文件時， 如貨物已運至車站，應予接受。如須申請輸出許可證及付貨物出口稅捐時，應由買方負責。

(三) FAS (Free alongside Ship)

FAS 係指船邊交貨之貿易條件。 賣方須負責在約定之日期或期間內將 貨物運至 指定之港口及 買方指定靠船之碼頭 （quay） 或駁船 (lighters) 交貨，且立即通知買方，並提供船邊交貨收據 (provide an alongside receipt)。 買方應負責指定裝貨之船隻及支付運費。如須取得輸出許可證並付貨物出口稅捐時，應由買方負責。買方接貨後，即須負擔所有費用及貨物滅失或損害之一切風險。

(四) FOB (Free on Board)

FOB 係指船上交貨之貿易條件。 賣方㈠必須負責在約定日期或期間內將貨物運至買方指定港口及指定之船舶上交貨；㈡必須取得輸出許可證並繳納其他規定之出口稅捐；㈢提供船上交貨之清潔收據（a clean on board receipt）；㈣負責裝船費用（loading cost）。但必要時，得徇買方要求，由買方負擔風險及費用，協助其取得提貨單（Bill of Lading）。買方應負責㈠在適當時指定及通知裝貨之船名、港口、停泊地及交貨日期（give due notice of the name, loading berth of and delivery dates to the vessel）；㈡擔負貨物至指定港越過船舷（ship's rail）後之一切風險及費用；㈢與船方簽訂貨物裝運合約，負責支付運費。

（五）C&F（Cost and Freight）

C&F 係指包括成本及至目的港運費之貿易條件。 賣方㈠必須訂立運輸合約，支付船公司運費及所收在卸貨口岸之任何卸貨費用，將貨運至指定目的港；㈡在約定日期或 期間內必須將貨 物裝載船上， 一俟貨物越過船欄後，一切風險即轉移買方；㈢必須擔負風險及費用取得輸出許可證，並繳付所需出口稅捐；㈣負擔裝船費；㈤提供買方發票及清潔提貨單；㈥裝貨後，立卽通知買方。買方㈠接受賣方運輸單據及提貨；㈡負擔貨物在海運過程中所發生之一切費用（海運費除外）， 包括卸貨費用（如運費不包括此項費用時）。

（六）CIF（Cost, Insurance and Freight）

CIF 係指包括成本 、 保險費及運費 將貨物運至目的 港之貿易條件。所有條件基本上與 C&F 相同， 賣方祇需增加投保海上貨物保險一項，以承保運輸途中貨物滅失或損害之風險，所需投保費亦由賣方負擔。如係以 CIF Landed 條件交易者，賣方尚須負擔卸貨費用，包括駁艇費及碼頭費。（本條僅規定提供最低限度之 F.P.A. 平安險，買方如須提高保險責任，應在契約內訂明）

（七）Ex Ship（named port of destination）

Ex Ship 係指在目的地港船上交貨之貿易條件 。 ㈠賣方必須負擔全部費用及風險將貨物運至合約指定之目的港船上交貨; ㈡賣方必須提供買方提貨單據 (包括提貨單或交貨單 delivery order), 俾買方可在船上提貨; ㈢卸貨費用由買方負擔; ㈣買方從貨物確實交其處理起, 負擔一切風險及費用。

(八) Ex Quay (Duty Paid or Duty on Buyer's Account)······(named port of destination)

Ex Quay 係指目的港碼頭交貨並付關稅或關稅由買方負擔之貿易條件。賣方㈠須負擔一切費用及風險, 將貨物依照約定之時期運至合約指定之目的港碼頭放妥交買方處理; ㈡並提供提貨單據 (包括交貨單) 交買方提貨; ㈢如屬 Ex Quay (Duty Paid) 條件者, 賣方且須自行負擔費用及風險取得輸入許可證, 並繳付關稅、通關費及其他因進口所需繳付之稅捐及費用; 如係以 Ex Quay (Duty on Buyer's Account) 條件交貨者, 所有該項費用風險由買方負擔; ㈣買方從貨物確實運放碼頭交其處理起, 負擔一切風險及費用。

(九) Delivered at Frontier (named place)

Delivered at Frontier 係指賣方須負責將貨物運至輸往國家海關關卡邊境交貨之貿易條件 (本條係一九六七年增訂)。 本條原爲鐵路或公路運送貨物而訂定, 但亦可適用於各種運輸方式。

依照本條規定, 賣方㈠必須擔負一切費用及風險, 將貨物在約定日期或期間內運至指定之邊境地點; ㈡提供買方一套習用之運輸文件、棧單、碼頭存貨憑單或提貨單等, 並予背書, 或將貨物運交買方抑提供買方爲收貨人之邊境交貨提單; ㈢提供輸出許可證或其他轉運所必需之文件; ㈣負擔出口所需關務費、國內稅捐等。買方㈠自接受賣方貨物交其處理後, 卽擔負一切風險及費用, 並負責在指定之邊境地點提貨; ㈡支付繼續轉運費用。

（十）Delivered Duty Paid（named place of destination）

Delivered Duty Paid 係指賣方須在目的地交貨，並付進口稅捐之交貨條件（本條係一九六七年增訂）。也卽是說，賣方所負的風險及費用，已由"Ex Works"超越"Customs border"而至買方國境指定之交貨地點。因此，此項貿易條件，有類買方國內之內銷交易。依照此條件，賣方㈠須負一切風險及費用，在約定日期及期間內將貨物運往輸入國家買方指定之地點交與買方處理（at the disposal of the buyer）；㈡提供買方一套習用之運輸文件、棧單、碼頭存貨憑單或提貨單等，並加背書，或將貨物運交買方抑提供買方為收貨人之目的地指定地點交貨的提單；㈢提供輸入許可證，並擔負進口關稅及稅捐，（包括通關費及其他稅捐或與輸入有關費用）。

　　賣方如不願負擔買方國家之附加價值稅及其他類似之稅捐，應在合約內註明"exclusive of VAT（value added tax）and/or taxes"。

（十一）FOB Airport

　　FOB Airport 係一九七六年依照 FOB 主要原則發展之新貿易條件。其內容如下：

(A)賣方之義務：

1. 供應與銷售合約相符之貨物，並檢附合約所需之符合證件。

2. 將貨物運交買方指定之航空公司、代理人或其他任何人收管。如未指定航空公司、代理人或其他人時，則可交賣方選擇之航空公司或其代理人收管。上項貨物，必須在合約規定日期或期間內依照機場慣常方式運至買方指定之啓飛機場交貨。

3. 除買方或賣方給予對方相反之迅速指示外，賣方應為買方洽訂運貨契約，由買方負擔運費。賣方應依照下列 B.1 條買方之指示簽訂運貨契約，並按通常運價將貨物空運至最接近買方營業所之指定目的地機場交貨。此項飛機，必須取道通常航線，並使用通常空運貨物之機型。

4. 賣方負擔風險及費用取得輸出許可證或其他貨物輸出必需之官方許可。

5. 除依照下列B.6及B.7條之規定外，支付有關貨物輸出徵收之任何稅捐及費用。

6. 除依照下列B.6及B.7之規定外，負擔任何有關空運之額外費用，直至依照以上A.2條規定將貨運交時為止。

7. 除依照下列B.6及B.7之規定外，負責貨物之一切風險至交貨時為止。

8. 賣方負擔費用提供適於空運貨物之適當保護包裝，但貿易習慣不用包裝運送者，不在此限。

9. 支付交貨必需之任何查核工作費用，包括核對品質、丈量、過磅及計數等。

10. 應自費立即電知買方貨已照交。

11. 如發生下列 B.6及B.7 條所列事件，應迅即以電傳電報通知買方此項事件發生之情況。

12. 提供買方適當格式之商業發票，以配合其規定要求。並徇買方要求由買方負擔費用，提供產地證明書。

13. 除上述 A.12 條之文件外，得徇買方要求協助其取得因貨物輸入目的地國所需之啓飛國或原產國發給之其他任何文件，但此項風險及費用，應由買方負擔。

14. 徇買方要求並由買方負擔風險及費用，依照下列B.6條之規定，給予買方一切協助向航空公司或其代理人提出關於貨運賠償之要求。

(B)買方之義務：

1. 適時通知賣方交貨之目的地機場，並給予適當之指示（如有必要），俾利貨物從指定之啓運機場運出。

2. 如賣方不願簽訂運貨契約時，買方必須自費安排將貨物由指定之啓運機場起運，並適時通知賣方此項安排。該項買方通知，必須說明負責裝運之航空公司或其代理抑其他任何人之名稱，以便賣方可將貨物交其負責裝運。

3. 除上述A.5條之規定外，須負擔依A.2條規定從賣方交貨時起有關貨物應付之一切費用。

4. 支付發票依據合約所列貨款及空運費（如後者已由賣方代付）。

5. 依照上述A.2條之規定，負擔從賣方交貨時起之一切貨物風險。

6. 如買方指定之航空公司代理人或其他任何人在賣方送貨時不予接管，其所發生之額外費用應由買方負擔，並從交貨時起負擔一切風險，但應以貨物經正式撥歸該合約，亦即明白提出保留或證明爲該合約所定貨物者爲限。

7. 如買方未適時對賣方提供適當之運貨指示時，其因此所發生之額外費用由買方負擔，並自約定交貨日期起或約定交貨期限之終了時起，負擔貨物之一切風險，但應以貨物經正式撥歸該合約，亦即明白提出保留或證明爲該合約所定貨物者爲限。

8. 負擔上述A.13條賣方因取得其他文件所需一切費用（包括領事文件及產地證明書費用）。

9. 負擔賣方代向航空公司或其代理爲追訴或索賠貨物所發生之一切費用。

（十二）Free Carrier（named point）

Free Carrier 係指貨物運送至買方指定地點交與指定之運送人接收處理的最新貿易條件。此項交易條件，係爲適應現代運輸之需要而於一九八〇年訂立的，尤其在近十餘年來複合式運輸 (multimodal transport) 已為國際運輸業所普遍採用後，貨櫃在駛進駛出型 (roll-on-roll-off type) 之拖車及渡船上轉駁運送已極普遍。因此，乃以 FOB 主要原則為基礎另訂此新條件，但賣方之責任界限祇負責至將貨物交與指定地點之指定運送人 (carrier) 保管處理為止。如合約未指定明確之地點 (precise point)，則當事人可說明地點之範圍，使運送人能提貨保管。對貨物滅失或損害的風險，則于貨物從賣方運交買方指定之運送人時起即轉移買方，並非在超過船舷欄杆之時。本條所稱運送人 (carrier)，係指承接公路、鐵路、航空、海運或複式聯合運輸之任何簽約人。賣方之義務祇須提供買方此項提單 (Bill of Lading)、空運提單或運送人之收據，即已完成提供裝運文件 (shipping documents) 之責任。茲將本條內容逐項譯述如次：

(A)賣方之義務：

1. 供應與銷售契約符合之貨物，並檢附契約所需之符合證件。

2. 在約定之日期或期間內，將貨物依照同意或習慣方式運至買方指定地點交與買方指定之運送人接收管理。如未指定明確之地點或有幾個地點均可交貨時，賣方得選擇其中最適當之地點交貨。

3. 自行負擔風險及費用，取得輸出許可證及其他貨物輸出必需之官方許可。

4. 除下列 B.5 條之規定外，支付貨物出口之稅捐及費用。

5. 除下列 B.5 條之規定外，依照上述 A.2 條規定負擔貨物一切費用至運交指定地點之運送人時為止。

6. 除下列 B.5 條之規定外，依照上述 A.2 條規定負擔貨物一切風險至運交指定地點之運送人時為止。

7. 自費提供貨物之慣用包裝 (customary packing)，但依照商業習慣無須使用包裝者，不在此限。

8. 支付交貨必需之任何查核工作費用，包括核對品質、丈量、過磅及計數等。

9. 應以電傳電報立即通知買方貨已運交，不得延遲。

10. 如發生下列 B.5 條所列事件，應以電傳電報立即通知買方此項事件發生之情況。

11. 自行負擔費用，並依上述 A.2 條之規定按照習慣提供買方提貨所需通常單據或其他證明文件。

12. 提供買方適當格式之商業發票，俾可符合有關規定；並徇買方要求，由買方負擔費用提供產地證明書。

13. 應買方要求，協助其取得上述 A.12 條規定以外之其他貨物在目的地進口及轉運途中必需之有關起運或原產國家所發的文件，但其風險及費用應由買方負擔。

(B)買方之義務：

1. 自行負擔費用簽訂自指定地點起運之運送合約，並適時通知賣方該運送人之名稱及交貨日期，以便賣方將貨物逕交運送人。

2. 除上述 A.4 條規定之費用外，應負擔依上述 A.2 條規定從賣方交貨時起之一切費用。

3. 支付合約規定貨款。

4. 自賣方依照上述 A.2 條規定交付貨物時起，負擔貨物之一切風險。

5. 負擔因未於約定時間指定運送人或運送人未及時提貨所發生之任何額外費用，以及自規定交貨期屆滿時起一切貨物風險，但應以貨物經正式撥歸該合約，亦即明白提出保留或證明為該合約所定貨物者為限。

6. 負擔取得 A.13 條規定之文件費用，包括領事文件及產地證明書費用。

(十三) Freight or Carriage Paid to (named point of destination)

"Freight or Carriage Paid to" 係指賣方須負擔運費將貨物運至指定目的地之貿易條件。此係配合現代運輸於一九八〇年訂定的。此項條件有類原有之 C.&F. 條件，但其對貨物滅失或損害之風險，不是在貨物超越船舶欄杆時轉移買方，而是在貨物運交第一個運送人 (first carrier) 接收時即已轉移買方。賣方祇須提供載明貨物運至指定目的地之提貨單、空運提單或運送人之收貨收據，賣方即已完成其交貨義務。

茲將本條內容逐項譯述如次:

(A)賣方之義務:

1. 提供與銷售契約符合之貨物，並檢附契約所需之符合證件。

2. 自行負擔費用簽訂運送合約，將貨物依照習慣方式經由通常路線運往目的地之指定地點交貨。如未約定地點或不能依習慣決定者，賣方得選擇目的地之最適當地點交貨。

3. 除下列 B.3 條之規定外，負擔貨物風險至運交契約指定之第一個運送人 (first carrier) 時為止。

4. 應以電傳電報立即通知買方貨物已運交第一個運送人接收，不得延遲。

5. 自費提供貨物之慣用包裝 (customary packing)，但依照商業習慣無須使用包裝者，不在此限。

6. 支付裝運貨物交與第一個運送人接收所需之查核工作費用，包括核對品質、丈量、過磅及計數等。

7. 自費提供買方習慣上通常需要之運輸文件。

8. 負擔風險及費用，取得輸出許可證及貨物出口所必需之官方許可，並支付有關貨物輸出之稅捐及費用，包括任何出口稅及爲完成貨物裝運所需之任何手續費用。

9. 提供買方適當格式之商業發票，俾可符合有關規定，並徇買方要求，由買方負擔費用提供產地證明書。

10. 應買方要求，協助其取得前條規定以外之其他貨物轉運時必需之有關起運國或原產地國家所發文件。

(B)買方之義務:

1. 在目的地約定之地點收貨，並依約支付貨款及除運費以外之其他運輸途中所發生之一切費用](包括卸貨費)，但已包括在運費以內或已由運送人在收運費時已繳付者，不在此限。

2. 自賣方依 A.3 條規定將貨物交與第一個運送人時起負擔一切貨物風險。

3. 如買方有權保留貨物一段時間，以決定貨物是否逕運交其本人或運交其選擇之目的地點時，買方如未適時給賣方指示，其所發生之額外費用及限期屆滿後之一切風險，應由買方負責，但應以貨物經正式撥歸該合約，亦卽明白提出保留或證明該合約所定貨物者爲限。

4. 負擔取得 A.10 條規定之文件費用，包括領事文件及產地證明書費用。

5. 支付進口時或因進口所需繳納之關稅及其他稅捐。

(十四) Freight or Carriage and Insurance Paid to (named point of destination)

此係一九八〇年新增訂之貿易條件。此項交易條件與 "Freight or Carriage Paid to" 之條件相同，祇增加賣方應投保標的物在運輸途中之減失或損害的風險及負擔其保險費而已。

在此條款下，賣方之風險於貨物運交第一個運送人接收時卽已轉移買方，所以買方主要依靠運輸保險條款以求保障。買方亦有權向運送人索賠，但此項權利往往價值不大，因運送人有除外責任及賠償金額的限制。因此，買方如遇投保之貨物發生滅失或損害時，往往轉向保險公司索賠。其投保金額通常係按 CIF 貨值加百分之十。

　　貨物一經投保運輸保險（transport insurance），買方可從保險公司得到貨物之損失賠償，故必須放棄其對運送人之索賠權利給保險公司（卽債權之代位權）。但買方仍須向運送人提出損失賠償之要求，以便保險公司取得代位權後向運送人索賠（卽追索權行爲）。

　　由於"Freight or Carriage and Insurance Paid to"之運輸風險遠較過去傳統之 CIF 爲基礎的範圍大，其保險金額自應加大，蓋保險範圍業已脫出海上保險（marine insurance）之範疇也。因此，買賣雙方必須先行就貨物性質及可能發生之風險情況加以考慮，以便決定其應投保之適當保險條款。同時，賣方投保後應卽電報通知買方，如遇買方認爲合約原約定之保險條款及金額不足以包括可能發生之風險時，得增加投保。

4-1-2　國際商會與美國之貿易條件的比較

　　玆擬就國際商會與美國之各種貿易條件純粹與外銷有關者，從買賣雙方之義務及費用負擔與風險之分界，作一比較如下。除以中文說明外，爲使讀者易於直接了解起見，特再就原文摘要列表如次，俾讀者可增加體會其原文眞諦。

　　FAS——國際商會所稱 FAS，係 Free alongside Ship 三字之縮寫，而美國定義之 FAS，則指 Free along Side 三字之縮寫，故依照美國定義必須在 FAS 之後另加 Vessel 一字，始與 INCOTERMS 之意義相同。依據國際商會 INCOTERMS 之解釋，在 FAS 條件下，商品必須送至船邊，並安放在船邊之碼頭（quay or dock）或靠船之駁艇中（in lighters）；而美國定義則須送至碼頭或由駁艇送至船邊索具可達之範圍內。後者規定駁艇靠船必須在裝貨索具可達範圍內，其定義似較前者更為明確。INCOTERMS 規定賣方得應買方要求代辦出口文件，費用由買方負擔。美國定義亦規定所有申領出口文件之費用由買方負擔，但在 FAS 評註，則說明在美國 FAS 條件下，雖規定洽取海運船位及購買海上保險與兵險係買方責任，惟實務上頗多交易係洽由賣方代辦，故究應由誰辦理，買賣雙方應先有所了解。又賣方為保護其本身權益，宜指定買方投保標準之倉庫至倉庫海上保險（standard warehouse to warehouse coverage），希業者多加注意。

FOB——國際商會之 FOB 條件，係指 FOB Vessel 而言，乃從大英國協歷史性之解釋，而美國習慣所謂 FOB，係指 FOB Carrier or Point of Place 之統稱，其中相當于國際商會條件者祇 FOB Vessel 一種。按照此種條件交易者，內銷商可將商品以內銷或外銷計價方式售與國內之出口商，而出口商再轉售國外商人。買方之責任，在指定輪船或預定艙位及通知賣方其所定之船名、裝船地點及日期；賣方之責任，在依照指定之日期或期限，將商品運往指定港口裝船。依照國際商會 INCOTERMS 之解釋，賣方負擔之費用及風險，祇負責至將商品裝上船舶超越船舷之欄桿為止（effectively passed the ship's rail），並以 Ship's Rail 為交貨之分界點（point of delivery），商品超越欄桿後之滅失或損害風險即轉移買方負擔。而美國解釋，賣方之費用及風險，必須負責至將商品實際放置在船上（loaded on board the vessel）為止，因此其承擔之風險，乃延長至安放妥當始告終止。此為兩者解釋不同之一。又 INCOTERMS 規定，賣方須負責領取輸出許可證及支付所有出口稅捐，但美國解釋則應全由買方負責。此為兩者解釋不同之二。依

Table 1

Compared items	FAS—INCOTERMS	FAS Vessel—American Defination
Seller's obligation & risks	Deliver the goods at his own risks & expense alongside the vessel at the loading berth (on the quay or in lighters) named by the buyer at the named port of shipment on the date or within the period stipulated. notify the buyer without delay that the goods have been delivered alongside the vessel.	Delivered the goods at his risks and expense alongside the overseas vessel within reach of its loading tackle or on the dock designated and provided by, or for, buyer on the date or within the period fixed
Buyer's obligation & risks	Nominate carrier & give the seller due notice of the name, loading berth of and delivery date to the vessel. Bear all the charges & risks of the goods from the time when they have been effectively delivered alongside the vessel at the named port of shipment at the date or within the period stipulated. If failed to name the vessel or to give instruction in time, bear the additional cost & all risks of the goods from the date of expiration of the period stipulated for delivery.	Give seller adequate notice of the name, sailing date, loading berth of and delivery time to, the vessel. Responsible for any loss or damage, or both, while the goods are on a lighter or other conveyance alongside within reach of its loading tackle, or on the dock awaiting loading, or until actually loaded on board the vessel & subsequent thereto.
Expenses for:		
1. Customary packing	Seller's responsibility	seller's responsibility
2. Checking operation(such as checking quality, weighing, measuring, counting)	—do—	—do—
3. Loading	Buyer's responsibility	Buyer's responsibility
4. Export duties & taxes	—do—	—do—
5. Insurance	—do—	—do—
6. Documents:		
a. Export Licence	Obtain at buyer's request & expense	obtain at buyer's request & expense
b. Commercial invoice	Provided by seller	provided by seller
c. Alongside or dock receipt	—do—	—do—
d. Bill of Lading	Buyer's responsibility	Buyer's responsibility
e. Consular invoice	—do—	provided by seller at buyer's request & expense
f. Certificate of origin	Provided by seller at buyer's request & expense	—do—
h. Documents required for importation and/or for transit thru another country	Assist to obtain at buyer's request & expense	assist to obtain at buyer's request & expense.

Table 2

Compared items	FOB-INCOTERMS	FOB Vessel-American Defination
Seller's obligation & risks	Deliver the goods at his own risks & expense on board the vessel named by the buyer at the named port of shipment on the date or within the period stipulated.	Place the goods at his own risks & expense actually on board the vessel designated & provided by, or for, the buyer on the date or within the period fixed.
Buyer's obligation & risks	Charter a vessel or reserve a shipping space on board a vessel and give the seller due notice of the name, loading berth & delivery date.	Give seller adequate notice of name, sailing date, loading berth of, and delivery time to, the vessel.
	Bear all costs & risks of the goods from the time when they have effectively passed the ship's rail.	Responsible for any loss or damage, or both, after goods have been loaded on board the vessel.
	If failed to name the vessel or to give instructions in time, bear the additional costs & all risks of the goods from the date of expiration of the period stipulated.	Bear the additional costs & all risks of the goods from the time when the seller has placed them at his disposal if the vessel named by him fails to arrive or to load within the designated time.
Expenses for:		
1. Customary packing	Seller's responsibility	Seller's responsibility
2. Checking operation (Such as checking quality, measuring, weighing, counting)	—do—	—do—
3. Loading	—do— (according to custom of the port)	—do—
4. Export duties & taxes	—do—	—do—
5. Insurance	Buyer's responsibility	Buyer's responsibility
6. Documents:		
a. Export licence	Seller's responsibility	Buyer's expense
b. Commercial invoice	Provided by seller	Provided by seller
c. Customary clean receipt (mate's receipt)	—do—	Seller provides ship's receipt or on board B/L with ocean freight to be borne by buyer
d. Bill of lading	Obtain at buyer's request, risk & expense	
f. Consular invoice	Provide at buyer's request & expense	Provide at buyer's request & expense
g. Certificate of origin	—do—	—do—
h. Documents required for importation and/or for transit thru another country	Obtain at buyer's request & expense	Obtain at buyer's request & expense

照 INCOTERMS 之規定, 船方之清潔收貨單 (clean receipt) 由賣方提供, 但裝船提單得協助買方向船方領取, 費用由買方負擔。美國定義則規定賣方必須提供船方清潔收貨單或裝船提單; 換句話說, 領取裝船提單之單證費仍應由賣方負擔。此為兩者解釋不同之三。

C&F and CIF ── 國際商會之 C&F 及 CIF 條件, 雖均負擔商品至目的港之運費, 但其風險之分界點 (division of risk) 則仍以船舷之欄桿 (ship's rail) 為準, 又所謂 "On Board" the Vessel, 係指 "Shipped on Board"的意思, 如係 Received for Shipment 者, 祇提供 Received for Shipment Form of B/L 仍不足, 必須俟商品裝上船, 經船方或其授權人加蓋 "Shipped on Board" 膠章轉變為 "Shipped on Board B/L" 後始有效; 換句話說, 在商品仍在備運期間, 尚未裝上船舶者, 其風險仍歸賣方負擔。但依照美國定義, 凡以提供 On Board B/L為交易條件者, 其風險之分界點仍以商品交送至船上 (delivered on board the vessel)為止, 而在提供備運海運提單 (received for shipment B/L) 的場合, 則賣方之風險祇負責至將商品運交海運運送人保管 (delivered into the custody of the ocean carrier)為止, 無須俟裝船後加蓋"Shipped on Board" 之膠章即可。此為兩者不同之處。在 CIF 條件下, 國際商會規定海上保險祇須按 CIF 貨值加百分之十投保 F.P.A. 平安險即可, 如買方不要求代保兵險, 則無此代保義務。至美國定義, 在海上保險方面雖無特別規定, 但在兵險一項, 則特別規定, 除非賣方同意買方購買, 否則必須由賣方代為投保, 費用由買方負擔。

Ex Quay/Ex Dock ── 國際商會之 Ex Quay 條件, 常用者有兩種: 一種係 Ex Quay (Duty Paid), 一種是 Ex Quay (Duty on Buyer's Account); 而美國之 Ex Dock, 則規定除非另有協議, 賣方必須繳納進口國家必要之進口稅及其他稅捐。又依照國際商會 Ex Quay 之規

Table 3

Compared items	C&F-INCOTERMS	C&F (named point of destination)—American Defination
1. Seller's obligation & risks	(a) Contract at his own expense for carriage of the goods to the agreed port of destination by the usual route. (b) Load the goods at his own risks & expense on board the vessel at the port of shipment and at the date or within the time fixed. (c) Notify the buyer without delay after the goods have been loaded on board the vessel.	(a) Provide and pay the transportation to the name port of destination. (b) where received-for-shipment B/L is required be responsible for any loss or damage, or both, until the goods have been delivered into the custody of the ocean carrier; where on-board clean B/L is required, be responsible for any loss or damage, or both, until the goods have been delivered on board the vessel.
2. Buyer's obligation & risks	(a) Bear all risks of the goods from the time when they have been effectively passed the ship's rail at the port of shipment. (b) Bear all costs & charges incurred in the course of transit until their arrival at the agreed port of destination.	Responsible for loss of or damage to goods, or both, from the time and place at which seller's obligations under (b) above have ceased.
3. Expenses for:		
1) Customary packing	Seller's responsibility	Seller's responsibility
2) Checking operation	—do—	—do—
3) Loading	—do—	—do—
4) Export duties & taxes	—do—	—do—
5) Insurance	Buyer's responsibility	Buyer's responsibility
6) Documents:		
a. Export licence	Seller's responsibility	Seller's responsibility
b. Commercial invoice	Provided by seller	provided by seller
c 1. on-board/shipped B/L or	—do—	—do—
2. received-for-shipment B/L	(with "shipped on board" endorsement).	(need not endorse or stamp the words "shipped on board")
d. Consular invoice	Provided by seller at buyer's request and expense	Provided by seller at buyer's request & expense
e. Certificate of origin	—do—	—do—
f. Documents required for importation and/or for transit thru another country	Assist to obtain at buyer's request & expense	Assist to obtain at buyer's request and expense

Table 4

Compared items	CIF—INCOTERMS	CIF (named point of destination)—American Defination
1. Seller's obligation & risks	Bear all costs & risks as mentioned in above C&F terms and cover marine insurance on F.P.A. terms at his own expense	Bear all costs & risks as mentioned in above C&F terms and cover the agreed marine insurance(W.A. or F.P.A.)at his own expense with war risk coverage to be borne by buyer.
2. Buyer's obligation & risks	(a) Bear all costs & risks as mentioned in above C.&F. terms. (b) If a policy of marine insurance is required to cover additional special risks, the charges will be borne by buyer.	(a) Responsible for loss of or damage to the goods, or both, from the time and place at which seller's obligations have ceased. (b) Pay for war risk insurance covered by seller.
3. Expenses for:		
1) Customary packing	Seller's responsibility	Seller's responsibility
2) Checking operation	—do—	—do—
3) Loading	—do—	—do—
4) Export duties & taxes	—do—	—do—
5) Insurance	Covered by seller	Covered by seller
6) Documents		
a. Export licence	Seller's responsibility	Scller's responsibility
b. Commercial invoice	Provided by seller	Provided by seller
c.1. on-board/shipped B/L or	—do—	—do—
2. received-for-shipment B/L	(with "shipped on board" endorsement)	(need not endorse or stamp the words "shipped on board")
d. Consular invoice	Provided by seller at buyer's request and expense	Provided by seller at buyer's request & expense
e. Certificate of origin	—do—	—do—
f. Documents required for importation and/or for transit thru another country	Assist to obtain at buyer's request & expense	Assist to obtain at buyer's request & expense

Table 5

Compared items	Ex Quay-INCOTERMS	Ex Dock (named port of importation)-American Defination
1. Seller's obligation & risks	Place the goods at his own costs & risks at the disposal of the buyer on the quay or wharf at the agreed port of destinaton and at the time as provided in the contract	(a) Bear costs & risks to place the goods on the dock at the named port of importation. (b) Responsible for any loss or damage, or both, until the expiration of the free time allowed on the dock at the named port of importation.
2. Buyer's obligation & risks	Bear all risks & expense of the goods until such time as they have been effectively placed at the disposal of the buyer.	Bear the costs & risks of the goods if delivery is not taken within the free time allowed.
3. Expenses for:		
1) Customary packing	Seller's responsibility	Seller's responsibility
2) Checking operation	—do—	—do—
3) Loading & unloading charges both at ports of shipment & destination	—do—	—do—
4) Export & import duties & taxes(including customs clearance)	—do— (If the seller doesn't want to pay import duties & taxes, he has to add words "duties on buyer's account")	—do—
5) Insurance	Covered by seller	—do— (provide & pay for war risk insurance)
6) Documents:		
a. Export & import licences	—do—	Seller's responsibility
b. Commercial invoice	Provided by seller	Provided by seller
c. Delivery order &/or any other documents	—do—	—do—
d. Consular invoice	Provided by seller at his expense	Provided by seller at his expense
e. Certificate of origin	—do—	—do—

定，賣方所負擔之費用及風險，應負責至將商品送至指定之進口港碼頭交買方處置（at buyer's disposal）時爲止；換句話說，賣方將商品放置碼頭後，其風險即已轉移買方。而美國之 Ex Dock，則規定賣方應負責將商品運送至進口港碼頭，直至容許免費期限屆滿時（until the expiration of the free time allowed on the dock）爲止，其所負之風險時限自較 INCOTERMS 爲長。再者，INCOTERMS 以賣方須負一切風險將商品運至買方之進口國家碼頭交貨，自可視運途有無戰爭情況自行決定是否須加保兵險，故無必要硬性規定賣方必須投保兵險。而美國之 Ex Dock，依其評註解釋，主要在供進口貿易使用，目的在保護其進口商，故在賣方義務之第(4)款規定，除非另有協議，賣方必須投保兵險，並支付保險費。

Delivered Duty Paid (named place of destination in the country of importation) /**FOB** (named inland point in the country of importation)——此係進口國家內陸地點交貨之貿易條件。INCOTERMS 規定，賣方必須負擔風險及費用將商品在約定日期或期限內運至進口國家買方指定之內陸地點交由買方處理，並將運輸文件提供買方。其交貨方式，可交由第一運送人（first carrier）將商品運至指定目的地或自備運輸工具將商品逕運該指定目的地。一旦完成上項義務，商品之一切風險即已轉移買方。美國定義則規定賣方必須負責將商品裝由運輸工具運至進口國家買方指定之內陸地點交貨爲止（指明until arrival of goods on conveyance）。前者所謂交貨地點範圍較廣，而後者指明在運輸工具上交貨，似有多少區別。

Table 6

Compared items	Delivered Duty Paid—INCOTERMS	FOB (named inland point in country of importation)—American Defination
1. Seller's obligation & risks	(a) Deliver the goods at his own costs & risks at the disposal of the buyer, duty paid, at the named place of destination in the country of importation on the date or within the period stipulated. (b) Notify the buyer that the goods have been placed in the custody of the first carrier for despatch to the named place of destination or they have been dispatched to that destination by his own means of transport.	(a) Deliver the goods at his own costs & risks to the named inland point in the country of importation. (b) Responsible for any loss or damage, or both, until arrival of goods on conveyance at the named inland point in the country of importation.
2. Buyer's obligation & risks	Bear all the risks of the goods & pay any expenses whatsoever incurred in respect thereof from the time when they have been put at his disposal at the named place of destination.	(a) Take prompt delivery of goods from conveyance upon arrival at destination. (b) Bear any costs and be responsible for any loss or damage, or both, after arrival.
3. Expenses for:		
1) Customary packing	Seller's responsibility	Seller's responsibility
2) Checking operation	—do—	—do—
3) Export & import duties & taxes	—do—	—do—
4) Insurance	—do—	—do— (including war risks unless otherwise agreed upon)
5) Landing, discharged or landed charges (including lighterage, wharfing, warehousing & handling charges)	—do—	Seller's responsibility
6) Documents:		
a. Export & import licences	—do—	—do—
b. Commercial invoice	Provided by seller.	Provided by seller
c. Delivery order, warehouse warrant, dock warrant or the like	—do—	—do—
d. Consular invoice	Provided by seller at his expense	Provided by seller at his expense
e. Certificate of origin	—do—	—do—

4-1-3 國際商會 INCOTERMS 與華沙牛津規則之比較

國際法學會於一九三二年修訂華沙牛津規則，爲專供 CIF 契約使用之規則，故其英文名稱爲"Warsaw-Oxford Rules for CIF Contracts"。國際商會在一九三六年制定國際統一貿易條件之 INCOTERMS 時，其 CIF terms 卽係採納其定義。該華沙牛津 CIF 契約規則共二十一條，其中十條重要條款，均已納入 INCOTERMS 之 CIF terms。其餘條款爲：㈠約定之特定船舶種類不得任意代替；㈡貨物所有權於單證交予買方後，卽轉移買方占有；㈢買方有義務接受適當之單證，不得拒付貨款；㈣買方在貨物裝運前或抵達目的地後，有權在適當之機會（a reasonable opportunity）下檢查，一旦發現有隱藏缺陷與固有瑕疵時，並享有救濟權利等❼。茲將兩者具有相同原文條款列后，以供讀者作比較參考：

4-2 契約之履行

賣方出售商品，爲履行其契約義務，必須經過三個階段，卽交付商品，轉移商品之所有權，並轉移商品之風險。買方之義務，在接受賣方商品，並支付價款。茲擬分別敍述買賣雙方所應盡之契約義務如下。

4-2-1 賣方義務

4-2-1-1 應有權出售商品

商品買賣之首要條件，爲賣方必須具有出售商品之權力（seller's right to sell the goods）。英國一九七三年之商品供應(默示條款) 法

---

❼ 國際貿易局與司法行政部民事司編譯「國際貿易法規暨慣例彙編」第一册
張錦源教授譯「華沙牛津規則」, pp. 621–637.

國際商會 INCOTERMS 與華沙牛津規則 CIF 條款之比較

INCOTERMS-CIF Terms	*Correspond to:* Warsaw-Oxford Rules for CIF Contract
A. Seller must:	
1. Supply the goods in conformity with the contract of sale.	Rule 2
2. Contract on usual terms at his own expense for carriage of the goods to the agreed port of destination by the usual route in a seagoing vessel.	Rule 7(1)
3. At his own risk and expense obtain any export licence.	Rule 14(1)
4. Load the goods at his own expense on board the vessel at the port of shipment and at the date or within the period fixed or, if neither date or time has been stipulated, within a reasonable time.	Rule 2 Rule 3(1)
Notify the buyer, without delay, that goods have been loaded on board the vessel.	Rule 13
5. Procure, at his own cost and in a transferrable form, a policy of marine insurance against the risks of carriage involved in the contract (cover min. F.PA. terms). Shall provide war risk insurance when required by the buyer and at the latter's expense.	Rule 12(1) Cover risks by the usage of trade
6. Bear all risks of the goods untill such time as they shall have effectively passed the ship's rail at the port of shipment.	Rule 5
7. At his own expense furnish to the buyer a clean negotiable bill of lading for the agreed port of destination, as well as the invoice of goods shipped and the insurance policy or a certificate of insurance.	Rule 7(1) Rule 16(1)
11. Provide the buyer, at the latter's request and expense with certificate of origin and the consular invoice.	Rule 14(11)
12. Render the buyer, at the latter's request, risk and expense, every assistance in obtaining any documents, other than those mentioned in the previous articles.	Rule 15
B. Buyer must:	
1. Accept the documents when tendered by the seller, if they are in conformity with the contract of sale, and pay the price as provided in the contract.	Rule 18(1)

Sect. 12(1)(a)曾有下列規定:

賣方必須有權出售商品 (has a right to sell the goods)，如將來有權出售 (will have a right to sell) 商品，必須在轉移此財產 (商品) 時具有所有權●。

美國統一商法 Sect. 2-707(1) 對賣主之地位，曾作概括之定義如下:

任何人具有賣主地位者，除賣主本身外，包括代表賣主已付商品價款或可代表賣主出價之代理人，抑或對商品具有保證權益或其他類似權利之人，均得稱為賣方。

上面所稱「權」(right)，即「權力」(power) 的意思; 也即是說，賣方在出售商品時，必須有處理商品的權力。賣方如非商品所有權人時，必須取得商品所有權人之授權或同意 (under the authority or with the consent of the owner)，方可出售; 否則必須對商品具有保證權益之權利人，在處理債務人之商品時出售其商品。

其次，所售商品必須係第三者不能提出任何權利或要求之商品，否則其所有權就有問題。關于此點，英國一九七三年之商品供應法 Sect. 12(1)(b)亦規定:

在簽約時，默示條款保證賣方在商品所有權轉移前，並無設定抵押於第三者及其他任何費用者，買方可安靜地取得商品 (quiet possession of the goods)，除非已知賣主或第三者因享受設定抵押等利益可能引起干擾。

譬如 Niblett v. Confectioners' materials Co. 一案，被告 (美國公司) 向原告 (英國公司) 洽售奶水3,000听，迨該貨抵達英國後，遭英國海關扣留，因該批貨物冒用某英國著名廠牌之商標，由該廠取得法院禁令扣留發售，因此賣方乃無權在英國售貨。這是第三者對賣方提出權

● P. S. Atiyah: *The Sale of goods*, ch. 8, p. 48.

利的一個例證 ❷。

　　關于賣方不應交送第三者有任何權利或要求之商品一節，聯合國之國際商品買賣公約第四十一、四十二及四十三條有下列規定：

　　第四十一條：賣方所交付的貨物，必須係第三者不能提出任何權利或要求的貨物，除非買方同意在這種權利或要求的條件下，收取貨物。但是，如果這種權利或要求是以工業財產權 (industrial property) 或其它智慧財產權 (intellectual property) 爲基礎的，賣方的義務應依照第四十二條的規定。

　　第四十二條：(1)賣方所交付的貨物，必須係第三者不能根據工業財產權或其他智慧財產權主張任何權利或要求的貨物，但以賣方在訂立合同時已知道或不可能不知道的權利或要求爲限，而且這種權利或要求係根據以下國家法律規定以工業財產權或其它智慧財產權爲基礎者：

　　(a)如果雙方當事人在訂立合同時預期貨物將在某一國境內轉售或作其他使用，則根據貨物將在其境內轉售或作其他使用之國家法律；或者

　　(b)在任何其他情況下，根據買方營業地所在國家的法律。

　　(2)賣方在上一款中的義務不適用于以下情況：

　　(a)買方在訂立合同時已知道或不可能不知道此項權利或要求；或者

　　(b)此項權利或要求的發生，係由于賣方須遵照買方所提供的技術圖樣、圖案、程式或其他規格。

　　第四十三條：(1)買方如果不在已知道或理應知道第三者的權利或要求後一段合理時間內，將此一權利或要求的性質通知賣方，就喪失援引第四十一條或第四十二條規定的權利。

　　(2)賣方如果知道第三者的權利或要求以及此一權利或要求的性質，就無權援引上一款的規定。

　　上述工業財產權應包括商標 (trade mark)、新型 (utility models)、工業新式樣 (industrial designs)、商號名稱 (trade name)；至智慧財產權亦可譯爲智慧所有權，應包括專門技術知識 (technical know-how) 及製造之程式或程序 (production formula or process) 等。此係政府對發明人 (inventor) 核准賦予一定期限之合法的專利特權，以排斥他人製造、使用或銷售其已專利之產品、商號標誌、名稱或

---

❷　P. S. Atiyah: *The Sale of Goods*, ch. 8, p. 48-49.

使用之製造方法或程序。

各國政府爲保護發明人之合法特權，均訂有專利法（Patent Law）以保障其權益。目前全世界已有八十餘國家設有專利機構。我國之專利法係於民國卅三年公佈，於卅八年實施，並於民國四十八年及四十九年兩度修正。

目前的國際專利制度（International Patent System），係依據一八八三年巴黎聯盟公約創設之國際工業財產權保護聯盟（International Union for the Protection of Industrial Property）而建立的。自巴黎公約通過後，曾經數度修訂，迄今已有六十四個工業發達及低度開發之國家參加巴黎聯盟，但我國始終未加盟。

4-2-1-2 交付商品與風險之移轉

賣方之交貨與買方付款，爲買賣雙方相對及同在之條件（counter and concurrent condition）；換句話說，賣方必須準備及願意將商品之所有權轉移買方，以換取買方之價款，而買方則準備及願意付款，以換取商品之所有權。依照一般契約規定，賣方有交付商品之義務，惟交付方式有那幾種？貨物風險及所有權之移轉，其界限又如何劃分？似有再加說明的必要。茲分述如次。

1. 交付之定義

Delivery（交貨）除具交送商品之意義外，在法律上還具有「自願轉移占有」（voluntary transfer of possession）的意思。我國民法第九四六條亦規定，占有之移轉，因占有物之交付而生效力。嚴格說來，交付商品在轉移商品之占有或管理（transfer of the possession or control of goods），並非實質上移轉所有權（passing of property），必須在象徵代表商品權利之提貨單（bill of lading）及其他類似證件移轉買方時，才算是所有權之眞正轉移。買方對賣方商品之眞正占有取決於所有權已否轉移；而所有權之移轉，又取決于買方是否準備及願意付款或賣方已否同意買方以寄售、承兌交單等付款方式交貨。

　　所謂交貨，有兩種型式：一是實質交付（actual delivery）；一是委託承運人運送，以交付提貨之運輸單據代替實際交付。玆分述之。

　　(1)實際交付商品（physical delivery of the actual goods）──最顯明的例子，係由賣方實地將商品運交買方或由買方實地在賣方指定地點直接提貨。如此均構成所有權之轉移。依照美國統一商法 Sect. 2-401(2)規定，除非另有協議，賣方在指定日期地點實地交付（physical delivery）商品，也構成買方對商品之實際占有（physical possession），所有權亦在交貨時轉移。

　　(2)交付商品之權利證券及其他貨運單據──由於國際貿易發達，商品之運輸型態及交運方式，亦日趨複雜。目前趨勢，除買方自行安排運輸者外，多由賣方安排運輸工具，賣方只要依照契約指定之交貨日期地點將商品交予運送人，並取得運輸提單背書後轉移買方，所有權卽告移轉買方。美國統一商法 Sect. 2-401(2)(a)曾規定，賣方商品依約無須在終點（目的地）交付者，其商品所有權在指定日期及地點裝貨時轉移買方。又同法 Sect. 2-503 及 2-504 規定，賣方應依照契約指定之方式、時間及地點交貨，如指示在特定目的地交貨並交付提貨單據者，可按一般習慣，經由銀行途徑轉送貨運證件；如同意將商品交運送人運輸者，其貨運證件之交付方式同。

　　玆以海上貨運為例，將商品交船東（運送人）裝上貨輪後，船東或其代理乃出具提貨單（bill of lading）。這種文件，在法律上及事實上均認為係代表商品（This document in law and in fact represents goods），故亦稱為商品之所有權證券（document of title），蓋運送人之接收商品，在代替接管及轉運商品，買方之取得代表商品所有權之權利證券，也可以認定買方已「推定占有商品」(constructive possession of goods)。英國1889年之 Factors Act, Sect. 1(4)，對商品之所有權證券曾作了一個很好的解釋。它說：提貨單 (bill of lading)、碼頭棧單 (dock warrant)、倉單 (warehouse keeper's certificate)、交貨單 (warrant or order for delivery) 及其他任何證件，在正常交易過程中足爲占有及管理商品之證明文件，或經證件所有人簽字後可以轉讓、交貨或收貨者，均屬之❸。

聯合國買賣公約第三十條對賣方交貨之義務有很明確之規定如下：

賣方必須按照契約與本公約之規定，交付商品，移交一切與商品有

關之單據，並轉移商品所有權 (transfer the property in goods)。

該公約第三十四條復規定，賣方有義務在契約規定之時間、地點及方式將貨運有關單據移交給買方。這裏所稱貨運單據，除各種提貨證件外，包括發票、保險單、裝箱單、領事簽證發票、產地證明書、重量單及品質或化驗單等。至提貨單據，依照國際商會一九七四年之信用狀統一慣例第二十四條規定，除一般所熟知之海運提單 (marine bill of lading) 及聯合貨運單據 (combined transport documents) 外，其他貨運單據應包括鐵路或內陸水路之提單或運貨通知單、雙聯式提單、郵包收據、投郵證明書、航空郵政收據、空運提單、航空貨運通知單或航空收據、卡車公司之提單或其他類似單據。此等單據，凡經運送人或其代理人加蓋收訖戳記或具有簽字，銀行均認其爲合格。其提貨證件之認定範圍更爲擴大了。

(3)交付商品給買方之代理人

賣方得依買方之指示，將商品交付買方之代理人轉移其所有權給買

---

❸ P. S. Atiyah: *The Sale of Goods*, ch. 9, p. 62.

方。　依照英國商品供應法 Sect. 32(1) 條規定，　交付商品給運送人，　實質上亦視同交付商品給買方。茲摘譯其條文如次：

依照契約規定，買方授權或要求賣方將商品送交買方或賣方爲買方運送商品而將該商品送交運送人（carrier），　不拘該運送人是否由買方指定，　實質上亦視同交付買方❹。

2. 商品風險之移轉

普通特定之商品（specific goods），事先必須過磅或丈量、試驗、包裝及標嘜，然後如期送至指定地點交付買方之運輸工具或運送人。交付時，必須保持商品交付之完整情況，買方接收後，商品之風險卽轉移買方。

關于商品風險之轉移,聯合國國際商品買賣公約第六十六、六十七、六十八及六十九條有下列詳細之規定：

第六十七條：(1)如銷售合同涉及貨物的運輸，但賣方無義務在某一特定地點交付貨物者，自貨物按照銷售合同交付第一運送人轉交買方時起，　風險即移轉買方承擔，如賣方有義務在某一特定地點把貨物交付運送人，在貨物于該地點交付運送人前，風險不移轉到買方承擔，賣方授權保留控制貨物處置權的單據，並不影響風險的移轉。

(2)在貨物上加標記、或以裝運單據、或向買方發出通知或其它方式清楚地注明有關合同以前，風險不移轉到買方承擔。

第六十八條：對于在運輸途中銷售的貨物，從訂立合同時起，風險即移轉到買方承擔。但是，如果情況表明有此需要，從貨物交付給簽發載有運輸合同單據的運送人時起，風險就由買方承擔。儘管如此，如賣方在訂立合同時已知道或理應知道貨物已經遺失或損壞，而又不將這一事實告知買方，則這種遺失或損壞應由賣方負責。

第六十九條：(1)在不屬于第六十七條和第六十八條規定的情況下，從買方接收貨物時起，或貨物已交買方處置，而買方不在適當時間內受領，則在買方違約不提貨時起，風險即移轉買方承擔。

(2)如買方有義務在賣方營業地以外的某一地點接收貨物，當交貨時間已到而買

---

❹　P. S. Atiyah: *The Sale of Goods*, ch. 9, p. 63.

方知道貨物已在該地點交給他處置時，風險方始移轉。

(3)如合同所指貨物尚未加識別，則這些貨物在未清楚注明有關合同以前，不得視爲已交給買方處置。

第六十六條　貨物在風險移轉買方承擔後遺失或損壞，買方支付價款的義務並不因此解除，除非這種遺失或損壞是由于賣方的行爲或不行爲所造成。

爲使讀者更了解買賣雙方對商品交付與收受之風險分界起見，特根據國際商會 INCOTERMS 之規定列示如次，以供參考:

1. Ex Works——賣方依契約規定時間負責將貨物交至指定或通常交貨地點由買方處置時爲止，以後風險由買方負擔。

2. FOR,FOT——凡不滿整車之零擔貨物，賣方負責在指定日期或期限內，將貨物送交起運車站收管時爲止，整車者于裝上車輛交路局收管後風險卽歸買方。

3. FAS——賣方負責在規定日期或限期內，將貨物運至指定港口買方指定之船隻停泊處的船邊爲止，以後風險由買方負擔。

4. FOB——賣方負責在規定日期或限期內，將貨物運至指定裝船口岸，並裝上輪船越過船舷欄杆爲止，以後風險由買方負擔。

5. FOB Airport——賣方負責在約定交貨日期或期限內，將貨物運交啓飛機場買方指定之航空公司或代理收管爲止，以後風險由買方負擔。

6. ①*C&F* ②*CIF*——其風險之分界與 FOB Ship 同。

7. ①Freight or Carriage Paid to ②Freight Carriage & Insurance Paid to——賣方負責在契約規定時間，將貨物送交第一運送人收管爲止，以後風險由買方承擔。

8. Ex Ship——賣方負責在契約規定時間內，于指定目的港之通常卸貨地點，在船上將貨物有效交由買方處置爲止，以後風險由買方承擔。

9. *Ex* Quay——賣方負責在契約規定時間，將貨物運往約定港口之碼頭上交由買方處置為止，以後風險由買方負擔。

10. Deliver at Frontier——賣方負責在契約規定日期或期限內，將貨物運至邊境指定交貨地點交由買方處置為止，以後之風險由買方負擔。

11. Delivered Duty Paid——賣方負責在契約規定日期或期限內，將貨物運往指定輸入國內目的地交由買方處置為止，以後風險由買方負擔。

12. Free Carrier (named point) ——賣方負責在契約規定日期或期限內，將貨物運交買方約定地點及指定之運送人收管為止，以後風險由買方負擔。

4-2-1-3　依照約定地點及日期交貨

1. 依照規定地點交貨

任何商品買賣契約均有交貨地點之規定，賣方有義務照指定地點交貨；如賣方無義務在任何特定地點交付商品者，依照聯合國國際商品買賣公約第三十一條之規定，賣方之交貨義務如次：

(a)如果銷售合同涉及到貨物的運輸，賣方應把貨物移交給第一運送人，以運交買方。

(b)在不屬于上一款規定的情況下，如果合同指的是特定貨物或從特定存貨中提取或尚待製造或生產的未經特定化的貨物，而雙方當事人在訂立合同時已知道這些貨物是在某一特定地點，或將在某一特定地點製造或生產，賣方應在該地點把貨物交給買方處置。

(c)在其它情況下，賣方應在其訂立合同時的營業地把貨物交給買方處置。

又該公約第三十二條復規定：賣方如有義務安排貨物運輸時，必須訂立必要之運輸合約，按照通常運輸條件，用適合情況之運輸工具將貨物運達指定地點。英國之商品買賣法 Sect.-32(1)亦有類似之規定。

2.依照規定日期交貨

聯合國國際商品買賣公約第三十三條對於交貨日期有下列明確之規定：

(a)如契約已規定日期，或從契約規定可以確定日期者，應在該日期交貨；

(b)如契約已規定交貨之一定期限，或從契約規定可以確定其交貨之一定期限者，除非情況指明應由買方指定日期外，賣方可在該限期內任何時間交貨；

(c)在其它情況，賣方應在訂約後之合理時間內（within a reasonable time）交貨。

交貨日期為契約之必要條件，賣方如不能如期交貨，卽違反契約條件，買方得拒絕收貨。但買方如放棄此條件，縱使賣方提前交貨，亦得先徵求買方同意。關于賣方之提前交貨，聯合國買賣公約第37條曾作下列規定：

如賣方在交貨日期前交付貨物者，得在到達日期前交付任何缺漏部分或補足所交貨物之不足數量，或交付替換不符契約規定之貨物，或對不符貨物予以補救。但此種權利之行使，不得使買方遭受任何不合理之不便或承擔不合理之開支。買方如因此遭受損失，得保留要求損害賠償之任何權利。

買方如不堅持契約原訂之「交貨日期」條件，依照聯合國買賣公約第四十七條之規定，得另定額外之合理期限，通知賣方履行其交貨義務，屆期如仍不交貨，得拒絕收貨，但買方並不因此而喪失其對賣方延遲履行義務之要求損害賠償權利。茲列舉英國 Charles Richards Ltd.

v. Oppenhaim 一案說明如次:

原告同意供應被告 Rolls Royce 型汽車底盤一個，訂明在一九四八年三月二十日交貨。但屆期並未製就交貨，雖經被告繼續催促，仍未見製交，被告乃於同年六月二十九日通知原告，限期最遲在同年七月二十五日交貨，逾期不收，第直延至同年十月十八日始製就送貨，但爲被告拒絕，於是原告提出控訴。

法庭判決，認爲被告已正式通知原告一個延期交貨之合理期限，原告仍不能如期製交，自可拒絕收貨。❺

4-2-1-4　依照規定數量交付

賣方必須依照契約規定交付正確數量 (right quantity) 之商品，在聯合國買賣公約第三十五條(1)款亦有「賣方交付貨物必須與契約數量相符」之規定。如交付數量少于契約之規定數量，買方得拒絕收貨。又賣方所交數量如大于契約規定，買方得全部拒收，或僅照契約數量接收，其餘退回；倘全部接收，則超過契約部份應照價付款。譬如甲出售100噸小麥給某商乙，甲可能運送 100噸小麥和50噸大麥或50噸小麥和50噸大麥。乙商對第一種情形，可能祇接收契約規定之小麥100噸而將誤送之50噸大麥退回；對第二種情形，可能祇收50噸小麥而退回不合規格之50噸大麥。❻

再者，契約如規定整批交貨時，絕不容許賣方在發現短交後再補交之情形，因買方無義務接收分批交貨。如 Behrend & Co. Ltd. v Produce Brokers Co. 一案，賣方同意訂售一定數量之棉子在倫敦之 Inglis 港交貨，承裝貨船於倫敦卸交部份棉子後立即開往 Hull 卸貨，嗣於14天後

---

❺　P. S. Atiyah: *The Sale of Goods*, ch. 10, pp 65-66.

❻　P. S. Atiyah: *The Sale of Goods*, ch. 11, p. 68.

再駛回倫敦繼續卸交其餘棉子。買方僅接收第一次卸交之棉子而拒絕回程第二次卸貨。法官認爲買方有權拒絕第二次交貨，蓋依據英國商品供應法 Sect.-30(1) 規定，除非另有協議，買方無義務接受整批之分批交貨。 ❼

4-2-1-5 依照規定品質交付

依照規定之品質交付，係一般契約之默示條款。如在契約中加以明確規定，則構成契約之明示條款。這些默示條款，早年見諸英國一八九三年之商品買賣法 (The Sale of Goods Act, 1893)，旋於1973年再納入英國之商品供應（默示條款）法 (The Supply of Goods (implied terms) Act, 1973)，而美國之統一商法則納入商品默示保證條款內。至聯合國之買賣公約第三十五條，規定似較籠統。茲就有關條文抄列如次：

⑴賣方交付之貨物，必須與契約規定之數量、質量及規格相符，並須按照契約規定之方式裝箱或包裝。

⑵除雙方當事人另有協議者外，貨物除非符合下列規定，否則卽爲與契約不符：

(a)貨物適于同一規格貨物通常使用的目的；

(b)于訂約時，買方曾明示或默示通知賣方，貨物須適用於任何特定目的，除非情況顯示，買方並不依賴賣方之技能及判斷力或無正當理由使其信賴者；

(c)貨物品質與賣方向買方提供之貨物樣品或式樣（模型）相同；

關于商品品質之默示條件，可分爲下列三點：

⑴必須符合買方之規格說明、樣品或模型 (conformity to description, sample or model)；

---

❼ P. S. Atiyah: *The Sale of Goods*, ch. 11, p. 67.

(2)必須適于銷售（merchantability）；

(3)必須適用于特殊目的用途（fitness for a particular purpose）。

玆再解說如次：

1. 商品必須符合規格說明、樣品或模型

英國商品供應（默示條款）法 Sect.13(1)有下列規定：

凡銷售商品以規格說明（sale by description）為條件之契約，其默示條款為：商品必須符合規格說明；如憑樣品及規格說明銷售者，其所交商品如規格不符，雖表面上大部份與樣品符合，亦不足構成符合條件。❽

由此可知，凡商品銷售以「規格說明」為條件者，符合規格說明是一個重要條件。玆舉一九六七年 Beale v. Taylor 之案例以說明之：

被告登廣告洽售汽車，其廣告指明其汽車係"HERALD, Convertible, White 1961"，原告依照廣告說明向被告購入後檢驗，發現該車係由兩部份零配件焊接而成，僅一部份屬1961年車型。英國上訴法庭認為廣告說明 "1961 HERALD" 應屬契約條件（contractual term），非祇是一個說明（a mere representation）而已❾。

又如 Re Moore & Co. Ltd. v. Landauer & Co. 案：

甲商某同意向乙商某訂購每箱30听裝澳洲水果罐頭 3,000 听。交貨後，發現約半數係每箱24听裝，而總听數仍為3,000听。英國上訴法庭認為：買方在價格上雖無損失，但已不合其包裝方面之要求，自可拒絕收貨。❿

再者，契約之規格說明必須實際明確，不得含糊不清或失之太籠

---

❽　P. S. Atiyah: *The Sale of Goods*, ch. 12, p. 71.

❾　P. S. Atiyah: *The Sale of Goods*, ch. 12, p. 72.

❿　P. S. Atiyah: *The Sale of Goods*, ch. 12, p. 76.

統。如使用 Fair Average Quality 或 On a Pure Basis 等詞,極易引起解釋上的糾紛。茲試舉規格說明不明確之 Peter Darlington Partners, Ltd. v. Gosho Co. Ltd. 案例如下:

賣方洽售 Canary 草種子50噸,規格訂明"On a Pure Basis"。交貨時,買方發現所交種子純度僅達98%,乃予拒絕接收。事實上,任何東西均無100%之純度,該類種子可能達到之最高純度亦僅98%,賣方照貿易習慣交付最高純度之草種,應屬符合要求。因此法官判決買方拒收98%之種子係屬錯誤。 ⓫

凡憑樣品銷售 (sale by sample) 者,在契約內祇可訂明參考「樣品」字樣,並無任何有關品質之記載,因此英國商品供應法 Sect. 15(2) 規定:凡憑樣品銷售商品者,其默示條款爲: (a)大部份商品之品質必須與樣品相符; (b)買方可在合理之機會下與樣品比較; (c)所交商品之外表與樣品合理比較檢驗,必須全無缺陷,以免遭致不適銷售 (free from any defect, rendering them unmerchantable)。 ⓬

美國統一商法 Sect. 2-313關于商品銷售依照規格說明與樣品之「明示保證」(express Warranty) 條件者,其規定如下:

(1)賣方之明示保證如下:

(a)賣方對買方所作任何關于商品之事實確認或承諾(any affirmation of fact or promise),構成契約基礎之一部份,而爲賣方之明示承諾者,其所交商品,必須與所作確認或承諾相符。

(b)任何商品之規格說明構成契約基礎之一部份而爲賣方之明示承諾者,其所交商品,必須與規格說明相符。

(c)任何樣品或模型構成契約基礎之一部份而爲賣方之明示保證者,

⓫ P. S. Atiyah: *The Sale of Goods*, ch. 12, p. 80.
⓬ D. W. Greig: *Sale of Goods*, ch. 5, p. 203.

其所交商品，必須與樣品或模型相符。

依照普通貿易習慣，買方僅憑視覺檢驗（visual examination）者，祇能從表面上檢視大宗商品是否與樣品或模型相符，無法察知其內在品質是否有物質上之不同（material difference）。英國一九七三年修正之商品供應法，已明確規定「必須全無缺陷，以免遭致不適銷售」，似已考慮到保護買方權益，是一項比較進步的立法。

2. 商品必須適於銷售

英國商品供應法 Sect.14(2)關于商品必須適於銷售之默示條件，有下列規定：

在經銷商品期間，其默示條件為：必須依約交付適於銷售之品質（merchantable quality）商品，除非(a)訂約前，商品之缺點經特別指點買方注意，(b)如買方在訂約前已檢驗商品，其缺點業經檢視顯露者。❸

所謂「適於銷售」（merchantability），必須考慮商品之規格及其目的用途。Salmond 在 Taylor v. Combined Buyer, Ltd. 一案說得好：「適于銷售」一詞，並非指品質好、尚好或平均（good, fair or average quality）的意思，也可能是品質較差或不好（inferior or bad quality）的商品，但在市場上照樣都可以銷售。在銷售商品時，默示條件並無規定它們屬于那種等級或標準。如買方須保障自己權益，必須在契約上表明其所需之特殊等級或標準。如不出此，除非另有保證，買方必須接受任何合乎規格說明之劣質商品。由此看來，任何商品只有合乎正常規格及品質之條件，雖較之同類其他產品低劣，仍屬可銷商品。茲舉下列 H. Beechana & Co. Pty, Ltd. v. Francis Howard & Co. Pty, Ltd. 一案以說明之：

---

❸　P. S. Atiyah: *The Sale of Goods*, ch. 12, p. 80.

被告向原告購針樅木材一批，訂價每百呎80先令，契約訂明係供製造鋼琴之用。被告在原告之存貨中選購，事後發現該批木材大部份受乾枯影響，無法使用。此項乾枯情形，普通在合理之表面檢視下無法察覺。原告辯稱，該批木材經常在市面售供製造木箱之用，爲適合銷售之商品。法官裁判，認爲此類木材雖可銷售供作製箱用途，但每百呎之售價僅30先令，如供製造鋼琴，則爲不適銷售商品。 **⑭**

美國統一商法 Sect.2-314對商品之適銷性，曾作下列規定：

(1)除非另有更改或免責限制，賣方在其契約中之默示保證，必須保證其商品在該類商品中爲適于銷售貨品。依本條規定，所有在室內或任何場所供應飲食用之消費品均屬之。

(2)凡適於銷售之商品，最低限度：

(a)必須依照契約之規定說明，無異議地通過該業的檢查；

(b)如係彙類商品，必須係契約之平均中等品質；

(c)必須適合該商品之普通用途；

(d)所有商品每一單位品量的容許變異必須平均；

(e)必須依照契約要求，加予適當之包裝及標貼；

(f)所有包裝容器或標貼之製作，必須依照承諾及確認之事項辦理。

3. 商品必須適用於特殊目的用途

美國統一商法 Sect. 2-315 規定：

賣方在訂約時，有理由了解買方所需商品之任何特殊目的，並依賴其技能或判斷，以選擇或提供適當之商品。除非對默示保證有所變更或免責限制，所有商品必須保證適用於該項特殊目的。

英國之商品供應法 Sect. 14(3)曾有類似規定，但仍不如其商品買賣法 Sect. 14(1)來得明確。茲將後者之原文迻譯如下：

---

⑭ P. S. Atiyah: *The Sale of Goods*, ch. 12, p. 88.

買方必須明示或暗示使賣方了解其所需商品之特殊目的，並依賴賣方之技能或判斷，從而確定其在經營期間可能供銷買方之需要規格。

默示條件規定: 賣方所交之商品，必須合理地適於該項目的用途。如契約訂售之商品爲具有專利或商標名稱之特定產品，則無應適合特殊目的之默示條件。從上述條文涵義，可歸納爲下列五個要件:

a. 買方須通知賣方其所需商品之目的;

b. 依賴賣方之技能或判斷;

c. 賣方必須係經營是項商品之商人;

d. 賣方所提供商品，必須合理地適應買方之特殊目的之用途;

e. 指定廠牌之附帶條件。

關于買方應通知賣方其所需商品之特殊目的問題，玆擬舉 Griffith v. Peter Conway Ltd. 一案例以說明之:

> 某婦人具有皮膚敏感毛病，某日向皮衣店購買 Harris Tweed 外衣一件，但未向店方透露其皮膚敏感毛病。該婦人購穿皮衣後，發覺因皮衣影響發生皮膚炎，乃向賣方控訴。英國上訴法庭判決，該婦人所購皮衣係供一般正常人穿著，該婦人在購買前如說明其患有皮膚敏感症，賣方自會告知其不適穿着。第該婦人事前並未正確透露其目的及情況，賣方自無須負責。❻

關于「依賴賣方之技能或判斷」一節，玆再舉 Cammell Laird & Co., Ltd. v. Manganese Bronze and Brass Co. Ltd. 一案例以說明之:

> 原告（船主）向被告訂製其輪船所需之螺旋槳一只，當檢送該螺旋槳之部份圖樣，其餘則依賴被告憑其技能或判斷完成之。交貨後，

---

❻　D. W. Greig: *Sale of Goods*, ch. 5, p. 189.

原告發現該螺旋槳由於部份缺陷，不適應用。法官判決，被告製造技術有問題，應負完全責任。 ❿

關于賣方提供商品應爲其經常經營之項目一節，特再舉 Spencer Trading Co. Ltd. v. Devon 一案例以說明之：

某經營樹脂及膠着劑等商品之零售商，接客戶訂購製捕蠅紙用膠水一批，因該商從未經營是項商品，致所交膠水不適製造捕蠅紙之用。旋經法官判決，該商應負責賠償。 ❼

4-2-2 買方義務

賣方有義務交付商品，買方卽有義務接受及付款。此係買賣契約雙方之同在條件 （concurrent conditions） 所構成之相對義務，故聯合國買賣公約第三十五條有「買方必須按照契約與本公約之規定，支付價款及收取貨物」之規定。

4-2-2-1 支付價款

1. 支付方式及日期

任何商品買賣契約均有付款方式及日期之規定，因此買方爲支付貨款，有義務採取一應步驟及手續，使價款如期支付。聯合國買賣公約第五十四條曾規定：「買方爲支付價款，有義務根據契約或任何有關法律規章之規定，辦理一切應採步驟及手續」。

關于付款日期方面，則在該公約第五十九條規定：「賣方必須按契約與該公約規定之日期或從契約及該公約可以確定之日期支付價款，無須賣方提出任何要求或辦理任何手續」。

假如買方無義務在任何其他特定時間內支付貨款時，該公約第五十

---

❿　Robert Lowe: *Commercial Law*, ch.3, p. 164.

❼　Robert Lowe: *Commercial Law*, ch. 3, p. 165.

八條規定其付款方式如下:

(1)如買方無義務在任何其它特定時間內支付價款，必須在賣方按照契約與本公約規定將貨物或控制貨物處置權之單據交予買方處置時支付價款。賣方可以支付價款爲移交貨物或單據之條件。

(2)如契約涉及到貨物之運送者，賣方得依照條件交運，並以買方支付價款爲移交貨物或移交控制貨物處置權之運輸單據爲條件。

2. 支付地點

普通買賣契約均有付款地點之規定，如買方無義務在任何其他特定地點支付貨款時，該公約第五十七條有下列規定:

(1)如買方無義務在任何其它特定地點支付價款時，必須在以下地點向賣方支付價款:

(a)賣方之營業地;

(b)如憑交付貨物或移交單據支付價款者，則在交付貨物或移交單據地點支付。

(2)賣方必須承擔因其營業處所在訂約後變動而增加之付款方面的費用。

凡賣方以接受支票、滙票、期票或承兌交單等方式爲付款條件者，一般視爲「有條件之付款」（conditional payment）。 如上述支付工具或承兌承諾無法兌現時，賣方有權訴請買方支付價款。

4-2-2-2　收取及檢驗商品

1. 收取商品

收取商品係買方之契約義務，聯合國買賣公約第六十條對買方收取商品之義務有下列規定:

(a)採取一切合理措施，使賣方能交付商品; 並

(b)接收商品。

依照一般國際慣例，買方之收取商品如非在交付前檢驗者，並不認爲在交付時卽已「接收」商品（not deemed to have accepted the goods on delivery），除非買方已給予適當之機會去檢驗商品，以確定是否符合契約之規定（given a reasonable opportunity of examining the goods for the purpose of ascertaining whether they are in comformity with the contract）；換句話說，買方如發現不符契約規定時，得拒收所交商品。這點在英國商品買賣法 Sect. 34 已有明白之規定。

2. 商品之檢驗

賣方交送貨物給買方，買方應於何時檢驗？在何地檢驗？在收到後如發現所交貨物與合約規定不符時應於何時通知賣方？在實際收到貨物之若干時期內如未將不符合契約之實際情形通知賣方是否將喪失其聲稱貨物不符之權利？茲特列舉國際有關公約及英美法律之有關規定與判例，以供參考。

依據國際法學會一九三二年修訂之 CIF 契約華沙牛津規則（Warsaw - Oxford Rules for CIF Contracts）第十九條規定，商品於運抵買賣契約所規定之目的地時或裝船前（依前者抑後者，由買方之意思決定），除非給予買方合理之機會（a reasonable opportunity）或合理之時間（a reasonable time）檢查，不得視爲買方已接受該商品。該商品縱係共同檢查，買方應於檢查完成後三天內，將其主張貨物不符契約之事實通知賣方。若買方怠於此項通知時，不得行使拒收商品之權利。惟因該商品隱藏缺陷或固有瑕疵而遭受滅失或損害者，買方所享有一切救濟行爲之權利，不受本條之影響。⑱

---

⑱　國際貿易局與司法行政部民事司編譯「國際貿易法規暨慣例彙編」第一冊 p. 637; Warsaw-Oxford Rules for CIF Contracts, art. 19.

　　美國統一商法（Uniform Commercial Code）Sect. 2-513 (1)(2)對買方之貨物檢驗權利曾規定：除非買賣雙方另行協議，所有依照合約規定交送之貨物，買方均有權在付款或接受前之任何合理地點、時間以任何合理方法檢驗貨品。如賣方被要求或授權將貨物運至買方者，得于抵達後檢驗。上項檢驗費用由買方負擔，惟所交貨物如發現與合約規定不符被拒時，賣方應負擔該項檢驗費。⑲

　　英國商品買賣法對于買方檢驗貨物之地點並無一定之限制，所以在該法 Sect. 34 規定，如非在交貨前檢驗者，必須給買方適當之機會檢驗。所謂「適當機會」，應視(1)所運貨物是否于抵達目的地後應直接轉運買方之客戶所在地？(2)買方之交貨地點（港口）是否適於檢驗？(3)基於貨物之性質及包裝是否適於在買方之交貨地點（港口）檢驗？依照英國一般案例，認爲 FOB 契約須在裝船前或抵達目的地後檢驗，並無一定限制，可由雙方按當時情況協定。一般而論，買方在裝貨港口既無檢驗設備，亦無機會驗收，自無在裝船前檢驗貨物之義務。至 CIF 契約，自然只有在目的地卸貨後才有機會檢驗了。至於應何地檢驗，則要看商品之型態及個案之特別情況而定。譬如 Van den Hurk v. R. Martens & Co. Ltd. 一案，賣方同意售與買方桶裝 Sodium Sulphate 一批，運往 Manchester 交貨。賣方事前已知此批貨物須轉運買方在 Lyon 及 Genoa 之客戶，于貨到 Manchester 後必須立卽運出。基於該貨之性質，買方不可能在碼頭開桶檢驗。迨貨到 Genoa 及 Lyon 後，買方客戶發現該批貨物有劣質之 Caustic Soda 誤裝在內，于是客戶隨卽退貨，要求賠償。法官 Bailhache 認爲：賣方既預知該批貨物係轉售

---

⑲　U. S. Uniform Commercial Code, (1972 Official Text) art. 2 Sales, Sect. 2-513.

其客戶，且基於該貨性質無法預作檢驗，則買方根據其客戶要求轉向賣方索賠，應屬合理。⑳

又假如貨物已運抵目的港之倉庫儲存，買方在轉售第三者前，自有適當之機會先行檢查貨物。但貨物之在目的港轉運倉庫儲存，係純爲候船轉運客戶，則須考慮是否有適當之機會檢驗？該批貨物之性質及包裝是否適於在碼頭檢驗？假如此係密封包裝之鹹肉，則須立卽轉運，在碼頭檢驗旣非適當時間，亦非適當場所。

從上面所述，可知英美貿易發達國家對買方之貨物檢驗權利，均採取較具彈性之規定，可視貨物之性質與個別之交運情形在合理之環境及時間情況下進行。聯合國在一九八〇年訂定之國際商品買賣公約卽依此原則規定如下：

第三十八條：(1)買方必須在實際可行之情況下以最短之時間內檢驗貨物或由他人檢驗。(2)如契約涉及貨物之運輸，檢驗可延遲至貨物到達目的地後進行。(3)如貨在運輸途中改運或買方須再發運貨物，致無合理之機會加以檢驗，而賣方在訂立契約時已知或應知此種改運或再發運之可能性，檢驗可延遲至貨物到達新目的地後進行。

第三十九條：(1)買方對貨物之不符合約，必須在發現或理應發現不符情形後一段合理時間內通知賣方，說明不符情形之性質，否則將喪失其聲明貨物不符合約之權利。(2)無論如何，買方如不在實際收到貨物之日起兩年內將貨物不符合約情形通知賣方，則將喪失其聲稱貨物不符合約之權利，除非此一時限與合約規定之保證期限不符。(Unless this time-limit is inconsistent with a contractual

---

⑳ D. W. Greig: *Sale of Goods*, ch. 4, pp. 139-143.

period of quarantee)。

第四十條: 如賣方已知或理應知道貨物之不符合約情形而未將此事實告知買方, 則賣方無權援引第三十八條及三十九條之規定。

4-3 違約之救濟

國際間之商品買賣, 依照國際公約及一般貿易習慣之規定, 賣方有交付商品、移交貨運單據、並移轉商品所有權之義務; 買方則有支付價款及收取商品之義務。惟一旦任何一方違反契約之規定時, 受害一方, 自有採取正當措施, 以謀求救濟之權利。茲就聯合國買賣公約有關規定, 以及英美兩國之有關是項立法; 闡述如次。

4-3-1 買方違約時之救濟方法

4-3-1-1 買方不按時通知商品規格之救濟方法

依照聯合國買賣公約第六十五條規定:

(1)如買方未依約在議定時間或在收到賣方要求之一段合理時間內, 將所需商品之形狀、大小或其他特徵等訂明通知賣方時, 賣方得在不損害其享有之任何其他權利下, 依照其所知之買方需求, 自訂規格。

(2)如賣方自訂規格, 必須訂明規格細節通知買方, 並規定一段合理時間, 讓買方可提出其不同之規格。如買方收到賣方之通知後並未表示異議, 則賣方所訂規格即具約束力。

普通商品之買賣可分為兩種型態: 一種為依據年度生產計畫自製商品, 即經常所謂自製備銷品 (ready-made goods); 一種係接受客戶定貨, 依買方指定規格之特製商品 (specially manufactued goods)。後者必須依據買方規格說明或藍圖製造，但也可依據買方之需求，憑其製造技術及經驗，自行設計。賣方為免影響其生產程序，必要時得徵求買方同意後逕行製交。此係聯合國公約為救濟買方延誤通知之一項救濟措施，實未可厚非。

4-3-1-2 買方不依約付款提貨之救濟方法

1.延緩買方付款提貨期限

依照聯合國買賣公約第六十二條之規定，賣方得首先要求買方履行其契約義務，儘速支付價款及收取商品。如買方無法在契約規定時間內履行義務時，並得依照第六十三條之規定，另行規定額外之合理時限，要求買方付款提貨。倘買方具有誠意付款提貨，並經通知賣方寬限時限，如賣方對其所提時間可以接受，則不得在此期間採取任何補救措施。但賣方並不因此喪失其對延誤履行義務可能享有之要求賠償權利。

溯一九六四年之海牙統一國際商品買賣法，亦曾在其原約第六十一條規定，賣方得首先要求買方履約付款提貨，如買方之不按契約規定期間內付款提貨尚不致構成嚴重損害時，賣方得再按原約第六十二條第二款及第六十六條第二款之規定，寬限其履約時限，屆時如再不付款提貨，始予解約。足見先後國際立法之精神，均屬一致。

2.對買方不付款之貨物救濟措施

支付貨款與收取商品，乃貿易上之相關義務。依約付了貨款，就有義務去提取商品；如無意付款，即表示不願提貨。因此買方如不履約付款，賣方唯有扣留交貨或被迫採取各項可行之救濟途徑，以攫回在運送中之貨物。

英國商品買賣法及美國統一商法對于買方之不付貨款，有頗多類似之救濟規定，而聯合國公約之有關規定，似嫌過于籠統，遠不若英美法之週全。茲試分述如次。

(1)留置商品

聯合國對買方之不履行付款提貨義務而賣方尚擁有貨物或仍具控制貨物之處置權時，得採取合理措施，以保全貨物。其第八十五條之規定如下：

如買方推延收取貨物或在支付價款與交付貨物須同時履行而買方並未付款時，賣方得在擁有貨物或控制貨物處置權之際，按情況採取合理措施，以保全貨物，直至買方償還其合理費用爲止。

依照英國商品買賣法 Sect. 39(1)a 及(2)規定：凡未獲付款之賣方，如仍掌握貨物或所有權尚未移轉買方時，得爲貨物之保全，行使貨物留置權(right of lien on the goods)或貨物扣交權(right of withholding delivery)，以留置或扣留貨物。

所謂「未獲付款之賣方」(unpaid seller)，依照該法 Sect. 38(1)之解釋，凡全部貨款未付、押匯證券 (negotiable instrument，指信用狀等) 未收到或匯票遭拒絕支付者均屬之。惟賣方之行使貨物留置權，必須具備下列三個必要條件： (a)貨款規定 必須在交貨 前支付者； (b)貸售貨物 (goods sold on credit) 之付款日期已屆或賒帳 期間買方已破產者； (c)貨物仍在賣方掌握中者。

以上(a)(c)兩點對賣方之行使留置權均無問題，惟(b)點貸售貨物，除非交貨日期尚未洽定，貨物猶在手中，或貨物正在運輸途中仍保留處置權或在委託代理人保管中，自可予以扣留或追回外，倘一旦已交予買方或買方之代理或受託人 (bailee) 抑買方或其代理業已「合法」取得貨物者，則賣方已喪失貨物留置權。又貨物已送交運送人 (carrier) 或其他受託人，目的在交其運往買方而未提及保留貨物之處置權 (without reserving the right of disposal of goods) 者，亦將同樣喪失其貨物留

置權。❶

　　依據一般國際慣例，貨物雖已交運送人（common carrier）運送，但提單收貨人用賣方名字或不填收貨人名字而代以"To order"字樣、于背書後交銀行洽收貨款者，則賣方仍保有貨物處置權(right of disposal of goods)。在 CIF 契約中，賣方所開匯票連同貨運單據經由銀行轉送而未經買方接受前，縱使賣方業經讓售銀行預先取得貨款，但在買方未付款前，賣方居於開票人地位仍為第二債務人（secondary liability），故貨物之所有權仍屬賣方，得作為付款之保證。倘賣方在交運時提單未作上項安排或其他適當之預防措施者，則賣方難免喪失貨物之留置權。依照英國法律，在訂約時容許在 General Conditions 內預先插入「保留所有權條款」(Reservation of Property Clause)，規定「賣方保留貨物之法定所有權直至收到購貨之現金價款為止；如買方處理賣方之財產（指貨物）時，則買方應以賣方代理及委託人之身分保管其處理貨物所得之價款」（The seller retains the legal property in the goods until he receives the purchase price in cash and entitled to the proceeds if the buyer disposes of the seller's property, the buyer holding those proceeds as an agent and trustee for the seller)❷。此係英國一八九三年商品買賣法 Sect. 19　為保障賣方權益所訂「有條件移轉商品所有權」之規定。德國及荷蘭亦有此共同之規定。在荷蘭發生之Aluminium Industrie Vaassen BV v. Romalpa Aluminium Ltd. 一案例，即係採用「保留所有權條款」而經由英國法庭審判支持的。本案當事人 Alu-

---

❶ P. S. Atiyah: *The Sale of Goods*, ch. 24, pp. 248-259; D. W. Greig: *Sale of Goods*, ch. 8, pp. 292-301; Schmitthoff:*Export Trade*, pp. 103-105.

❷ Schmitthoff: *Export Trade*, p. 53.

minium Industrie Vaassen BV（AIV）係荷蘭一私人公司，經向英商 Romalpa Aluminium Ltd. 洽售鋁箔一批，交貨條件為 Ex Works，在荷蘭之 AIV 工廠交貨，價款按荷幣計算，並由買方指定收貨人在荷蘭驗收，因買方未依約付款，乃引起賣方在英國控訴。本案契約之成立，與荷蘭法律有密切關係，但未要求引用，故審判時根據英國法律。由於訂約時列有上述「保留所有權條款」，英國上訴法庭認為荷蘭 AIV 公司對其供應之商品仍享有所有權。至 Romalpa 之再售該貨，應視為 AIV 之代理關係，保管其處理後所得價款。❸

一般說來，賣方交貨方式可能有三種情形：第一，賣方可能已將商品運出而提單仍載明 "To the order of the seller or his agent"，如此，賣方可保留其貨物之所有權直至買方付款交貨。第二，賣方可能已將商品交運並將滙票及貨運提單經由銀行向買方提請付款或提示承兌中，在所有權未移轉或提單未交付買方前，賣方得將提單退回。第三，賣方可能已將提單載明 "To the order of the buyer or his agent" 而未在契約內規定「有條件之移轉所有權」，則商品之命運將決定于提單是否已轉移買方。按提單載明買方之名字，並不足以表示賣方已有意將所有權轉移買方；如賣方將該提單交與買方或其代理，則可無抗拒地推斷，賣方已願意將商品之所有權轉移買方。以上「有條件保留所有權」之規定，如能列入契約條款，則可否定移交提單即表示已移轉所有權予買方之認定，將使買方變為賣方之代理或受託人，使賣方仍有權處理買方出售該批商品之所得。❹

兹試舉賣方對貸售及分批交貨契約行使留置權之案例以說明之：

譬如賣方係茶葉進口商，將進口茶葉存入保稅倉庫。買方以記帳方

---

❸ Schmitthoff: *Export Trade*, pp. 79-80.
❹ Schmitthoff: *Export Trade*, pp. 77-81.

式向賣方訂購若干箱茶葉，當由賣方發給提貨單，訂明茶葉仍暫存保稅倉庫，俟若干日後付款提貨。不久買方宣告破產涉訟，法官判決：賣方雖已將提貨單給與買方，但賣方仍享有留置權占有貨物，如同買方之代理人保管貨物。今買方破產，無力付款，自可行使其留置權。

又如 Re Edwards, ex parte Chalmers 一案，賣方同意送交買方漂白粉330噸，分批交貨，由二月起至十二月止，每月交30噸，于交貨14天付現。在十二月二十日買方宣告破產，致十一月份之貨款亦未交付，賣方乃停止交送。法庭判決，認為賣方之停止繼續交貨極為合理，蓋買方在未完全履行契約前即先破產，賣方在舊欠未清及未交部份付款前自可拒絕繼續交貨。❺

美國統一商法 Sect. 2-703(a) 對買方不依約在交貨時或交貨前付款，亦有扣交商品 (withhold delivery of goods) 之規定，如遇發現買方破產時，並得依照該法 Sect. 2-702(1)之規定，拒絕或停止交貨。

(2)停止商品之交付

依照英國商品買賣法 Sect. 44 規定：賣方如遇買方破產但貨已運出時，得行使停止貨物運送權 (right of stoppage in transit)；換言之，賣方得在運輸途中恢復占有其貨物，直至買方付款時止。

查停止在運輸途中之貨物，係賣方取回貨物之一種擴張行為。此種行為，在國際貿易中較留置權更具實際價值而又為賣方所常採用的途徑，同時也往往為法院所同情而容易得到有利的裁判。惟此項權利之行使，依照英國商品買賣法之上項規定，必須在買方破產時為之。這裏所謂 "IN TRANSIT"，係指貨物已離開賣方掌握，尚未抵達買方或其代理，但仍在運送途中之中立的第三者手中（如運送人之代理貨運公司及

---

❺　D. W. Greig: *Sale of Goods*, ch. 8, p. 300.

其他獨立之中間人)。依照英國商品買賣法 Sect. 44 規定，在買方宣告破產仍未付款前，賣方得行使其停止運送權 (right of stoppage)，要求運送人中止運送。惟賣方在行使停止運送權時，須先向運送人或運送人之總公司提出要求，並必須在貨物仍在其掌握中之運輸工具，且能及時通知其船員或代理者採取有效之制止行動，方可收效。惟在執行上，應注意下列數點：

a. 賣方將貨物運交買方 指定之運送人或代理，並不足以使賣方喪失其停止運送權。假如運送人或代理僅是買方轉運貨物之代理人，則賣方仍可要求行使其對貨物之中止運送權，除非這些貨物仍在代理手中；反是，如代理已受買方委託按照合約條件提貨，並依照買方指示將貨物出售，則賣方之上項權利即告喪失。又在 FOB 合約下賣方將貨物交船裝運，雖提單之收貨人爲買方，但貨物仍在運送途中，故賣方亦保有停止運送該批貨物之權。不過，一旦貨物抵達目的地，並由船方將貨物轉交買方或其代理人，甚或由其轉運其他地區，則"TRANSIT"即告終了。

b. 以買方具名之提單，或原爲賣方具名之提單轉交買方，並不表示賣方已喪失其停止運送權，祇要買方仍未付款，賣方即仍然保有其貨物之處置權。不過尚須經過一段法律程序罷了。

c. 如買方未付款，但提單已交買方，並由買方背書轉讓給善意之第三人 (third party in good faith)，則情形不同，縱使貨物仍在運輸途中，賣方之行使停止運送權就不無問題。❻

　茲列舉 Kemp v. Ismay & Co. 一案以說明行使停止貨物運送權之實例如下：

---

❻ Schmitthoff: *Export Trade* pp. 105–108.

英國某出口商代表澳洲商人向賣方訂購貨物一批，訂明該貨須標示 N.X.Z. 嘜頭，由利物浦裝 Suevic 輪運往澳洲之 Adelaide 交貨。該出口商于貨物運出後宣告破產，賣方乃立即行使停止貨物運送權。法官 Lord Alverston 依據 Lord Esher 對 Bethell v. Clark 一案判例，認爲賣方依照契約條款或買方對賣方之指示，得行使該停止運送權，故判決賣方之行爲有效。❼

美國之統一商法 Sect. 2-705(1) 對于賣方之行使停止貨物運送權，則有較寬之規定。玆逐譯如下：

賣方在發現買方破產時，得停止在運送人或其他代理人控制中之貨物交付；又在交貨前，如買方拒絕或不能如期支付貨款，賣方有權扣留整個車廂、卡車、飛機及大批貨物之交付或要求歸還貨物。

查運送人承運之貨物種類繁多，而包裝大小不一，除非因買方破產、必須運送人及時救濟者外，如買方不付款時亦麻煩運送人概予停止運送，實不勝其負荷，故美國立法，對未付價款之貨物行使停止運送權，僅限於整批或大宗貨運，實極合理。較之英國買賣法之行使停止運送權僅適用於買方破產時，似又進步多矣。

賣方行使停止運送權，旨在恢復貨物之占有，因此也連帶發生改運裝卸等費用以及再賣與更換貨運單據等複雜問題，業者不可不注意及之。

(3)再售收回之商品

賣方之行使貨物留置權或停止運輸途中之貨物交付，目的在再賣收回之商品，而該項再賣品之承購人，則希望從原購人手中得到完整之所有權，故賣方必須正視在尚未再掌握該批貨物時之再售可能性。英國商品買賣法 Sect. 48 規定在下列四種情況下，賣方得再售其商品：

(1)賣方無明確之義務交付買方任何特定之貨物時；

---

❼ D. W. Greig: *Sale of Goods*, ch. 8, p. 303.

(2)賣方對買方之拒絕收貨及廢止契約表示可以接受時；

(3)依照契約規定，如遇買方違約，賣方得保留對貨物之再售權時；

(4)凡屬易腐貨物，經通知買方如不在規定之合理時間內付款則擬再售時。❽

在此必須一提者，賣方一旦通知買方決定再售其商品時，依照英國商品買賣法 Sect. 48 之規定，在再售後，賣方不得再訴請買方支付貨款，賣方如有損失，只能訴請第一買方（first buyer）賠償其因不領受貨物而再售之差價等損失。關于賣方轉賣商品與契約差價之損失應由買方賠償一節，在聯合國買賣公約第七十五條亦有同樣之規定。至關于賣方之再賣商品權，則規定較爲籠統，僅於第八十八條規定：在買方延遲提取貨物或延遲支付貨款與保管費時，賣方得採取任何適當辦法，出售該批貨物，但此項意向必須事先通知買方。

美國統一商法 Sect. 2-703 及 2-706 亦有關再售商品之規定，惟對商品之再售，必須採取誠實態度與商業上合理之方法，以公開或私自洽銷方式處理之。除賣方得向買方要求賠償其契約價格與再賣價間之差額損失外，並得依照同法2-710之規定，要求買方賠償中止運交之回程運什費、保管及手續費等附帶損失。

4-3-1-3　買方拒絕付款收貨之法律救濟

未獲付款之賣方，依照英國商品買賣法之規定，可採取兩項個人救濟（personal remedies）：一是依該法 Sect. 49 之規定，訴請支付價款（action for the price）；一是依該法 Sect. 50(1) 之規定，訴請賠償損失（action for damage）。玆分別節譯如次：

1. Sect. 49(1)及(2)：訴請買方支付價款：

(1)依照契約條款，商品之所有權已移轉買方，由于買方之不當疏

---

❽　P. S. Atiyah: *The Sale of Goods*, ch. 24, pp. 267-270.

忽或拒絕付款，賣方得繼續向買方採取法律行動，要求支付貨款。

(2)依照契約規定，不拘商品交付與否，價款必須在確定之日支付 (payable on a day certain irrespective of delivery) 者，由於買方之不當疏忽或拒絕付款，縱使貨物之所有權尚未轉移或仍未撥交貨物，賣方亦得繼續向買方採取法律行動，要求支付價款。

2. Sect. 50(1): 訴請買方賠償損失:

由於買方之不當疏忽或拒絕收貨付款，賣方得繼續向買方採取法律行動，要求賠償因拒絕收貨所遭受之損害。

從 Sect. 49 及 Sect. 50(1)分析，賣方可能採取之法律行動有下列三種情形:

a. 在貨物所有權業已轉移，買方且已領受貨物時，可要求支付貨款;

b. 在貨物所有權尚未轉移而買方拒收貨物時，可要求賠償損失;

c. 在貨物所有權業已轉移而買方拒收貨物時，要求支付價款或賠償損失。

假如貨物所有權業已轉移或貨款已指定支付日期而買方拒絕提貨付款，賣方得按 Sect. 49 之規定要求付款或按 Sect. 50 要求賠償損失。賣方在採取行動前，得衡量一下究採取那一種途徑較爲有利。

「損失」之估計，依 Sect. 50(1)之規定，可包括買方違約後賣方所遭受之直接及自然損失。Sect. 50(3)更作進一步規定，賠償商品價格，可按貨物應接收時或在買方拒絕接受之市場價格計算。在 CIF 契約，買方如拒絕接受貨運單據，賣方實不甚方便在交貨之目的地處理貨物的卸載、存倉、及轉售，其可採途徑，似仍以追索價款爲宜 ❾。

美國統一商法 Sect. 2-709 關于訴請買方支付貨款 (action for

❾ P. S. Atiyah: *The Sale of Goods*, ch. 25, pp. 271-283.

the price）之規定，似較英國立法進步。玆逐譯如次：

(1)買方如到期不付貨款，賣方得向買方追索下列貨款以及 Sect. 2-710所規定之任何附帶損失：

a. 在風險轉移買方 後合理時間內有 關已收貨物之價款 或確認之貨物損失或損害；

b. 鑑定貨物價格， 如賣方在合理之 情況及努力下仍 無法按合理之價格作有效之出售時。

(2)賣方訴請買方支付貨款，必須鑑定貨物符合契約之規定並仍在其掌握中。如可再售，得在法院裁決催收前之任何時間轉售。此項轉售之所得記入買方帳項，任何未售貨品由法院裁定催收。

(3)由於買方之不當拒收貨物、不如期付款或取消契約 （Section 2-610），賣方如已依前條款要求賠償損失者，則不得在本條款下要求支付價款。

以上所謂賣方之附帶損失 （seller's incidental damages）， 依美國統一商法 Sect. 2-710 之規定，包括運輸、停止交付及保管期間發生之一切費用及手續費，以及買方違約後退貨與再賣等所產生之費用。

聯合國買賣公約第六十一條關于買方不履行契約義務時賣方可能採取之救濟措施爲： (a)首先得依照該約第六十二條之規定， 行使其法律上賦予之「要求買方支付價款及收取貨物」之權利； (b)買方如不照辦， 得再按該約第七十四及七十七條之規定，行使其法律上賦予之「要求損害賠償」之權利。該條原文(a)(b)兩款使用 "Exercise the right" 及 "Claim damage" 等字， 均係法律用語，意在要求者（claimant）在行使其(a)款權利無效時，有權採取(b)款步驟提出法律要求， 訴之于法， 尋求法律上的救濟。又該公約第六十四條復規定，如買方不履行其契約及本公約內之任何義務， 卽等於根本違反契約，賣方得宣告契約無效， 並要求損害賠償。此係賣方採取救濟措施之必然步驟。在宣告契約無效之一段合理時間內，如賣方已依照該公約第七十五條之規定以合理方式將貨物轉賣，其轉售價格與契約所訂價格之不足差額，得要求買方補償，並按該公約第七十四條之規定，可取得任何其他因買方違約而遭受之損失（包括利潤在內）；如賣方未將貨物轉售，得依照該公約第七十六條之規定，要求賠付原契約價格與宣告契約無效時之市價差額，並照該公約第七十四條及第七十八條之規定要求任何其他損害賠償（包括延遲付款利息）。

4-3-2 賣方違約時之救濟方法

4-3-2-1 賣方延遲交貨之救濟方法

買方對賣方之延遲交貨 (late delivery)，普通有兩種處理方式：一是拒絕接受，在買方認爲「交貨時間」係契約之必要條件時多採用之；一是接受交貨，在買方認爲賣方之延遲並不影響其使用或銷售時多採用此種寬容措施。惟後者情況之處理方式，極似普通違反契約保證之處理。

依據一般契約法之規定，賣方之延遲交貨將構成買方之嚴重損害時，買方得立即解除契約，並要求賣方賠償損失。買方對賣方之延遲交貨如可寬容，其寬容之要求及時限得由賣方提出，亦可由買方自動提出。茲列舉聯合國買賣公約第四十七條之有關規定如下：

(1)買方得規定一段合理之額外時限，讓賣方履行其義務；

(2)除非買方已收到賣方之通知將不在其寬限之時間內履行其契約義務，買方不得在此時間內採取任何對賣方違約之救濟措施。但買方並不因此喪失其對賣方延遲履行義務所享有之要求損害賠償權利。

又該公約第四十八條 (2) 及 (4) 款復規定：如賣方已通知買方提出要求，將延遲至其要求之指定時間內履行義務，而買方不在一段合理之時間內答復時， 則賣方可按其 指定之時間內 履行義務， 同時買方亦不得在此時間內採取與賣方履行義務相牴觸之任何救濟措施。賣方之上項要求，必須在買方收到後始能生效。

如賣方之違約純爲延遲交貨，則買方之接受貨物，訴請賣方賠償損失， 有不同之規例可循。 一般情形， 損害賠償之計算， 係按依約交貨時與實際交貨時之市場價格差額核計。倘實際交貨時之市場價格高于應依約交貨時之價格， 則買方之所謂損失， 祇是「有名無實」（merely nominal） 而已； 反是， 假如市場之行情下跌， 實際交貨時之市價已較依約應交貨時之市場價格下落不少，則應以兩者差價之實際損失爲準。惟買方在預測市場價格卽將下跌而將貨物先行轉售時，其損失差額自較按實際交貨時市價減少，因此損失之計算，自應改按依約應交貨時之市價與買方轉售價格之差額核算方較合理，以避免買方取得不正當之利益。至買方在賣方延遲交貨期間萬一遭受幣制貶值之損失，除非訂約時有協議， 否則不得向賣方要求賠償❶。關于特製品（special manufacture）之賠償， 因非大宗貨品， 極難在市場購得， 如買方之轉售價格尙在賣方核算之合理範圍， 亦可作爲買方損害賠償之計價依據。

現代之國際貿易， 貨物往往在訂約後或運輸途中卽已由買方轉售他人。故在市價下跌時， 其轉售價格往往較貨物抵達時之市價爲高。依照英國法院判例，如遇賣方延遲交貨而買方仍接受貨物時，其損害賠償之計算， 應以依約應交貨時市價與買方轉售價格之差額爲準，不得從賣方之違約圖取不正當之利益。玆列舉 Wertheim v. Chicoutimi Pulp Co. 一案例以說明之：

賣方訂約售與買方 3,000 噸潮溼之木漿一批，訂明 FOB 買方之運輸工具爲每噸25先令， 在一九〇〇年之九月十日至十一月一日內交

---

❶ Robert Lowe: *Commecial Law*, ch. 3, p. 233.

貨，由買方安排車輛將貨物送交 Manchester 之客戶約需運費13先令，合計銷貨成本爲38先令。在契約訂定之交貨期間木漿價格已漲至每噸70先令，惜賣方無法如期交貨，迨實際交貨時，木漿市價已跌至42先令6辨士。惟買方在與賣方訂約前後早已以每噸65先令陸續出售，事實上已獲多少利潤。因此陪審團一致同意援照加拿大魁北克國王法庭之 Bench 法官判例，應按契約規定交貨日期之市場價格與買方轉售價格之差額計算，爰裁決買方之實際損失爲5先令❷。

本案買方之銷貨成本爲38先令，市價縱跌至42先令6辨士，尚有多少利潤，況買方已按65先令先行轉售，其利潤已相當可觀。假如買方無轉售之貿易行爲，則買方自可按契約規定之交貨日期市價70先令與實際交貨時市價42先令6辨士之差價27先令6辨士要求賣方賠償損失。第買方在與賣方訂約前後已陸續以65先令之價格轉售他人，其中65先令與42先令6辨士間之差額損失22先令6辨士，已從轉售中得到補償，如買方再按27先令6辨士計賠，則其中之 22 先令6辨士無異重複計算，似有失公允，故法院判決祇按實際損失之5先令計賠，實極合理。

4-3-2-2　賣方不交貨之救濟方法

1. 要求退回貨款及賠償損失

買方如遇賣方不交貨或拒絕交貨（non-delivery or refusal to deliver）但已付清貨款時，得向賣方追回貨款，並要求特別損害賠償（special damage）。在英國商品買賣法 Sect. 54 曾規定，買方由於賣方未履行其「對待給付」之義務，得在任何情況下，有權要求賣方賠償其利潤或特別損失，並追還價款。

關于損害賠償方面，依照聯合國買賣公約第四十九條之規定，賣方發生不交貨情況，如經買方按照該公約第四十七條(1)款之規定寬限其交

❷　D. W. Greig: *Sale of Goods*, ch. 7, pp. 287-289.

貨日期，但賣方仍表示不能在所規定之寬限期間交貨時，得宣告契約無效。在契約宣告無效後，如貨物已有市場價格，買方得依該公約第七十六條之規定，按契約規定價格與宣告契約無效時之市價差額，要求賠償，並按該公約第七十四條之規定取得其他已知及預料之損害賠償，包括利潤損失。

依照美國統一商法 Sect. 2-713(1) 有關賣方不交貨或拒絕交貨之損害賠償，則規定如下：

賣方不交貨或拒絕交貨之損害賠償，應按買方已知賣方違約時之市場價格與契約價格之差價連同 Sect. 2-715 規定之其他任何附帶及後果損失合併計算，但必須減除賣方違約後為其所省之費用。

英國商品買賣法對賣方不交貨之損害估計，在該法 Sect. 51 有下列規定：

(1)由於賣方之不當疏忽或拒絕交貨，買方得繼續控訴賣方，要求不交貨之損害賠償。

(2)其損害之計算，可按賣方違約後一般情況之直接及自然損失計算。

(3)如該批貨物有適當之市場價格，則損害之計算，可照契約價格與規定交貨期之市場價格的差價核實估計；如未定交貨日期，則按拒絕交貨時之市價核計。❸

以上條文，事實上係一個「市場價格規則」(Market Price Rule)。假如市場價格低於契約價格時，買方除追回貨款外，祇能要求價格以外之其他正常損害 (normal damage)。

2. 另購代替品並要求賠償損失

賣方不履約交貨買方另購代替品(procurement of substitute goods)

---

❸ P. S. Atiyah: *The Sale of Goods*, ch. 28, p. 305.

者，約有兩種情況：一爲購買純爲自用，賣方如不交貨，買方只得另購代替品；一爲購買在轉售圖取合法利潤。凡從事國際貿易者，往往在訂約後或貨物猶在運輸途中，卽已將貨物轉售客戶。一旦賣方不交貨或拒絕交貨時，勢須另覓貨源，如係特定商品（special goods），則一時不易在市場上覓得代替品；如係一般商品，可在市場上覓購補充，但難免有價格漲跌之差價損失。如無法覓得同等商品，而以較高級品代替時，則差價之損失更大。此外，買方再售應得利潤之損失，勢必向賣方要求賠償。關于此點，聯合國商品買賣公約第七十五條曾作補充規定：買方在宣告契約無效後，得以合理方式購買代替品，並要求賣方按照契約價格與代替品間之差價補償損失，同時照該公約第七十四條之規定取得任何其他損害賠償。此殆參考美國統一商法 Sect. 2-712 訂定之。茲摘譯美國商法該條內容如下：

(1)賣方違約後，買方得在不過度延遲之情況下，以誠實合理方式現購或訂約採購代替品。

(2)買方得按代替品價格與契約價格之差價連同 Sect. 2-715 規定之其他附帶或後果損失，一併要求賣方賠償，但須減除自賣方違約後爲其所節省之費用（上項 Sect. 2-715 所謂附帶或後果損失，係指買方因賣方違約所遭受之一切損失，包括檢驗、收貨、搬運、倉儲、保管、佣金等及其他合理之臨時費用）。

美國立法規定 買方得以購買代 替品之價格作 爲計算損害 賠償之基礎，似較英國法進步多矣。蓋英國之「市場價格規則」，在執行上買方難免遭受不合理之損失。譬如買方向賣方訂購一批商品，每噸價格爲十英鎊，其轉售客戶價格爲每噸十二鎊，依照當時市價預計可賺二鎊。如賣方不能交貨向市場採購同樣代替品之價格爲十一鎊，則買方照上項市場價格與契約差價計算，祇能得到 每噸一英 鎊之賠償，似將損失利潤一鎊。如照轉售價格與契約價格之差價計算，則有二英鎊之差額，其原有之合理利潤可得到實質之補償。因此英國法官在處理該類案件時，不能不將 Sect. 51及Sect. 54兼顧採用，俾不致有所偏失，因 Sect. 51(1)之規定，僅能估算賣方違約後所遭受之直接與自然的損害，但對轉售之損失却並不重視，法官審理案件時，迫得加引 Sect 54.所授予買方之特別損害賠償要求權，使買方應得之轉售利潤及其他特別損失，得到合理之補償。茲試舉 Re R. & H. Hall, Ltd. and W. H. Pim（Junior）& Co. 之仲裁案例以說明之：

　　賣方治售買方特定之玉米一批，由指定之特定輪船裝運，每夸特售價51先令9辨士，買方之轉售價格為每夸特56先令9辨士，當該輪抵達時，國際市場價格已跌至每夸特53先令9辨士，但賣方並未將該批特定玉米運來。

　　以上案情，顯示兩種事實：第一，在指明此項交易係特定商品，指定由特別輪船裝運，並經買方將該批特定商品轉售第三者；第二，該契約條件，業訂明該批商品係供轉售之用。依據英國商品買賣法 Sect. 51(1)之規定，雖可在市面上另購代替品，但此類進口之特定商品在當地市場實不易覓購，如再按該輪抵達時之市價向國外進貨，必須較原訂契約多付二先令之價款，雖可由賣方補償（依照市場價格規則），但買方原有利潤即告損失，且將損失其他一應轉運等費用，殊不合理；如賣方能照原約價格51先令9辨士與買方轉售價格56先令9辨士之差價5先令計賠買方之損失，則買方原應得之利潤仍可得到補償❹。

4-3-2-3　賣方違反契約條件或保證之救濟方法

1. 拒收貨物並要求賠償

　　賣方如違反契約條件（breach of conditions），不按時交貨，或所

---

❹　P. S. Atiyah: *The Sale of Goods*, ch. 28, pp 305-310.

交貨物之品質數量不符契約規定而構成基本違約時，買方得解除契約並有權拒收貨物（right reject the goods）。如未付款，可拒絕支付；倘已付清價款，則可追還貨款，並要求賠償損失。但買方有下列任何一種情形者，卽喪失其拒絕貨物權。

(1)買方已向賣方表明接受（express acceptance）。——此種情形，表示已有適當機會驗收了貨物。

(2)買方保留貨物已超過適當時間尚未對賣方表示拒絕者。——此種情形，雖未將驗收結果通知賣方，但未表示拒絕，卽默示已經驗收了貨物。

(3)買方于賣方交貨後在未有適當機會驗收前，卽已採取若干行爲變更賣方之所有權（如將貨轉售並交付第三者），則視同已接收貨物。

以上之認定，係英國商品買賣法 Sect. 35之規定，而此項認定，又以同法 Sect. 34規定以「買方已有適當機會檢驗（has had a reasonable opportunity of examining）貨物，以確定是否與契約符合」爲基礎。

按照上述第(1)(2)種情形，買方于接收貨物後，卽喪失其拒絕貨物之權利，依照上項規定 極爲明顯，惟第(3)種情形，以現代國際貿易情況論，似不合潮流，玆不妨舉兩個案例如下，以供參考：

(1) **Perkins v. Bell 案**

買方在 Leicester 市場賣方貨攤取樣訂購大麥一批，訂明該批大麥必須送往距買方農場二英哩半火車站路邊交貨。賣方推想，買方可能貨已轉售，其中部份大麥須轉運客戶。由於所交該批大麥品質低劣，遭客戶退貨，買方請求取消與賣方契約。法官判決，認爲買方已喪失退貨權，因火車站應是貨物之檢驗地點，除火車站以外，並無其他更適當之檢查地點，亦無其他顯明之事實可否定車站卽係貨物檢驗地點之假定❺。

(2) **E. & S. Ruben v. Faire Bros. & Co.** 案:

賣方售貨與買方，而買方再售與C君，買方並通知賣方將貨物逕送交C君，賣方業予照辦。在此種情形之下，買方當無適當之機會驗收貨物。交貨後，C君發現貨物與契約規定不符退貨，買方乃轉向賣方索賠。法官 Hilbery 判決，認爲: (a)以上述情形論，其交貨驗收地點應爲賣方之營業處所; (b)當買方通知賣方將貨逕交 C君時，推定買方已從賣方提貨 (had constructively taken delivery from the seller); (c)買方之轉售行爲業已轉變賣方之所有權; (d)依照英國商品買賣法 Sect. 35之規定，買方不得拒絕收貨。❻

從上面兩個案例，可知其判決係以買方轉售貨物而推定買方業已驗收爲依據。揆諸現代貿易環境與運輸進步情況，上述英國商品買賣法 Sect. 35 之第(3)種規定實有未合，蓋目前工商社會，爲爭取貨運時效，頗多係委託賣方將貨物直接運往買方之客戶者，況貨物以罐頭及其他密封式包裝者，彼彼皆是，買方確有時無法有適當之機會在轉售前先行檢驗，再行出售。凡此情形，卽認爲放棄其驗收權，並認定其業已接收貨物而剝奪其退貨權，確有未當。因此，英國在一九六七年之 Misrepresentation Act 已將一八九三年之商品買賣法 Sect. 35 加一括弧句 "(except where section 34 of the act otherwise provides)", 使 Sect. 34 成爲主宰條文而涵義更趨明晰。其原文如下:

(a) When he intimates to the seller that he has accepted them, or

(b) (except where section 34 of the act otherwise provides) when the goods have been delivered to him, and

---

❺　D. W. Greig: *Sale of Goods*, ch. 4, p. 138.

❻　Robert Lowe: *Commercial Law*, ch. 3, pp. 149–150.

(i) he does any act which is inconsistent with the ownership of the seller; or

(ii) when, after lapse of a reasonable time he retains the goods without intimating to the seller that he has rejected them. ❼

目前問題之焦點仍在買方是否「已有適當之機會檢驗貨物」？ 如買方事實上確有適當之機會檢驗貨物却未加檢驗而售交第三者，則其退貨權仍將喪失。譬如在 Perkins v. Bell 一案，賣方售與買方大麥一批，訂明送至車站交貨，當時買方確有適當之機會檢驗貨物，但買方並不檢驗而直接將貨送交某客戶。嗣後，客戶發現規格不合退貨。法官判決，認為買方已喪失退貨權，主要理由為所有權已由買方再轉移客戶，賣方不可能自客戶之倉庫提回貨物。❽

晚近英國法院判例，頗多因貿易情況及運輸方式之變遷，認定送往買方之交貨地點，不一定是驗收貨物之合理地點。所以在這種情形之下，凡買方已將貨物轉售客戶而須立即轉交者，在無適當機會檢驗即予轉運時，並不見得即喪失其退貨權。譬如 Molling & Co. v. Dean & Son 一案，原告接受被告訂印40,000冊書籍，訂約時已知道該批書籍業轉售美國書商，須依照美商原稿排印，並印美商名稱地址，包裝後運交被告。迨印就交被告時，被告未予檢驗即轉運美商。第抵達後，美商發現印刷不合契約規定退貨，乃由被告將書自費運回英國。法官判決，認為被告確無適當之機會驗收，該書之驗收適當地點 (proper place) 應在送達美國美商之指定地，被告應該仍享有退貨權，其退貨費用並可要求原告賠償❾。此項判例，與前面 Perkins v. Bell 一案之判決完全不同，蓋前案係

---

❼ P. S. Atiyah: *The Sale of Goods*, ch. 26, p. 290.

❽ P. S. Atiyah: *The Sale of Goods*, ch. 26, p. 291.

❾ P. S. Atiyah: *The Sale of Goods*, ch. 26, p. 292-293.

在 Misrepresentation Act 通過前依據原商品買賣法 Sect. 35 之規定，買方如轉售貨物給第三者卽喪失其退貨權，而後者則依據 Misrepresentation Act 之修正條文酌情裁判，自能兼顧事實作合情合理之判斷，確已進步多矣。關于買方是否確無適當之機會驗收貨物及買方是否未經檢驗卽將貨物轉運其客戶？又買方之客戶退貨費用是否應由賣方負擔？這些問題，賣方必須事先詳加調查分析，再作適當之應付及處理，方不致吃虧。

買方拒收貨物之決定，必須通知賣方。除非接受賣方委託或另有協議，買方並無義務爲賣方退運貨物，但買方必須隨時準備提供賣方退運貨物之便利。如貨物業已轉售第三者並已收貨，則買方喪失拒收貨物權，祇可向賣方要求賠償損失。

依照聯合國買賣公約第八十六條之規定，買方如已收到貨物，在行使退貨權時，必須按照當時情況採取合理措施，代爲保全貨物，直至賣方付清其所支付之合理費用爲止。在買方通知賣方退貨後，契約卽告廢止，買方僅居於賣方之代理人地位，負合理保管之責。如賣方不付還貨款或所墊之合理保全費用，買方得依該公約第八十八條之規定，于事先通知賣方後出售該貨，以求補償。

2. 要求違反保證之損害賠償

關于已交付並接受之貨物，如發現違反品質、規格或商品適應性之保證 (breach of warranties as to quality, fitness or description of goods) 時，買方可採取之途徑爲：(1)要求賣方減價或(2)要求賣方賠償損失。

依照聯合國買賣公約第五十條之規定，如賣方所交貨物品質與契約規定不符，買方得要求減低價格。其減價方式，可按實際交付貨品在交貨時之價值與符合契約貨品當時之價格比例計算。

依照英國商品買賣法第五十三條(1)款規定:

如遇賣方違反保證或賣方違反任何契約條件、買方選擇或被迫按違反保證處理時，得:

(a)對賣方之違反保證，提出減少或消滅價格之要求;

(b)對賣方之違反保證，要求損害賠償。

關于上項損害賠償之計算，依據該法第五十三條(2)款評估原則之規定，在正常情況下，可按直接或自然產生之損害情形測定之。而對違反品質、規格或商品適應性之保證，則在同法第五十三條(3)款規定，可按賣方交貨時所交商品之價值與符合契約保證之商品價格差額，計算其損害賠償。

事實上，賣方所交商品如有缺陷，不一定可在交貨時發現，頗多係在買方轉售第三者時始發現。在此種情況，法官很可能在賣方確知買方未經檢驗卽轉售第三者時，裁定照轉售時之當地市價與符合契約品質價格之差額計賠。依一般情形論，在市場價格下跌時，買方將採部份退貨措施，拒收不符品質之貨品，使貨價損失歸賣方負擔;如對品質缺陷情況有所了解時，則不妨要求違反品質保證之損害賠償。惟如何從品質之缺陷程度估計損失，則屬技術上之困難問題，極易引起爭端。

依照美國統一商法 Sect. 2-714 規定，買方如已接收貨物，可在發現所交貨物與契約有任何不符或違反契約無法補救抑有侵犯專利及假冒商標等情事引起訴訟時，得在合理之時間內通知賣方，要求賠償違反保證之一切損失。其貨物之損害賠償，可按保證貨品之市價與所交貨物之當時價值差額計算。在正常情況下，其他 Sect. 2-715 規定之附帶及後果損失，亦應計賠。

3. 要求違反保證之後果損害賠償

由於商品之品質缺陷，在使用時，人體或財產遭受損害為極平常的事。此項違反品質保證之商品，不拘爲自用或轉售，依照英國商品買賣法 Sect. 54 之規定，其後果損失，得按特別賠償（special damage）處理，照實質損害（physical damage）之實際損失賠償。

4. 要求修理或更換

依照聯合國買賣公約第四十六條(2)(3)款規定，如發現所交商品不符契約規格時，得要求賣方交付替代商品（substitute goods）或就原交商品之缺點予以修理或補救。但必須按該公約第三十九條之規定，在發現不符（lack of conformity）後之合理時間內提出。

4-4　影響契約履行之因素

在買賣當事人簽訂契約後，往往由於意外之突發事件發生，使一方當事人無法達成契約之目的，或由於無法預測之情勢變化，使契約之履行變爲不可能（impossibility）、違法（illegal），甚或因契約標的物之毀滅，使當事人陷于實質上的無法履行。爲處理這些問題，英國之 Law Reform（Frustrated Contract）Act, 一九四三年乃創制所謂「商業挫折原則」（Doctrine of Commercial Frustration），以解決此困難。依此原則，契約之一方當事人，如事實證明其「不履行」（non-performance）爲正當時，可得到原諒。

契約之一方當事人實際上「不可能履行」（imposibility of performance）契約義務，與外在環境之變化，使其履行「增加困難」（additional hardship），兩者之意義截然不同。譬如供應商由於天災、罷工，使其增加採購原料之困難，或因滙率下跌，使原料成本增加，從而增加其履行之困難。凡此種種，祇在增加其履行契約義務之困難及費用而已，並不足以構成基本情勢之變化，使賣方之履行契約義務變爲客觀上

的不可能（objectively impossible）。因此，所謂「不可能」，應該是
「實質上和客觀上的不可能」（physically and objectively impossible）。
此類可促使契約一方當事人不可能履行契約義務之事態，約可分為下列
五種：

4-4-1 特定標的物之毀滅

契約之履行，必須特定（specific）標的物之繼續存在，如訂約後，
該標的物非由於任何一當事人之過失而在風險轉移前滅失，則契約即告
失效。譬如在 Howell v. Coupland 一案，買方向賣方訂約預購其在
Whaplode 農地所產之馬鈴薯200噸，不幸大部份為蟲害所毀。英上訴
法庭認為此係特定農作物，既非賣方之過失所毀，契約應可失效❶。但
如製鞋商因工廠失火，所製皮鞋全部焚毀，仍不得免除履約責任，因所
需皮鞋仍可向其他來源購得，祇增加其履約上之困難及費用而已。倘訂
製之鞋為特定工廠所出，其機器及產品因火災全毀，致不可能履行其契
約義務，自可原宥❷。

依照上述商業挫折原則，商品在所有權未轉移買方之前即已滅失或
變壞（perish or deteriorate）則賣方須負擔該項損失，並不得向買方
索取價款，同時買方也可不付貨款，賣方亦無交貨責任；反過來說，如
商品在風險轉移買方後滅失或毀損，則買方仍應照付貨款。又如買方業
已全部付款或部份付款，但標的物在所有權及風險未轉移買方前已全部
滅失而賣方不能完全給付（a total failure of consideration）時，則賣方
應完全退還貨款，如係分批交貨契約，且係部份不能給付者（a partial

---

❶ D. W. Greig, *Sale of Goods*, ch. 6, p. 215.

❷ Robert N. Corley & William J. Robert:*Principles of Business Law*,
ch. 14, p. 259.

failure of consideration)，則可不必全部退款，其未交貨部份亦不得適用商業挫折原則。上項商業挫折原則所指損失，係屬特定商品之意外滅失或變壞 (accidental destruction or deterioration)，但不包括基於商品本身品質缺陷之損失。

依照 Law Reform (Frustrated Contract) Act 之規定，下列三種情況不得引用商業挫折原則:

(1)在銷售特定商品 (specific goods) 之契約，如商品在所有權及風險轉移買方後滅失或毀損，買方仍應照付貨款，並不得引用該法訴請救濟。

(2)在銷售特定商品之契約，商品在所有權尚未轉移而風險業已轉移買方時發生滅失或毀損。其最顯明之例子爲 CIF 契約，商品很可能在風險業已轉移買方後提單尚未轉移前即告滅失。在此種情況下，買方仍應照付貨款，亦不得引用該法訴請救濟。

(3)商品之所有權已轉移買方，但風險仍在賣方，則是項商品之滅失或毀損，應由賣方負責，不得轉移買方❸。

以上對商業挫折原則之適用規定，極爲合理，似值得參探。

4-4-2　政府之干預

在契約訂定之後，突然政府公佈法令，禁止契約有關之特定商品的進口或出口，使契約當事人無法在契約規定期間內履行其契約義務，得予免責。但並非任何政府禁令可使契約無效或履行爲非法 (illegal)，有時政府之停止特定商品的進出口是有時間性的，契約仍可在雙方協議下延期至政令開放時履行。又如廠商製售之特定商品，在運輸途中突爲政

---

❸ P. S. Atiyah: *The Sale of Goods*, ch. 18, pp. 174-175.

府充公徵用，賣方自可免責，並解除其契約責任❹。 又如 C. Czarnikow Ltd. v. Rolimpex 案，波蘭國家貿易公司於一九七四年五～七月間，訂售英商其所產波蘭甜菜糖一批，訂明照倫敦精糖協會 (Refined Sugar Association) 之標準合約規定，于同年十一月至十二月交貨。按照 RSA 之 Force Majeure Clause 規定，如遇政府干預 (government intervention)，得延長交貨期限或取消契約。同年八月間，波蘭因雨水過量歉收，波蘭政府爰於同年十一月五日公佈，從該日起至一九七五年止，禁止砂糖出口，因此波蘭國家貿易公司之輸出精糖變爲違法，乃引用 Force Majeure 條款，要求廢約。英國樞密院 (House of Lords) 認爲波商爲免引起國內社會政治之不安，引用該條款之 "government intervention" 定義，要求廢約，應屬合理❺。

4-4-3 戰　爭

具有甲國國籍之商人，訂約出售一批貨物給隸籍乙國之進口商，一旦甲國與乙國發生戰事時，與敵國通商變成違法，其所訂契約可免予履行。譬如 Fibrosa Spolka Akcyjna v. Fairbairn Lawson Combe Barbour Ltd. 一案，買方波蘭商人向英格蘭 Leeds 城之英商訂購 Flax-hackling Machine 一批，訂明在一定時間內 CIF Gdynia, Poland 交貨，如遇戰事，可以延期交付，第訂約後，不久發生戰爭，Gdynia 爲德軍佔領。法官判決，認爲本案因戰爭發生，契約之履行已發生挫折，雖規定可以稍爲延期，但無法挽回契約之實質履行，因與敵國通商，將構成違法❻。

❹ Andrew J. Coppola, N. G. Totowa & Littlefield: *Law of Business*, pp. 124–125.

❺ Clive M. Schmitthoff: *Export Trade*, ch. 11, pp. 113–114.

❻ Clive M. Schmitthoff: *Export Trade*, ch. 11, pp. 112.

4-4-4　天　　災

天災（act of god）之發生，可使契約之履行變爲不可能。但天災並非時常可構成契約當事人之免責。譬如甲商訂售其農場所產之豆類10,000蒲式耳（bushel），如農場爲洪水或暴風雨所毀滅，可以免責；惟契約如不訂明係其農場所產豆類，則甲商仍應設法在市面上購足10,000蒲式耳交貨，不得免責❼。

4-4-5　其他契約人之影響

契約當事人之一方，爲履行其契約得與第三者簽約，要求參與履行契約之全部份或一部份義務。譬如向第三者訂購特定之材料、設備等是。如訂約後該第三者拒絕或無法提供契約所需特定之材料、設備或服務時，該當事人得要求解除契約，但須擔負適當之損害賠償❽。

聯合國商品買賣公約第七十九條第(2)—(5)款亦有同樣之規定如下：

(2)如當事人不能履行契約係由於參與執行契約全部或一部份之第三者不履行義務時，該當事人只有在下列情況下可免責：

a. 按本條第(1)款規定，免除責任（第(1)款規定：當事人由於某種非其所能控制之障碍，使其不能履行契約之任何義務，而此種障碍又無法在訂約時預知、避免或克服其後果者，如能提出證明，得免負責任）。

b. 如該款規定亦適用於其所雇用之人員，則該批人員可同樣免責。

(3)上項免責，應以第(1)款所規定之障碍存在期間有效。

(4)不能履行義務之一方，必須將障碍及其對履行義務能力之影響情

---

❼ Coppola, Totowa & Littlefield: *Law of Business*, p. 127.

❽ Anderson & Kumpf: *Business Law*, ch. 14, pp. 232-233.

形通知對方。

(5)本條規定，不妨礙任何一方行使本公約規定之要求損失賠償以外的任何權利。

上述五種無法控制之事項，如發生在契約有效期間而無法如期履行其契約義務者，雙方當事人得就事態發生之情況加以分析，倘事態很快解決，或政府之禁令或管制有一定期限，則不妨協議以延期履行之方式解決之，其影響程度輕微者，更不妨協議適當之處理方式。如此項挫折事項，已使基本情勢變化，致嚴重影響其契約之繼續履行時，自可按照商業挫折原則，予以廢約，蓋延期履行可能涉及原訂價格之工資材料計算基礎改變，使賣方無法繼續履行。或在挫折事件發生前，賣方已花費不少人工材料等製造費用，必須求得合理之補償。凡此種種，買賣雙方唯有在廢約前設法調整其權利義務，以獲致妥善之解決辦法。

4-5　契約之適用法律

4-5-1　適用法律之選擇

4-5-1-1　法律選擇之自治原則

國際貿易之契約當事人，因所屬國籍、住所、標的物之所在地以及締約地與履行地等構成契約之事項不同，因此契約履行發生問題時，乃發生本國法律與他國法律競相適用之衝突現象。此項涉外案件之法律衝突，均發生在涉外法律適用之程序上。故現代國家，就特定涉外事項之有關法律，凡與外國法足以構成互相衝突者，乃規定其適用法律之選擇規範，以解決國際爭端。此種法律規範，就是一般所稱牴觸法（Conflict of Law）。

　　現代民主國家對一般對外貿易契約，均採用自治原則，尊重當事人之自由意志去選擇適用法律 (applicable law)，或稱契約之準據法 (proper law of contract)。我國涉外民事法律適用法第六條曾規定：「法律行爲發生債之關係者，其成立要件及效力，依當事人意思定其適用之法律」。可見我國立法，也是採用自治原則。

　　關于國際商品買賣之法律適用問題，一九五五年六月十五日在海牙召開之海牙會議，曾通過了一項「國際商品買賣之法律適用公約」，參加締約國有比利時、丹麥、芬蘭、法國、意大利、挪威及瑞典等歐洲國家，該約第二條規定如下：

　　買賣契約應受契約當事人合意選定國家之國內法 (domestic law) 支配。此項準據法之選定，可在契約中以明示條款 (express clause) 確定之。

4-5-1-2　法律選擇之方式及原則

　　適用法律之選擇 (choice of law)，有單元選擇及多元選擇。僅選擇一個國家之法律爲適用之法律者，稱爲單元選擇。如我涉外民事法律適用法第一條關于「人之行爲能力」之規定，係採「依本國法」，此卽適用法律之單元選擇。第六條規定：「法律行爲發生債之關係者，其成立要件及效力，依當事人意思定其適用法律；當事人意思不明時，同國籍者依本國法，國籍不同者，依行爲地法……」。可見對契約適用法律之選擇，有明示採自由選擇之國家法律及未明示採本國法及行爲地法之多種標準。

　　適用法律之選擇原則：(1)應公平合理；(2)主要利害國家之法律應列爲優先考慮；(3) 所選擇之法律應與交易有最密切及最眞實之關聯 (the transaction has its closest and most real connection) 爲原則。

4-5-1-3　明示選擇法律

所謂明示之選擇 (express choice)，係指契約之適用法律，由双方依據上述選擇方式及原則，自願共同選定後在契約內訂明條款。管轄法院乃依據所選定國家之抵觸法去分析發生糾紛事項之法律規範，以確定其所選法律是否與契約有密切關聯。如所選法律與契約毫無關聯，法院得拒絕受理。玆舉 Vita Food Products Inc. v. Unus Shipping Co. 一案說明如下：

> 在美國紐約註册之某公司與在加拿大 Nova Scotia 註册之某公司簽約，同意交由該 Nova Scotia 註册公司之輪船將靑魚一批自加拿大之 Newfoundland 運往紐約交貨，提貨單之印刷條款訂明「運輸契約由英國法律管轄」。Lord Wright 法官判決，認爲此項交易，從法律原則及事實觀點言，與英國法律毫無關聯，故不應選擇該法律爲適用法律❶。

所以自由選擇法律之意願表示，並非毫無限制，其所依據之原則，必須合法 (legal) 與符合事實 (bona fide)，使契約之解釋、履行、解除等均能與所選擇之法律有密切關聯。

談到契約之型式，一般人通常會提到這是英國契約 (English contract) 或那是法國契約 (French contract)。但事實上，依據契約之性質，有時契約之某種特殊部份仍須受到某些有關國家法律之管制，而大部份則受另一國之法律管轄。譬如英國伯明罕 (Birmingham) 之某製造商，經由其在澳洲 Melboune 之代理出售澳商工作母機一批，交易條件爲 FOB London，雙方當事人均同意其契約之成立及效力適用澳洲維多利亞州 (State Of Victoria) 之州法律，而契約之執行在英國伯明罕之製造商，故契約之履行則適用英國法❷。又如 A. V. Pound & Co.

---

❶ Schmitthoff: *Export Trade*, ch. 12, p. 129.
❷ Schmitthoff: *Export Trade*, ch. 12, p. 128.

Ltd. v. M. W. Hardy Inc 案，契約雖訂明適用英國法，但售貨條件為 FAS Lisbon，所需出口許可證，依照葡萄牙法律規定，必須由葡萄牙出口商申請發給，因此其契約之履行已受葡國法律之管轄❸。

以上都是契約適用多種國家法律的例子，因此，買賣雙方當事人在訂立契約時，必須考慮到契約履行之週邊情況再決定其契約之適用法律，因一國法律往往無法管轄所有影響契約履行之週邊實際情況，一旦發生糾紛訴諸仲裁或法院時，其判決之確定力及執行力就會遭受影響。因為選擇契約的適用法律並非無限制的，雙方當事人必須事先考慮其合約性質及所選準據法在執行上可能遭遇之事實問題，從而決定其最適當之準據法，以明示條款在契約中表明。

在此必須進一步說明者，契約中明示適用之法律，如僅規定受某國法律管轄，往往一般人會解釋為管轄僅及於「契約之成立及效力」(the formation and essential validity of the contract)，但「不涉及其契約之履行」(performance)。譬如英國出口商以 Free delivery 條件售與法國進口商貨物一批，契約僅訂明契約受英國法管轄 (The contract is governed by English Law)，法官很可能認為買方之貨物檢驗及拒絕權受法國法律管轄，因為依據契約之簡單說明，可解釋為英國法律僅能涵蓋契約之成立部份，而不包括契約之履行。因此頗多國際契約在訂明適用法律時，都加上本契約之成立、效力、解釋及履行等均受 (in all respects) 某某國法律管轄等字樣。此外，應特別注意者，準據法之適用，僅限於契約之成立、履行等實體法方面，至於訴訟程序與準據法無關，訴訟之進行，仍應依受理法院所在地法處理。

4-5-1-4　未明示選擇法律

依照一九五五年國際商品買賣之法律適用公約第三條規定：「在雙

❸ Schmitthoff: *Export Trade*, ch. 2, pp 23-24.

方當事人未選定適用法律時，買賣契約受出賣人受領訂單時之習慣居所地國家法律之支配。若訂單係由出賣人之分公司受領，則買賣契約受該分公司之所在地國家法律支配。但若訂單係於買受人習慣居所地國或其分公司所在地交付，則無論訂單受領人為出賣人或其代表、代理人或旅行推銷員，買賣契約均應受買受人習慣居所地國家法律或買受人分公司之所在地國家法律支配。」由於契約準據法之選擇問題頗為複雜，為求適當而公平合理，決非簡單之幾句條文可決定的。所以當時英國就首先不受該約之約束。這裏祇能提供大家參攷而已。

目前從事國際貿易之業者，頗多在契約內不訂明準據法的，一旦發生糾紛時，受理法院頗感棘手。因此，首先必須從契約當事人之行為能力（capacity）、契約之形成（formation）、效力（包括 formal validity, essential validity & illegality）、解釋（interpretation 一包括契約之條文意義及當事人之明示默示義務）及履約方式（manner of performance）等，一一加以審查，並就下列事項一併加予檢查，從而推定其適用之法律：

(1)合約訂立地點

(2)合約履行地點

(3)雙方當事人應用之文字及專門術語（指使用之國際貿易術語解釋規則）

(4)交易文件之形式

(5)雙方當事人之人格

(6)合約之標的物

(7)交付仲裁

(8)履行債務之金額或保證義務

(9)與過去交易之關係

⑽特別法律對該交易之影響❹。

　　推定契約締結地法律為適用法律——假如契約之履行與契約之訂立在同一個國家，則契約之形成、締結及效力自可屬同一個國家的法律管轄。通常出口貿易之買賣雙方，都不在同一個地方，應以契約確認接受地點為執行法律義務之所在地。例如，英國商人在倫敦接受印度商人CIF Calcutta 之定貨，法院可確定該合約受英國法律管轄，因為合約之訂立在英國，裝船交運義務之履行也在英國。

　　推定契約履行地法律為適用法律——頗多情形契約履行地與契約訂定地不在同一地方，因此應有強有力的理由推定：這個契約或至少契約的履行部份應受履行地之法律管轄。例如，馬爾他 (Malta) 商人向直布羅陀 (Gibraltar) 商人訂購一批貨物，交貨條件為 FOB Gibraltar。貨到後，買方已將貨轉售當地第二購貨商 (sub-purchaser)，嗣該商以品質低劣而由買方要求退貨，依據買方所在地之馬爾他法律，此項退貨行為是合法的。但依據合約規定，"FOB Gibraltar" 交貨義務之履行係在直布羅陀，依照該地法律，買方于到貨後再交第二購貨商，業已喪失其退貨之權利❺。

　　以上係契約的履行部份應受履行地法律管轄的實例，　可供讀者參攷。

4-5-2　外國裁判之效力與執行

4-5-2-1　裁判管轄之選擇

　　契約當事人之選擇法庭管轄，可影響法律之適用，如所選擇之法庭為排他管轄、不能依據合意選擇之法律作判決者，其訴訟勢將危害當事

❹ Schmitthoff: *Export Trade*, ch. 12, p. 130.

❺ Schmitthoff: *Export Trade*, ch. 12, pp. 130-132.

人之權利義務。故契約當事人在選擇適用法律及管轄法庭時，不可不慎重調查考慮。

依據一九五六年十月第八屆海牙國際私法會議擬訂之國際商品買賣合意選擇法庭管轄公約草案 (Draft Convention on the Jurisdiction of the Selected Forum in the Case of International Sales of Goods) 規定，買賣契約當事人得明白指定由一締約國之法庭管轄，其行使管轄權所爲之判決應予承認並聲明有效，毋須其他締約國作實質之審查。惟此項裁判，依據裁判國法律必須具有確定力及執行力，不得違背請求承認國之公共政策 (public policy)。當事人依據裁判國法律合法傳喚或通知其代表出席，如遇宣告缺席而作缺席判決時，該缺席之當事人應有充分時間爲防禦之抗辯；如判決因違反前項規定而被確定拒絕時，若原告無過失，並不排除原告以相同理由向拒絕承認及執行該判決之締約國法庭提起新訴訟的權利。

關于法庭管轄之決定，有三個原則：(1)自動管轄原則 (principle of submission)——由雙方當事人合意選擇法庭管轄，在契約中訂定之。該被指定之法庭卽有專屬管轄權，當事人應接受該國法庭之判決。(2)有效原則——管轄國對特定案件之事物，如不能判決並切實執行者，則不得就該案行使其裁判管轄；換句話說，選擇之法庭，必須對特定案件具有裁判及有效執行權者爲原則。此項案件，以涉訟當事人之住所及財產在管轄法庭可行使裁判管轄者居多，歐陸法系國家多採用之。(3)裁量管轄原則——管轄國得受理不在境內之被告所提案件，行使其裁判管轄，傳喚在他國之被告到庭應訴，如被告不到庭，仍得作有效判決，但其判決之行使性得由管轄國裁量之。契約當事人殆可按照上述三種原則參酌實際情況確定之❻。

❻ 劉甲一著：國際私法，pp. 303-306.

4-5-2-2　外國裁判之承認與執行

外國法院所作判決,由於各國之國情、風俗習慣及審判制度之不同, 殊難望其必能獲得承認, 並付諸執行。因此, 在手續上必須經過判決之 承認及執行之程序。經承認之外國判決, 必須再經過國內法院下列三種 方式付諸執行:

(1)再審後, 發給執行許可書;

(2)依據外國判決作成新判決;

(3)登記外國判決。

我國民事訴訟法第四〇二條對外國法庭之判決有下列各款情形之一 者, 不承認其效力:

(1)依中華民國之法律, 外國法院無管轄權者;

(2)敗訴之一造為中華民國人而未應訴者;

(3)外國法院之判決有背公共秩序或善良風俗者;

(4)無國際相互之承認者❼。

4-6　仲　　裁

4-6-1　採用仲裁解決貿易糾紛之優點

解決國際貿易爭端最好的辦法是調解 (conciliation), 其次是仲 裁 (arbitration), 最後才是訴訟 (litigation)。 一個從事國際貿易之 從業人員, 在準備與外商簽訂銷售合約時, 最好預先考慮萬一發生貿易 糾紛時應採用何種程序以解決爭端, 對自己權益才可得到最佳保障。如 爭端起因于品質與說明不符或貨不對樣, 這涉及技術問題之最好解決方 法是請專家或專業商會或團體來調解, 如涉及契約之構成或其他純粹法

---

❼　劉甲一著: 國際私法, p. 324.

律問題，自仍以訴請法院來解決較爲適當。惟國際商品買賣，往往牽涉到貨物之品質、運輸、保險與貨款之交付等複雜問題，其引起爭執事項的性質，多涉及各業之專業知識，如由專家參與調處或仲裁，自較法院純以法律觀點來處理，較易達成合理裁斷，且可縮短處理時間，節省費用，故爲業者所樂予採用。

4-6-2　仲裁之程序及執行

採用仲裁方式解決貿易糾紛，應事先在契約內 ㈠ 訂立仲裁條款（arbitration clause），並註明㈡仲裁範圍，㈢仲裁地點及仲裁規則，與㈣仲裁所依據之適用法律（applicable law）。依仲裁程序所作之仲裁判斷（arbitral awards），必須具備理由，作成之仲裁判斷書應送雙方當事人或送交管轄法院依民事訴訟之程序送達之。

仲裁人對當事人間之判斷，與法院之確定判決有同等效力，但須聲請法院執行裁定後方得强制執行。敗訴之一方如能依仲裁人之判斷自動執行，自無問題，惟萬一不服，勝訴之一方，仍得聲請執行地所在國之管轄法院予以裁定，方可執行。

仲裁判斷能否爲外國法院予以承認及執行，各國所採之寬嚴標準不同，有採立法方式，亦有採雙邊協定之互惠方式者，殊無統一準則。我國對外商務仲裁之效力，尚無明文規定，如兩國尚未簽訂互惠協定者，須由法院依據具體事件及各種糾紛之發生情況，分別酌情處理。要之，所作判斷如公平合理並不違背我國之公共政策（public policy），我國法院仍將作適當之裁判❶。

國際間以公約方式規律商務仲裁之執行效力，係於一九二三年六月

---

❶　柯澤東著：國際商務仲裁（參閱外貿協會出版之"國際貿易實務研習會第27-28期講義"）

在日內瓦簽訂「仲裁條款議定書」開始，於一九二七年九月復在斯地再簽訂「外國仲裁判斷之執行公約」，規定締約國對合意所爲之仲裁判斷，應承認其效力，且應依判斷作成國之程序規則予以執行，但須不違反請求執行國之公共政策或其法律原則。因此，締約國間往往仍須簽訂雙邊互惠協定，始能達到有效的執行❷。一九五八年在聯合國之努力下，又於同年六月十日在紐約召開之聯合國大會通過了「聯合國承認及執行外國仲裁判斷之國際商務仲裁公約」（United Nations Conference on International Commercial Arbitration Convention on the Recognition and Enforcement of Foreign Arbitral Awards），參加簽字國計52國，規定外國之仲裁判斷，無須再簽訂雙邊協定即可在締約國間予以承認及執行，但一方當事人向執行地所在國之主管機關提具證據證明有下列情形之一者，得依該造之請求，拒予承認及執行:

㈠契約當事人對其適用之法律有某種無行爲能力情形者，或契約當事人作爲契約準據法之法律係屬無效，或未指明以何法律爲準時依裁決地所在國法律係屬無效者;

㈡受裁決援用之一造未獲關于指派仲裁員或仲裁程序之適當通知，或因他故致未能申辯者;

㈢裁決所處理之爭議非爲交付仲裁之標的或不在其條款之列，或裁決載有關交付仲裁範圍以外事項之決定者;

㈣仲裁機關之組成或仲裁程序與各造間之協議不符，或無協議而與仲裁地所在國法律不符者;

㈤裁決對各造尚無拘束力，或業經裁決地所在國或裁決所依據法律之國家的主管機關撤銷或停止執行者。

---

❷　參閱司法行政部與國際貿易局編譯之「國際貿易法規暨慣例彙編」第二冊第1497及1502頁。

又聲請承認及執行地所在國之主管機關認定有下列情形之一者，亦得拒不承認及執行仲裁判斷:

（甲）依該國法律，爭議事項係不能以仲裁解決者;

（乙）承認或執行裁決有違反公共政策者❸。

4-6-3 國際商會及聯合國之仲裁規則

國際商會為協助各國商人解決國際貿易糾紛，擬採用契約當事人合意方式，約定在合約訂明以國際仲裁解決紛爭，儘量避免普通法院之管轄，曾於一九五五年訂頒「國際商會調解暨仲裁規則」一種，逮一九七五年，復另訂「國際商會仲裁法院仲裁規則」以取代之。當事人如在契約中引用該規則，得由該仲裁法院按規則所訂仲裁程序進行仲裁。該仲裁法院祇是一個行政機構，並非仲裁機構，當事人提付仲裁之爭議，係由指定之仲裁人所組成之「仲裁庭」仲裁之。爭議可由獨任仲裁人或由三仲裁人裁決之。由雙方當事人約定獨任仲裁人仲裁者，得以合意提名仲裁人，由仲裁法院確定之; 如雙方當事人對獨任仲裁人之提名無法協議時，該獨任仲裁人應由仲裁法院指定之。爭議由三仲裁人仲裁者，則由雙方當事人各提名一人由該法院確認，當事人之一方未提名者，由該法院代為指定，其第三仲裁人由該法院指定，並擔任仲裁庭長。仲裁地除當事人有合意者外，應由仲裁法院選定之。惟當事人提付仲裁者，應視其已承諾將立即履行判斷結果，以該仲裁判斷案件為終局裁決，並放棄其任何方式上訴之權利❹。

聯合國國際貿易法委員會(United Nations Commission on Inter-

---

❸ 參閱司法行政部與國際貿易局編譯之「國際貿易法規暨慣例彙編」第二冊第1509頁。Schmitthoff: *Export Trade*, ch. 26.

❹ 參閱司法行政部及國際貿易局編譯之「國際貿易法規暨慣例彙編」第二冊第1565頁。

national Trade Law）鑑于仲裁係解決國際貿易爭端之有效方法，乃於一九七六年訂立「聯合國國際貿易法委員會仲裁規則」，並請各國廣泛使用。依照該規則規定，雙方當事人可採用選任一個獨任仲裁人或三個仲裁人之方式處理提付交與承辦之仲裁案件。後者方式由雙方當事人各選一仲裁人，再由該兩仲裁人另選一仲裁人為仲裁法庭之主任仲裁人。雙方當事人得協議在兩造國家內決定仲裁地點，但仲裁法庭得在雙方同意之國家內決定仲裁場所。仲裁判斷對雙方當事人具有拘束效力及履行義務❺。

　　關于仲裁條款之決定，似可由一方洽請對方自下列各範例中酌情選定之：

　　例㈠：“Any controversy or claim arising out of or relating to this contract, or the breach thereof shall be settled by arbitration in（仲裁地）in accordance with the Rules of the （某國）Arbitration Association and judgement upon the award rend_ered by arbitrator (s) may be entered in any court having jurisdiction.”

　　例㈡：“All disputes arising in connection with the present contract shall be finally settled by arbitration. The arbitration shall be held at （仲裁地）, and conducted in accordance with the Rules of Conciliation & Arbitration of the International Chamber of Commerce. Judgement upon the award rendered may be entered in any court having jurisdiction or application may be made to such court for a judicial acceptance of the award and an order of enforcement, as the case may be.”

---

❺　參閱司法行政部及國際貿易局編譯之「國際貿易法規暨慣例彙編」第二冊第1590頁。

例㈢: "Any dispute or whatever nature arising out of or in any way relating to the contract or to its construction or fulfilment may be referred to arbitration. Such an arbitration shall take place in Taipei, Republic of China, in accordance with the Arbitration Regulations of the Republic of China."❻

4-7 契約之廢除

4-7-1 契約經履行後廢止 (Discharge By Performance)

一般買賣契約,均訂有雙方履行之條件,一俟賣方對契約之性質、數量、品質及履行時間業已完全履行 (full and complete performance),買方亦依約如期支付價款並提貨, 則契約雙方當事人之責任卽告終了,契約也自動廢除。但下列各種情形必須加予注意:

(1)部份履行 (partial performance) —— 如契約在簽訂時雙方當事人卽經明白表示或默示同意 (expressly or implicitly agreed) 此係不可分之整個契約 (entire contract) 者, 則一方當事人未完全履行其契約義務時, 不能解除其責任, 其已履行部份亦不能得到補償, 除非另一方當事人同意接受其部份履行、 並放棄原契約條件者, 自當別論。假如係屬可區分契約 (divisible contract), 則當事人已履行之部份契約, 應有權利要求合理之報酬。

(2)實質履行 (substantial performance) ——契約規定必須精確完成者, 如遇一方當事人實際完全履行契約義務後, 另一當事人發現

---

❻ 柯澤東著:國際商務仲裁 (參閱外貿協會出版之 "國際貿易實務研習會第27-28期講義")

尚有多少瑕疵或缺陷時，得要求對方補救，或自己逕予補救後扣除此項支出之補救費用。

(3)提供履行 (tender of performance) ——契約之一方當事人，由於另一當事人之拒絕或不同意而不克完全履行其契約義務時，該一方當事人可不負履行之責任，蓋此項「履行之提供」即等於「實際履行」 (Tender of performance is equivalent to actual performance)。

(4)履行時間 (time of performance) ——契約訂有履行時間，並規定「時間」為履行之要件者，則任何不依照規定時間履行契約者，應視為基本違約 (fundamental breach of contract)，受害一方得要求損害賠償。

4-7-2 契約經同意後廢除 (Discharge by Agreement)

(1)依照契約條款 (provision of original contract) ——經雙方當事人之同意，得在契約上預先訂明，如遇某種事故發生時，任何一方可依照契約原訂條款之規定，通知對方解除契約。

(2)雙方同意廢止 (recession by agreement) ——契約得經雙方當事人之同意廢止，各自退貨還款，雙方回復原狀。這叫做共同廢約 (mutual recession)。如因一方欺詐，受害一方向法院控訴而廢約，不得視為同意廢約。

(3)契約之一方棄權 (waiver) ——契約之一方當事人對另一當事人之不能依照契約規定履行義務，得放棄其依約追償之權利而同意解除另一方當事人之履約義務。這種情形，在法律上稱為棄權 (waiver)。如甲方已交貨，而乙方無能力付款，甲方得放棄其要求乙方付款之權利，將貨物收回，並同意廢約。

(4)更換契約 (substitution) ——契約雙方當事人如 認爲所訂契約並不適合，得隨時經雙方同意更訂新約。一俟新約成立，卽代替舊約，對雙方均發生約束力。

(5)和解及補償 (accord & satisfaction) ——契約之一方當事人得同意另一當事人和解，並同意其以補償方式補償其不履行契約所招致之損失，並取消契約。

(6)免除賠償 (release claim) ——契約之一方當事人對另一方當事人已提出損害賠償之要求，嗣後復免除其賠償責任而同意廢約。此所謂 Release, 係指一方已向對方提出賠償要求而復免除其賠償責任， 與上述 Waiver 之放棄追償權利，意義完全不同。

4-7-3　契約因不可能履行而廢止 (Discharge By Impossibility)

契約之不可能履行 (impossibility of performance)，可能基于商業挫折之多種因素，使一方當事人無法履行其契約義務，前章業經詳細敍述，在此恕不再贅。

4-7-4　契約因當事人之違約而廢止 (Discharge By Breach Of Contract)

契約可能由於一方當事人之完全不履行、部份履行或拒絕履行而廢止。茲分述之。

(1)完全違背(total breach) ——契約一方當事人之完全違背爲不可恕，受害一方得要求損害賠償，並立卽廢約及不再履行其契約義務。

(2)部份違背 (partial breach) ——契約一方當事人之部份違背，如受害一方情形嚴重，得廢止契約，要求賠償損失; 如一方當事人確已實際履行，但所受損害輕微，則受害一方仍應履行其契約義務，並接受對方有缺陷之履行 (defective performance) 而僅要求其賠償損失而已。

(3)拒絕履行（renunciation）——契約之一方當事人在契約規定限期內正式來文拒絕履行其契約義務，受害一方得視爲「提前違約」（anticipatory breach of Contract），可不再履行其契約義務，並俟規定履行期屆滿時訴請賠償損失。

參　考　書

1. Furmston: *Cheshire & Fifoot's Law of Contract*, Part VII, ch. 1
2. Anderson & Kumpf: *Business Law*, ch. 14 & 15
3. Coppola, Totowa & Littlefield: *Law of Business Contract*, ch. 13, pp. 115-128
4. Corley & Robert: *Principles of Business Law*, ch. 14, pp. 256-261 & ch. 15, pp. 274-279

第五章　國際商品買賣契約之主要條款

以上各章，係敍述契約構成之要素，契約當事人之權利義務，以及發生糾紛時之補救方法及處理程序。這些規例，歷經國際間貿易界多年之習用及逐步修訂而成為公認之一般習用規範，國家立法或國際商業政治組織祇集合專家意見及歷年流傳之慣例，加以編整及具體化而已。因此，契約之涉及上述各款，除必須受貿易慣例、一般成文法之默示條款、以及法院判例、國際公約與國內法之有關規定的約束外，普通國際商業契約之內容條款，其屬于一般性者，可列入「一般條款」（general conditions），在契約內以印刷方式訂明，其須雙方洽談協定者，始在主要條款內加以明確規定，俾雙方可遵照履行。茲特列舉如次，以供讀者參考。

5-1　品質條件

近年來，由於科技發達，人類對商品需求之水準提高，商品之類型及製造亦日趨複雜，因此商品買賣契約對品質之規定，亦因商品之性質及用途而異。大抵說來，買賣契約對品質之決定方式，可分為憑規格說明（sale by description）及憑樣品（sale by sample）兩大類。茲說明如次。

5-1-1 憑規格說明

凡憑品質或規格說明以決定商品之品質條件者，(1)可由賣方提供產品說明書、型錄、圖樣等由買方選擇決定；或由買方提供設計圖樣、技術說明，並指定使用材料，由賣方製供其所需產品。(2)由買方指定廠牌或商標 (brand or trade mark)，由賣方供應該特定品牌之產品。(3)憑標準規格交貨 (sale by standard)，如商品交易所、同業公會所訂之品質標準是。(4)按平均品質交貨 (fair average quality)，一般農產品多指定某地某季節或年期 (season or crop year) 之產品交貨，品質則按該季或年期所產之平均品質為準。

5-1-2 憑 樣 品

所謂樣品，係指品質樣本 (quality sample) 而言，即商品之大小、厚度、形狀、體積或容量固應與樣品相符,即品質亦應與樣品之品質相符 (correspond with the sample in quality)，且以無不可銷售之任何缺陷 (The goods shall be free from any defect rendering them unmerchantable) 為合格。——此係英國商品買賣法 Sect. 15 對憑樣品交易之介說，前面業經提過。所以說，這裏所謂憑樣品交易，不但指所交商品從表面檢視 (visible examination) 應與樣品相符，即品質亦應相符。

品質決定之時間及地點，有所謂裝運品質條件 (shipped quality terms) 及卸貨品質條件 (landed quality terms)。前者如 Ex Work, FAS, FOB, C&F, CIF 等多以起運地裝運時之品質為準，後者則以目的港卸貨時之品質為準者居多,如 Ex Ship, Ex Quay 是；但亦有 C&F CIF 契約以目的港卸貨時品質為準者，不可一概而論。品質之檢驗，究以廠商自行檢驗之報告為準，抑委由具有權威之公證檢驗機構在裝運地或卸貨地之品質檢驗報告爲準，得由買賣雙方協議，在契約內予以訂明之。

5-2　品質保證條件

凡買賣契約訂有品質保證條款（guarantee or warranty）及保證期限（guarantee period）者，其保證日期，可自通知貨物準備在工廠交運或貨物風險移轉至買方時開始，直至期滿時止，其有效時間可由雙方協議。在保證期間買方如發現有任何故障或缺陷，證明係由於設計疏忽、用料不當、偸工減料或粗製濫造所致者（resulting from faulty design, materials or workmanship），應以書面立卽通知賣方，並由賣方于接獲通知後依約負責照下列方式加以補救：

(a)修理發生故障或缺陷部份；

(b)將該項有缺陷之貨物或零件退回修理；

(c)將該項有缺陷或不良之貨物退換；

(d)更換不良零件，費用由賣方負擔。

賣方在接獲買方通知之相當時期內（within a reasonable period after receipt of notification）如不進行修換，買方得在合理方式下（in a reasonable manner）自行補救，費用由賣方負擔。上項缺陷或故障，應在契約規定條件下操作及正常使用情況下發生（Defects appear under the conditions of operation provided for by the contract and under proper use），賣方始可負責修換。如該項缺陷或故障係由於買方或自雇人員之安裝、保養或修理不當或未經賣方書面同意使用之其他方式所致，賣方可不負責。至正常之耗損（normal deterioration），自不包括在內❶。

5-3 價格條件

國際商品買賣之計價條件, 包括價格基礎 (basis of price) 及計價貨幣 (currency) 兩個要素。所謂價格基礎, 卽前述國際商品交易之價格條件, 其價格之結構, 包括商品之成本及所有費用、將商品運往買方指定地點之運送人 (carrier) 直至風險轉移買方時爲止。是項商品風險與費用負擔之分界, 可參閱前章 INCOTERMS 之解說。

依照一九七三年英國商品供應(默示條款)法 Sect. 8(1)規定,價格可在契約中訂定或訂明決定價格之方式❷。如採用淨價 (net price) 或含佣價格 (price with commission), 則可在報價時寫明, 如 US$100 net per kg. CIF New York or including 5% Commission on FOB value。如市場價格變動頗大, 且係商品交易所經常交易之大宗商品, 其計價方式則不妨採用平均價格 (average price) 或基準價格 (base price)。譬如十一月份交運之粗糖, 可按十一月份一日至卅日在倫敦砂糖交易所每日 L.D.P. (landed, duty-paid) 之公定盤價 (fixed official price) 平均計算該批粗糖之每噸價格, 或再加計其他計算因素, 以推算其應售價格。又如倫敦之 United Terminal Sugar Market Association, 其粗糖之計價係以96°爲基準, 超過或低於96°之糖度, 均分別照公定盤價之加減百分比予以補貼或減價。茲抄錄其計價方式如下:

Settlement of degrees above and below 96° mean outturn polari-

---

❶ *General Conditions of Sale for the Import and Export of Durable Consumer Goods and of other Engineering Stock Articles*, No. 730, art. 9 (publisrhed by U. N. Economic Commission for Europe)

❷ P. S. Atiyah: *The Sale of Goods*, ch. 2, p.18.

zation shall be calculated on the official price fixed by the Committee of the Association in London for the frist day of the month of tender as follows:

For every full degree:

above 96° to and including 97°, add 1.4%

above 97° to and including 98°, add an additional 1.4%

above 98° to and including 99°, add an addiitional 1.4%

below 96° to and including 95°, deduct 1.5%

below 95° to and including 94°, deduct an additional 2.0%

below 94° to and including 93°, deduct an additional 2.0%

(Fractions of a degree shall be calculated in the same proportion)

Any sugar below 93° outturn polarization shall not be rejected but invoiced at an allowance to be fixed by mutual agreement.❸

　　表示商品價值之貨幣，可就出口國貨幣、輸入國貨幣或第三國貨幣三者中選擇一種為計價標準。通常多採用國際金融市場比較通用而較具信用之強勢貨幣為計價工具。由於國際金融市場動盪不定，匯率變動頗大，一俟裝貨押匯時，如遇採用之貨幣跌價，出口商不免遭受損失。再說，CIF 報價包括運費及保險費在內，報價後之運價及保險費率亦難保不上漲，如裝船時一旦上漲，賣方亦受損失。凡此種種變動因素，出口商均無法事先控制。因此，貿易商為避免風險，頗多在報價單或簽訂合約時加列下列加價條款 (price escalation clause)，以資保障：

Unless firm prices and charges are agreed upon, the seller shall

---

❸ *Rules & Regulations of United Terminal Sugar Market Association*, London.

be entitled to increase the agreed prices and charges by the same amount by which the prices or charges of the goods (including the freight rate, insurance premium and/or exchange rate of foreign currency) to be paid or borne by the seller have been increased between the date of quotation and the date of shipment (delivery). ❹

惟上項條款, 必須在世界經濟不穩定及物價、運價與保險率等均在波動劇烈情況下始可勉予使用, 否則平時不易爲買方所接受, 希讀者注意及之。

5-4 數量條件

所謂數量, 係指個數 (number)、 重量 (weight) 及度量 (measurement) 如長度、 面積、 體積、 容積、 百分數等是。重量之計算單位, 常用者爲磅 (pound)、 噸 (ton)、 公斤 (kilogram)、 公克 (gram = 1/1000kg)、 匈特威(hundredweight= 1/20 ton, 英制112 lbs, 美制100 lbs)、益司(ounce= 1/16 lb); 個數(number)常用者如件(piece)、套 (set)、 打 (dozen)、 籮 (gross=12 doz.)、 捲 (roll or coil); 面積 (area) 如平方英呎 (square foot)、 平方公尺 (square meter); 長度 (length) 如碼 (yard)、 英呎 (foot)、 公尺 (meter); 容積 (capacity) 如蒲式耳 (bushel)、 加侖 (gallon)、 公升 (liter); 體積 (volume) 如立方英呎 (cubic foot)、 立方英吋 (cubic inch)、 立方碼 (cubic yard)、 立方公尺 (cubic meter); 百分數 (percentage) 如計算含量

---

❹ Schmitthoff: *Export Trade*, ch.3,p.53.

或純度之百分比。

數量決定之時間及地點，目前最常採用者爲起運地裝貨時之裝運數量爲準（shipped weight final）及目的地卸貨時之卸貨重量爲準（landed weight or outturn weight final）兩種。又一般貨物之包裝重量，則分毛重（gross weight）及淨重（net weight）兩種。前者包括包裝材料之皮重（tare）在內，可按貨物逐件過磅求其實際皮重；亦可從整批貨物抽取百分之十的皮重，求取其平均皮重；間或依商業習用之包裝材料及包裝方法，以推定其皮重。

依照英國商品買賣法 Sect. 30之規定，賣方有依約交付買方正確數量之義務（duty to supply goods in right quantity），因此，固定包裝貨物，原則上應依照契約規定數量交貨；如少交，買方得予全部拒絕接受，除非徵得買方同意，以後補交或分批交貨亦可不予接受；至交付數量大于契約數量者，買方得全部接受或拒收多交部份。如一旦全部接受，則多交部份應照契約價格付款❺。

凡國際貿易以重量計價者，多按淨重計算，例由公定重量檢定人（public weigher）出具重量證明書。重量之決定，得由買賣雙方協議按起岸重量（loading weight）或抵岸卸貨淨重（net landed weight）爲準。凡規定以裝貨港之裝船重量爲準者，如遇途中發生耗損，賣方可不負責任；但裝貨時，應有公定重量檢定人之公證報告爲準，並在契約內訂明 Survey Report at loading port final 字樣。

一般貿易商對散裝或液體抑容易揮發之貨物，非裝船時無法控制裝量致造成溢裝或少裝，卽因長途運送，致發生水份蒸發或沿途漏失，因此在訂契約時，大都在規定之契約數量前另加 "about" 字樣。頗多散裝貨物，由於承載重量係取決于船東，在傭船契約往往訂明 5-10% at

---

❺　P. S. Atiyah: *The Sale of Goods*, ch, 11, pp. 67-68.

owner's option, 因此買賣契約之交貨數量，亦應訂明 5-10% more or less at seller's option 字樣，以資配合。此種超裝或不足數量，依照一般商場習慣，買方應照價結付或由賣方退還溢收價款。

上項 About 一詞，依照國際商會所訂「信用狀統一慣例」之規定，其寬容差額不得超過10%或少于10%。除信用狀對數量另有指明不許超過或減少者外，普通裝量在增減 5％之伸縮應屬許可，但數量若以包裝單位或個別件數計數者，則上項伸縮額度並不適用。此類規定，最好在契約中加以訂明，以免引起糾紛❻。

5-5　交貨條件

交貨條件為賣方之重要契約義務，與買方之付款提貨同樣重要。交貨條件包括裝運日期及裝運條件。茲分述如次。

5-5-1　裝運日期 (Time of Shipment)

裝運日期得由買賣雙方協定後在契約內訂明。其日期之約定，可分為下列三種：

1. 指定裝運時間 (fixed a period of time)

貨物指定在特定之時間內裝運，為交易中最常見之交貨條件。如 Jan./Mar. shipment, 指定在1-3月間裝運；January shipment 在一月份裝貨；Shipment during first half or second half of January or in the beginning, middle or by the end of January, 指定在一月份上半月或下半月抑一月份之上旬、中旬或下旬裝運。亦有指定在收到信用狀或滙

---

❻ *ICC uniform Customs & Practice for Documentary Credits* (1983 revision), art. 43.

款後一個月或若干日內裝運者，如 Shipment within one month or 60 or 90 days after receipt of L/C, T/T, M/T, or D/D 是。前面所稱「上半月」、「下半月」、「上旬」、「中旬」、「下旬」，依國際商會一九八三修正之信用狀統一慣例第五十二條及五十三條解釋爲：「月之1至15日止」、「月之16日起至月底最後之日止」、「月之1至10日止」、「月之11日至20日止」、「月之21日至月底最後之日止」，起訖日均包括在內。

2. 即期裝運（Prompt shipment）

即期裝運，一般最常用之術語爲 Shipment prompt, immediately or as soon as possible，即立即、迅即或儘速裝運的意思。依照一九八三年修正之國際商會信用狀統一慣例第五十條(c)款規定，凡以上詞語用以表示即期裝運者，銀行將解釋爲應從開證銀行開立信用狀日起30天內裝運。

3. 指定裝運日期（Specified date）

指定裝運日期之例子很多，如 Shipment on or about September 10, 1984是。依照國際商會信用狀統一慣例第五十條(d)款之規定，凡以 "on or about" 及類似詞語用以表示裝運日期者，銀行將解釋爲應在指定日期前五天起至該日期後五日止之期間裝運，首尾兩日均包括在內。

5-5-2　裝運條件（Terms of Shipment）

裝運條件，包括裝運方式、航線及船舶等三項。即：(1)貨物是否可分批裝運（partial shipment allowed）或禁止（不准）分批裝運（partial shipment not allowed or prohibited）？如可分批裝運，其分批數量及裝運日期應如何規定？又如須航空運輸、海陸聯運或郵政包裹，均須一併訂明。(2)貨物如係海運，是否應指定航線？應否指定直航船運往（direct shipment by direct vessel）？可否轉運（transhipment allowed) 或不容許轉運 (transhipment not permitted)？均須加以訂明。

(3)如須指定船舶類型、艙位或指定某船公司之定期船 (liner)，得在契約中或信用狀內加以訂明，作為附帶條款。

5-6　付款條件

付款為買方履行契約之重要義務，其付款條件應如何訂定，應視買方信用狀況、進口國外滙制度、國家財政經濟狀況、以及交易標的物之金額與風險等情況而定。茲就付款時間及付款方法，列舉如次。

5-6-1　交貨前付款 (Payment in Advance)

所謂交貨前付款，係指買方在簽訂契約時或簽約後之交貨前，以現金支付全部貨款，但亦有交貨前先付若干預付金 (partial payment)，其餘於交貨時或交貨後付清者。

5-6-2　交貨時付款 (Payment against Delivery)

此卽係一般所稱「交貨付現」(cash on delivery or C.O.D) 之付款方式。

5-6-3　裝運或交貨後付款 (Payment after Shipment/Delivery)

此種型態，計有下列六種：

(1)卽期信用狀付款 (sight credit payment against L/C at sight upon presentation of documents)

(2)在目的地交單付款 (payment against documents at destination)

(3)在目的地承兌交單後付款 (documents against the buyer's acceptance at destination, payable—days after sight or date.)

(4)延期付款 (defferred payment)──一般係憑遠期信用狀 (Us-ance credit) 或由銀行擔保分期付款。

(5)寄售 (consigment)──貨物運交代理商委託代售，一俟售罄，由代理商扣除佣金、運雜費、倉儲租金等費用，餘額滙回賣方。

(6)記帳 (open account)──此係賣方將貨物運交買方後記帳，于約定之時間內收款方式。亦可稱爲信用銷貨 (credit sale) 之一種。

依照一般國際貿易慣例，買賣雙方對付款方式與付款時間，一經約定，買方必須遵照辦理，如買方延遲付款，賣方除得延遲交貨義務外，並得要求買方賠償延期付款利息❼。

凡以信用狀方式付款，並以"about"（大概）或其他類似用詞表示金額者，應解釋爲上下差額在10％者可以容許❽。又信用狀除須載明提示單據之有效期限外，並須規定在提單或其他貨運單據簽發日期後之一特定期間提示該單據以求付款、承兌或讓購，如無是項規定，銀行將拒絕接受遲於提單或其他貨運單據簽發日期廿一天後所提示之單據❾。如規定之有效期限適逢銀行停業，則該有效期限得順延一天 ❿。

5-7　包裝及標示條件 (Packing & Marking)

現代運輸型態已日趨複雜，其運輸使用之工具，亦因運輸途徑或貨

---

❼　*U. N. Sales Convention*, art. 78.

❽　*I.C.C. uniform customs & practice for documontary credits* (1983 revision)*, art 34.

❾　*I.C.C. uniform customs & practice for documontary credits* (1983 revision)*, art 41.

❿　*I.C.C. uniform customs & practice for documontary credits* (1983 revision)*, art 39.

物性質而有差異。尤其在貨櫃運輸取代傳統式之運輸後，對貨物之包裝方式起了很大的改變。由於海陸運輸與航空運輸之設備及貨櫃型態不同，其貨物之適用包裝亦異。要之，適當之包裝 (proper packing)，應以貨物性質、型態、交運途徑（取道海運、陸運、海陸聯運或空運，應先考慮）及目的地等各項因素，加以考慮。如海運之一般貨物，必須包裝堅固；易破損者，必須加用板條 (crate)；易受潮者，必須外加塑膠包裝保護。東歐國家經濟互助協會組織 (Council for Mutual Economic Assistance) 所訂 General Conditions of Delivery of Goods (GCD CMEA 1968)ch. Ⅵ, sect. 20有關包裝之規定，可供參考。茲抄錄如下：

If there are no special directions in the contract concerning packing, the seller shall ship the goods in packing used for export goods in the seller's country, which would assure safety of goods during transportation, taking into account possible transhipment, under proper and usual handling of the goods. In appropriate case, the duration and methods of carriage shall also be taken into account ⑪。

倘契約對包裝無特殊規定，賣方應依該國習用之出口包裝，並考慮可能之沿途轉運起卸，以確保貨物之安全運輸。在適當情況下，對沿途運輸方式及持續時間，亦應考慮。

第一，賣方如不依照貿易習慣或買方之指示包裝，買方依照國際慣例，有權拒絕接受。第二，包裝必須顧慮到船公司計算運費所依據之重量及尺碼與貨品價值，貴重貨物必須事先填報貨物性質及價值，因船公司之損失賠償有一定限度及規定。第三，包裝之標示必須依照輸往國家

---

⑪　*CMEA* 1968, ch, 6, sect. 20, p. 176 (Translation by UNCITRAL)

之法律規定，以免遭受禁止進口或限制⓬。

5-8 運輸保險條件

國際商品買賣之運輸保險條件，普通在報價（如 CIF 報價）或訂約時已予訂明。爲使業者對貨運保險之危險種類、承保範圍及保險條款有所了解，特不嫌麻煩，分節說明如次，俾業者投保時有所抉擇。

貨物運輸保險可劃分爲(1)海運貨物保險（marine cargo insurance）、內陸運輸保險（inland marine insurance）及空運貨物保險（air cargo insurance）三種。晚近因郵購業務發達，於是保險業乃增加郵政包裹之保險條款。

貨物之運輸保險，最早發源於海上保險（marine insurance），由保險人承擔海上危險事故所引起之損害賠償。由於海上保險業務，經數百年之發展，已建立一套完善之保險制度、規章及理賠辦法。逮近代運輸工具革新，陸上及航空運輸乃隨之發展迅速，使海陸空三方面之運輸工具可密切配合，蔚成一貫作業，因此陸空運輸，無異是海上運輸的延伸，是故頗多保險條款，仍沿用海上貨運保險之原有基本條款，祇增加若干特別條款以資適應而已。茲分述之。

5-8-1 海運貨物保險

5-8-1-1 海運貨物保險之海損型態

海運貨物保險之海損，可分爲下列三種型態，保險人依承保標的物之損害性質及程度，予以分別理賠。茲分述之。

1. 全損（Total Loss）──指保險之標的物由於遭遇(1)海上危險

⓬ Schmitthoff: *Export Trade*, ch. 6.

(perils of the seas)、(2)火災 (fire)、(3)海盜 (pirates & rovers)、(4)投棄 (jettison)、(5)船長或船員之惡意行為 (barratry of master or mariners) 等危險事故而全部滅失。 此係普通所稱 基本危險 (basic risks) 之海損。 依照貨物之損害情形, 可分為實際全損及推定全損兩種:

(1)實際全損 (Actual Total Loss) ——實際全損之發生, 有下列三種現象:

　a. 保險標的物之完全實際毀滅 (An actual total loss where the subject matter insured is destroyed);

　b. 保險標的物之完全實際毀損, 已使保險物之原體不復存在 (An actual total loss where the subject matter insured is so damaged that it ceases to be a thing of the kind insured), 亦稱「原形之損失」(loss of specie), 如水泥之變成混凝土是。

　c. 保險標的物之完全實際毀損, 已使被保人喪失其對標的物之回復原狀 (An actual total loss when the assured is irretrievably deprived of the subject matter insured)

(2)推定全損 (Constructive Total Loss)——指保險標的物遭受危險事故之損害, 雖未構成全損, 但其防止損害及施救費用或修復及運往目的地之費用, 將超過其標的物到達目的地時之本身價值。因此, 在這種情形之下, 乃予放棄, 並推定為全損。如被保人選擇放棄 (abandon) 所有物以推定全損要求賠償時, 保險人有權取得該殘存物。

　2. 共同海損及費用(General Average & Charges)——"AVERAGE"在「海上保險」 具有特殊意義, 與一般涵義不同。 係指 滅失或 毀損 (loss or damage), 來自法文 "AVARIE", 意指毀損。 所謂共同海損,係指船舶或貨物受海難或其他危險，船長必須自動犧牲（voluntarily sacrificed）船舶之財物或船上所裝貨物之一部份，以預防或施救此項威脅性或可能發生之共同危險。其所發生之貨物犧牲損失及損害防止與施救費用，均由貨主及船主按貨物之價值、船值及運費比例分攤之。該項費用，均列入基本保單（basic policy）內，依法得向保險人要求賠償。輪船公司已習慣在其提單上加入此項 "adjustment of general average losses" 條款。

3. 單獨海損（Particular Average）──依據海損之實質言，不是全損就是分損，亦稱部份損失（Partial Loss）。依據英國一九〇六年之海上保險法 Sect. 64(1)之解說，單獨海損係保險標的物遭受所保之一項危險事故引起之部份損失，但非共同海損（A particular average loss is a partial loss of the subject-matter insured, caused by a peril insured against, and which is not a general average loss）；換言之，單獨海損是貨主之某一被保險貨物已意外遭受一個危險事故引起部份損失之謂，其他貨主及船方並無對該項單獨損失給予單獨施救之犧牲。

5-8-1-2　海運貨物保險範圍

保險人依據海上貨物保險之危險範圍，其承擔之保險責任，可分為下列各項保險：

(1)全損險（Total Loss only or T.L.O.）

(2)單獨海損不賠險或稱平安險（Free from Particular Average or F.P.A.）

(3)單獨海損險或稱水漬險（With Average or W.A.; With Particular Average or W.P.A.）

(4)附加險（Extraneus Risks）

(5)全險或稱一切險 (All Risks or A.R.)

1. 全損險——被保險標的物，由於被保險事故所引起之全部滅失或毀損，不拘爲實際或推定全損，在一般貨物保險單上大都涵蓋此種基本危險。依照英國一九〇六年海上保險法 Sect. 56、57及58之規定，全損必須照全部損失賠償，不得有任何扣減 (A "deductible" is not applied to a total loss claim)。保險人對被保人所支付之共同海損分攤費用，亦應賠償。在實務上，貨物如分別包裝，並註明件數及其分別價值，則每件可視同單獨之個別保險 (Each package is to be deemed a separate insurance)，海難滅失時，得按每件之全損釐定賠償。

2. 單獨海損不賠（亦稱平安險）——保險人除全損、共同海損之犧牲及施救費用之分攤均予賠償外，對被保險標的物之單獨海損不賠，但如遇船舶擱淺、沈沒、火災或船舶、駁船及其他運輸工具與除「水」以外之任何外界物體之接觸、碰撞或在避難港卸貨所引起之單獨海損，得不計成份 (irrespective of percentage)，予以賠償。

3. 單獨海損賠償（亦稱水漬險）——保險人除全損、共同海損之犧牲及施救費用之分攤均予賠償外，對被保標的物因承保危險事故引起之單獨海損照保單規定之百分比率予以賠償。Lloyd 公司爲減輕其賠償責任，並避免計算小額單獨海損之麻煩，曾于其 S.G. 保單附列單獨海損之免賠額 (franchise clause) 如下：

"穀類、魚類、鹽、水果、麵粉及種子之單獨海損，除非係共同海損及擱淺，概不予賠償；砂糖、菸草、大蔴、亞蔴、生皮及皮革之單獨海損未達百分之五者不賠；其他貨物之單獨海損未達百分之三者不賠"。

上項穀類、魚類爲極易受海水毀損之貨物，砂糖、菸草等則極易在航行途中損壞，其他訂明在 3 % 以下不賠，則在避免計算小額賠償之麻煩。

事實上，免賠額百分比之高低，可由投保人在投保時按貨物之性質，向保險公司約定以加貼之附加條款爲準。如無此約定者，概照此規定處理。此項免賠額條款，普通規定單獨海損在未達免賠額之百分比者可以不賠，如到達或超過所定百分比時，應全額賠償。此外，亦有按約定之免賠額百分比扣除(% deductible)者，如是，則可按額扣除後再賠。如約定單獨海損不拘多少應全部照賠者，可在保險契約內訂明 "Particular Average, irrespective of percentage"字樣。

4. 附加險——以上保險人所承保之全損、單獨海損及共同海損，均屬基本保單所列保之基本危險範圍。惟頗多危險事故之發生，旣不包括在基本海險條款 (basic perils clause)，亦不包括在水漬險及平安險條款 (Particular Average & F.P.A. clauses) 內。這些意外之災害 (fortuities)，保險界稱爲基本險以外之附加險。最常見者如：(1)偷竊、挖竊及不能交貨 (thieft, pilferage & non-delivery)，(2)淡水及雨水 (fresh water & rain)，(3)破損 (breakage)，(4)正常之漏損及破損 (ordinary leakage & breakage)，(5)鈎損 (hook damage)，(6)油污 (oil)，(7)污染 (contamination)，(8)貨艙之汗濕及熱氣 (sweat & heating of the hold)，(9)發霉 (mildew & mould)，(10)鼠蟲損害 (rats & vermin) 等。其餘戰爭 (war) 及罷工、暴動及內亂 (strikes, riots & civil commotions)，則列入特殊之附加險。一般進出口商均得依其貨物性質、包裝情形以及運往地區之情況，另行加保所需之附加條款，加貼在水漬險或平安險之基本保單上，使貨物在運輸途中可能發生之基本險以外之危險，都可得到保障。

5. 全險（亦稱一切險）——在基本保單上加保所需之附加險，難免掛一漏萬。爲便利起見，如投保全險，除兵險及罷工暴亂險仍須另行投保外，其餘各項附加險幾可涵蓋在內。依據英國 1906 年之海上保險法

sect. 55之規定，凡投保全險者，其損害賠償應全額照賠，並無百分比之限制(payable irrespective of percentage)。但標的物由於延遲及固有瑕疵或標的物之本質所致之滅失、毀損或費用(loss damage or expense proximately caused by delay or inherent vice or nature of the subject-matter insured)，不在保險之列。

5-8-1-3 協會海運貨物保險條款

目前海運貨物保險使用之基本保單（basic policy），均沿用英國勞依玆（Lloyd）在一七七九年訂定之 S.G.（卽Ship & Goods 之簡稱）標準格式（如圖：**⓭**）爲依據，迄今已達二百餘年。在西曆17世紀末年，英國已是航海發達國家，倫敦爲世界航業中心，愛德華勞依玆（Edward Lloyd）係在一七八〇年十一月十七日開始在其經營之勞依玆公司(The Corporation of Lloyd's) 辦理海上船貨保險業務時使用的。英國在一九〇六年制定海上保險法時，並將該 S.G. 保單本文列入該法條文。此項保單格式條款，歷經多年之修改增刪，或附貼條款，以適應各項需求，並經法院判案時加以採用，迄今業有一定之解釋。目前使用之保單格式，大抵仍沿用當年格式，契約當事人祇就合意事項，略加增補或加貼條款而已。其增加補充之條款，則以印刷條款（printed clause）、圖戳、打字或書寫等方式附加在統一之基本保單上。

倫敦保險人協會（The Institute Of London Underwriters）于一八八四年成立後，爲配合海上運輸之發展，曾釐訂各種貨物運輸保險條款（Institute Cargo Clauses），爲世界各國所採用。近年爲配合發展海陸聯運，復于一九八二年修訂貨物保險條款之全險、水漬險及平安險三種爲(1)Institute Cargo Clauses (A) （原爲 All Risks）, Institute Cargo Clauses (B) （原爲W.A.） 及Institute Cargo Clauses (C) （原爲F.P.A.）。

⓭ J. K Goodacre: *Marine Insurance claims*, ch. Ⅲ, p. 52.

S. G.

Printed according to the Form revised and corrected at New Lloyd's, on the 12th Jan. 1779.

Sold by W. Mays, Stationer, &c.

IN the Name of God, Amen. .... Langston & Dixon .... as well in ...... own Names, as for and in the Name and Names of all and every other Person or Persons to whom the same doth, may, or shall appertain, in Part or in All, doth make Assurance, and cause Themselves .... and them, and every of them to be Insured, lost or not lost at and from

Plymouth to Guernsey

Upon any Kind of Goods and Merchandizes, and also upon the Body, Tackle, Apparel, Ordnance, Munition, Artillery, Boat, and other Furniture, of and in the good Ship or Vessel called the Richard

whereof is Master, under God, for this present Voyage, James Bennett or whosoever else shall go for Master in the said Ship, or by whatsoever other Name or Names the same Ship, or the Master thereof, is or shall be named or called; beginning the Adventure upon the said Goods and Merchandizes from the Loading thereof aboard the said Ship, Richard

upon the said Ship, &c. Commencing the Risk at Guernsey the 14 Nov. 1780. and so shall continue and endure, during her Abode there, upon the said Ship, &c. And further, until the said Ship, with all her Ordnance, Tackle, Apparel, &c. and Goods and Merchandizes whatsoever shall be arrived at Guernsey

upon the said Ship, &c. until she hath moor'd at Anchor Twenty-four Hours in good Safety; and upon the Goods and Merchandizes, until the same be there discharged and safely landed. And it shall be lawful for the said Ship, &c. in this Voyage, to proceed and sail to and touch and stay at any Ports or Places whatsoever without being deemed any deviation

without Prejudice to this Insurance. The said Ship, &c. Goods and Merchandizes, &c. for so much as concerns the Assured, by Agreement between the Assureds and Assurers in this Policy are and shall be valued at

Four Hundred Pounds upon the Ship

Touching the Adventures and Perils which we the Assurers, are contented to bear, and do take upon us in this Voyage, they are of the Seas, Men of War, Fire, Enemies, Pirates, Rovers, Thieves, Jettizons, Letters of Mart and Counter Mart, Surprizals, Takings at Sea, Arrests, Restraints and Detainments of all Kings, Princes and People, of what Nation, Condition or Quality soever; Barretry of the Master and Mariners, and of all other Perils, Losses and Misfortunes, that have or shall come to the Hurt, Detriment or Damage of the said Goods and Merchandizes and Ship, &c. or any Part thereof. And in case of any Loss or Misfortune, it shall be lawful to the Assureds, their Factors, Servants and Assigns, to sue, labour and travel for, in and about the Defence, Safeguard and Recovery of the said Goods and Merchandizes and Ship, &c. or any Part thereof, without Prejudice to this Insurance; to the Charges whereof we the Assurers will contribute each one according to the Rate and Quantity of his Sum herein Assured. And it is agreed by us the Insurers, that this Writing or Policy of Assurance shall be of as much Force and Effect as the surest Writing or Policy of Assurance heretofore made in Lombard-street, or in the Royal-Exchange, or elsewhere in London. And so we the Assurers are contented, and do hereby promise and bind ourselves, each one for his own Part, our Heirs, Executors, and Goods, to the Assureds, their Executors, Administrators, and Assigns, for the true Performance of the Premises, confessing ourselves paid the Consideration due unto us for this Assurance by the Assured   at and after

the Rate of Two Guineas & a half to return 25 P Ct if departs with Convoy for the Voyage & arrives

In Witness whereof we the Assurers have subscribed our Names and Sums Assured in London.

N. B. Corn, Fish, Salt, Fruit, Flour and Seed, are warranted free from Average, unless General, or the Ship be Stranded. Sugar, Tobacco, Hemp, Flax, Hides and Skins, are warranted free from Average, under Five Pounds per Cent. and all other Goods, also the Ship and Freight are warranted free of Average under Three Pounds per Cent. unless General, or the Ship be Stranded.

The following Insurance is upon the Brig Richard valued at £400

£100 R. Nicholson for Edward Higginson One hundred Pounds G. W. 17 Nov. 1780.

£100 Wm Daggs one hundred pounds ..... 17 Nov. 1780.

£100 J. Pickersgill, one hundred Pounds G. void 17 Nov. 1780.

£100 James Coats for R. Thanden One hundred Pounds G. Rd 17 Nov. 1780.

在新訂之(B)(C)條款，均增列「陸上運輸工具之傾覆或出軌 (overturning or derailment of land conveyance) 的危險損失」在內，該(B)條款並新增承保「地震、火山爆發或雷電 (earthquake, volcanic eruption or lightning)」及「海水、湖水、河水之侵入運送船舶、駁船、貨艙、貨櫃、運輸工具及儲貨處所 (entry of sea, lake or river water into the vessel, craft, hold, conveyance, container, liftvan or place of storage)」等危險事故所引起之損失條款。以上增訂之條款，顯係配合內陸運輸而設，即經保險業界所普遍採用。以上純為兼顧海陸兩用之保險條款，自不能與純為內陸運輸之保單，相提並論。茲將倫敦保險人協會所訂三種貨物保險條款之承保及不保範圍，列表如次頁，以供參考。

一般海上貨物運輸保險，多投保航程保險 (voyage policy)。該保單之生效日期，係從標的物離開所記載之起運地或港口倉庫時開始，並在正常之運輸途中繼續有效，直至下列任何一種情況下終止：

㈠至保單載明之目的地受貨人或其他最終倉庫或儲存處所；

㈡在抵達目的地或中途，應被保險人之要求將貨物卸存任何倉庫或地點儲存，或分配及分送；

㈢至保單所載最終卸貨港完全卸載後起算屆滿六十天。

被保貨物在最終卸貨港卸貨後，在保險失效前如將該批貨物再運往保單所載以外之目的地，在起運日起，保單即告失效。但在保險有效期間，被保險人因無法控制之延滯、船舶改航、被迫卸載、重裝或轉船及船東租用人行使自由運輸權所引起之危險變更者，得繼續有效。

5-8-2 空運貨物保險

在此國際市場競爭劇烈之八十年代，貨物之快速運送為爭取商機之必要條件，因此凡體積小而價值高之商品，多取道空運途徑，一則可縮

協會海上貨物運輸保險單承保及不保之危險範圍

（○表示承保及賠償；×表示不保及不賠償）

項目	危險事故引起之滅失及損害	Institute Cargo Clauses		
		(A)	(B)	(C)
1	全損或推定全損	○	○	○
2	船舶或駁船之擱淺、觸礁、沈沒或傾覆	○	○	○
3	火災或爆炸	○	○	○
4	陸上運輸工具之傾覆或出軌	○	○	○
5	船舶、駁船或運輸工具在遇難港與除水以外任何物體之碰撞或觸礁	○	○	○
6	在避難港卸貨	○	○	○
7	地震、火山爆發及雷電	○	○	×
8	共同海損之犧牲	○	○	○
9	投棄	○	○	○
10	波浪捲落	○	○	×
11	海水、湖水或河水之侵入	○	○	×
12	任何一件貨物在船舶或駁船裝卸時落海或掉落之整件滅失	○	○	×
13	偷竊及不能交貨（指漏裝、誤運或誤卸）、滲漏、破損、汗濡、受熱、油汚、汚染、發霉、鼠蟲害、鈎損及其他對被保險標的物之一切滅失或毀損之危險	○	×	×
14	共同海損與施救費用（除外危險引起之共同海損及施救費用，不予承保）	○	○	○
15	雙方過失碰撞	○	○	○
16	被保人之故意過失	×	×	×
17	正常滲漏、失重、失量或耗損	×	×	×
18	不良或不適當之包裝	×	×	×
19	固有瑕疵或本質	×	×	×
20	延滯	×	×	×
21	船東、經理人、租船人之破產或欠債	×	×	×
22	任何人員之不法行為引起被保險標的物之全部或部份蓄意性之損害或毀壞	○	×	×
23	原子、核子或其他類似武器引起之損害及費用	×	×	×
24	船舶或駁船之不適航及承載船舶、駁船、貨櫃、貨箱與其他運輸工具之不安全引起之損害及費用	×	×	×
25	戰爭	×	×	×
26	罷工、停工、工潮、暴動及騷亂	×	×	×

短運輸時間，以爭取市場機先，二則可加速資金運轉，以擴大經營利潤。

關于航空貨運，國際公約對運送人之責任賠償範圍，僅限於空運過程中及保管期間之危險事故，而航空貨運保險人之承保範圍，則遠及承保標的物離開其起運之倉庫、處所及儲存地點而至保單所載目的地之倉庫、處所及儲存地爲止。兩者密切關聯，玆分述如次。

5-8-2-1 航空運送人之責任限制

航空運送人對已登記交運之貨物，在運送人空運中及保管期間，不論係在航空站、在飛機上、或在航空站以外任何地點降落時，如發生滅失、毀損或遲延，均負賠償責任。空運期間不包括在航空站以外所從事之陸地、海洋或河流運送，但爲履行航空運送契約在陸地、海洋或河流所作之運送，係以裝貨、交貨或轉運爲目的者，除有反證者外，其任何損害，得推定爲空運期間之空運事故。

航空運送人對空運貨物之損害賠償，依據一九二九年十月十二日在華沙所訂之國際航空運送統一規則公約(Convention for the Unification of Certain Rules relating to International Carriage by Air, 簡稱華沙公約 Warsaw Convention) 第二十二條之規定，運送人對已登記貨物之毀損、滅失所生之損害，應負賠償責任，其賠償之責任限額，以每公斤250金法郎 (French Gold Francs) 爲限（每法郎含千分之九百純金65.5公毫），如託運貨物價值甚高，託運人得在交運時特別申報實際價值 (a special declaration of the actual value at delivery)，並加付補助費率 (supplementary sum)，其賠償責任將以不超過所報價值爲限。一九五五年華沙公約曾一度修訂，增加規定貨物之一部份或其中所裝之物件發生毀損、滅失或遲延時，在確定賠償限額時，應以該發生問題部份之總重量爲限。一九七五年九月二十五日復在蒙特婁第一號附加修正議定書第二條修訂該公約第二十二條之賠償限制爲每公斤17「特別提款權」(Special Drawing Rights)，並按判決日該國貨幣對「特別提款權」之價值折算之。如係非國際貨幣基金會之會員，則依該締約國所決定之方法計算之。又如該國法律不許適用公約第二十二條之規定者，則可聲明其國境內運送人在司法程序上責任限制爲每公斤250貨幣單位。此所稱貨幣單位，相當於含千分之九百純金65.5公毫。

　　事實上，航空運送人對貨物之空運危險，均連同旅客、行李及飛機本身一併向保險公司投保空險，並訂有最高之責任賠償限額，縱使對已申報價值之貨物，亦有最高責任限額之限制。

　　普通空運貨物在抵達目的地後，運送人均立即通知收貨人提貨。如發現貨物有損害時，應于收貨後十四日內書面提出索賠要求；如係貨物遲延，應於貨到後二十一日內提出；如係「不能交貨」(non-delivery)，應於空運提單發單日起一二○日內提出。貨物雖向保險公司投保，但亦應向航空公司直接提出索賠要求。

5-8-2-2　協會空運貨物保險條款

　　航空貨物運輸保險與海險不同，倫敦保險人協會之普通空運貨物保險，祇有空運條款一種 (Institute Cargo Claues-Air)，其保險範圍包括承保標的物在航空運輸過程中之一切滅失或毀損，故亦可稱爲協會航空貨運全險（即一切險）條款 (Institute Air Cargo Clauses-All Risks)，但不包括郵寄貨物 (excluding sendings by post) 在內。

　　上項空運貨物保險條款不包括兵險及罷工險條款，如有需要，應另行加保協會之航空貨運兵險條款 (Institute War Clauses—Air Cargo, excluding sendings by post)或航空貨運罷工險條款 (Institute Strikes Clauses—Air Cargo)。本保單生效日期，自所保標的物在保單所載起運地點之倉庫或儲存處所起運時開始，並在正常之運輸途中繼續有效，直至所載目的地送交受貨人或其他最終倉庫或儲存處所抑或運至目的地或中途之任何倉庫或儲存處所由被保險人用以轉運正常運程以外地區或予分配分送時終止。該保單之有效期，應自所保標的物從航空器在最終地點卸載完畢後三十天屆滿。

查航空貨運之保險條款，亦有「一般不保條款」(General Exclusion Clauses)不保下列各項損失及費用之規定：

1. 被保人之故意過失引起之損害或費用；
2. 被保標的物正常之滲漏、失重或耗損；
3. 被保標的物之不良或不當包裝或配製引起之損害或費用；
4. 被保標的物之固有瑕疵或本質引起之損害或費用；
5. 由於航空器之不適航或貨櫃及運輸工具之不適于安全運送引起被保標的物之損害或費用；
6. 近似遲延所引起之損害或費用；
7. 由於飛機所有權人、經理人、租機人或經營人之破產或財務困難所引起之損害或費用；
8. 任何使用原子或核子武器或其類似武器引起被保標的物之損害或費用。

5-8-3 郵寄包裹保險

目前倫敦保險人協會對郵寄包裹之貨物保險，似乎祇訂兵險條款(Institute War Clauses—sendings by post)一種，除此之外，似未另訂其他郵包保險條款。茲將該兵險承保之危險事故列舉如下：

1. 戰爭、內戰、革命、叛亂、暴動或其引起之內戰，或任何對抗交戰國武力之敵對行為。
2. 由於上述危險引起之捕獲、扣押、拘留、禁止或扣留及其結果，或其他任何威脅企圖。

3. 遺棄之水雷、魚雷、炸彈或其他遺棄之戰爭武器。

本保險並包括共同海損及施救費用 (General Average and Salvage Charges)，但不保「一般不保條款」(General Exclusion Clauses) 列舉之各項損失及費用。

目前我國之保險業者,大都按照協會F.P.A., W.A. 或 All Risks 條款接受外銷業者之投保。保單規定, 凡投保 F.P.A.之標的物, 自郵政局發給包裹收據日起至貨物遞交目的地收貨人止, 在經過水陸空運輸工具所遭遇之全損, 由保險人負責賠償; 如投保 W.A. 條款者, 並承擔水損之部份損失; 投保 All Risks 者, 則可承擔盜竊、挖竊、破損及水損等部份損失之賠償。保單之有效日期自郵政局發給包裹收據日起至貨物交達目的地收貨人或目的地郵政局通知貨到二十天後終止。惟在上述有效期間, 如收貨人已遷移地址, 必須轉送或退回原寄貨人時, 一旦該貨物已離開郵政局, 保險即告終止⓮。

⓮ 本節參考書及資料:

1) R. H. Brown: *Marine Insurance, Volume I—principles.*

2) Gerhard W. Schneider: *Export—Import Financing.*

3) Victor Dover: *A Handbook to Marine Insurance.*

4) William S. Shaterian: *Export—Import Banking.*

5) 孫堂福著: 海上保險學

6) 司法行政部民事司與經濟部國際貿易局編譯 「國際貿易法規暨慣例彙編」第二冊

7) *New Institute Cargo Clauses for insurance adopted by the Institute of London Underwriters & its Institute War Clauses for sendings by post.*

第六章　國際商品買賣契約之標準化

6-1　契約一般條款之標準化

國際商品買賣契約之明示條款，嚴格說來，可分爲「主要條件」如品質、價格、付款條件及交貨日期等，其餘條款爲交易商品所應注意履行之「一般條款」(General Conditions)。後者爲便利業者參考採用，似可考慮各國之法律制度，加以統一標準化。從進出口商之立場言，對于交易之商品，能就其商品特性、交易條件等訂定標準之一般條款 (Standard General Conditions)，則雙方極易根據此項明確之條件爲基礎，早日進行商談，並在主要條件如品質、價格、交貨日期等洽妥後，立即成交簽約。既省時又省事，實爲目前工商社會所共同追求之目標。

聯合國歐洲經濟委員會(The Economic Commission For Europe)有鑑及此，乃於一九五一年成立工作小組，從事於契約之「一般條款」之擬訂，迄一九六四年，已草訂八種標準一般條款 (Standard Genenal Conditions)。其中一九五三年所訂 Form 574「供應輸出廠房設備及機械之一般條款」(General Conditions for the Supply of Plant and Machinery for Export) 及一九六一年所訂 Form 730「耐用性消費品及其他工程用品之進出口一般條款」(General Conditions of Sale for the

Import & Export of Durable Consumer Goods and of other Engineering Stock Articles), 比較適合一般企業參考❶。前者條款，極適于
機器出口商使用，內容包括：(1)契約之成立、(2)圖表及說明文件、(3)包
裝、(4)檢驗及測試、(5)風險之移轉、(6)交貨、(7)付款、(8)保證、(9)免責、
(10)損害賠償之限制、(11)廢止契約權、(12)仲裁與適用法律，全文譯本，請
參閱司法行政部民事司與國際貿易局編譯之「國際貿易法規暨慣例彙編」
第一冊❷。後者條款，適於一般耐久性消費品之進出口商使用，內容包
括：(1)契約之成立、(2)使用及保養說明文件、(3)包裝、(4)風險之移轉、
(5)交貨、(6)付款、(7)買方拒絕收貨權、(8)保證、(9)免責、(10)仲裁與適
用法律❸。茲為便于讀者直接參考，特將該 Form 574 及 Form 730 原
條文抄錄如次：

---

❶ *Commentary on the General Conditions for the Supply of Plant and
Machinery for Export No. 574—Economic Commission for Europe
Industry and Materials Committee, United Nations, Geneva*

❷ 司法行政部民事司與國際貿易局編譯之「國際貿易法規暨慣例彙編」第一
冊第749至770頁。

❸ *General Conditions of Sale for the Import & Export of Durable
Consumer Goods and of other Engineering Stock Articles, No. 730
—United Nations Economic Commission for Europe, Geneva*

GENERAL CONDITIONS
FOR THE SUPPLY OF PLANT AND MACHINERY FOR EXPORT 574

Prepared under the auspices of the

UNITED NATIONS ECONOMIC COMMISSION FOR EUROPE

Geneva, December 1955

1. PREAMBLE

1. 1　These General Conditions shall apply, save as varied by express agreement accepted in writing by both parties.

2. FORMATION OF CONTRACT

2. 1　The Contract shall be deemed to have been entered into when, upon receipt of an order, the Vendor has sent an acceptance in writing within the time-limit (if any)fixed by the Purchaser.

2. 2　If the Vendor, in drawing up his tender, has fixed a time-limit for acceptance, the Contract shall be deemed to have been entered into when the Purchaser has sent an acceptance in writing before the expiration of such time-limit, provided that there shall be no binding Contract unless the acceptance reaches the Vendor not later than one week after the expiration of such time-limit.

3. DRAWINGS AND DESCRIPTIVE DOCUMENTS

3. 1　The weights, dimensions, capacities, prices, performance ratings and other data included in catalogues, prospectuses, circulars, advertisements, illustrated matter and price lists constitute an approximate guide. These data shall not be binding save to the extent that they are by reference expressly included in the Contract.

3. 2　Any drawings or technical documents intended for use in the construction of the Plant or of part thereof and submitted to the Purchaser prior or subsequent to the formation of the Contract remain the exclusive property of the Vendor. They may not, without the Vendor's consent, be utilised by the Purchaser or copied, reproduced, transmitted or communicated to a third party. Provided, however, that the said plans and documents shall be the property of the Purchaser:

　　(a) if it is expressly so agreed, or

　　(b) if they are referable to a separate preliminary Development Contract on which no actual construction was to be performed and in which the property of the Vendor in the said plans and documents was not reserved.

3. 3　Any drawings or technical documents intended for use in the construction of

---

These Conditions may be used, at the option of the parties, as an alternative to the General Conditions for the Supply of Plant and Machinery for Export prepared under the auspices of the United Nations Economic Commission for Europe, at Geneva, in March 1953 (General Conditions No. 188).

The English, French and Russian texts are equally authentic.

The observations of the experts who drew up these General Conditions, together with a description of the procedure followed, are embodied in the "COMMENTARY ON THE GENERAL CONDITIONS FOR THE SUPPLY OF PLANT AND MACHINERY FOR EXPORT No. 574" (document E/ECE/220)published by the Economic Commission for Europe. It can be obtained direct from the Sales Section of the European Office of the United Nations, Geneva, Switzerland, or through United Nations Sales Agents.

the Plant or of part thereof and submitted to the Vendor by the Purchaser prior or subsequent to the formation of the Contract remain the exclusive property of the Purchaser. They may not, without his consent, be utilised by the Vendor or copied, reproduced, transmitted or communicated to a third party.

3. 4　The Vendor shall, if required by the Purchaser, furnish free of charge to the Purchaser at the commencement of the Guarantee Period, as defined in Clause 9, information and drawings other than manufacturing drawings of the Plant in sufficient detail to enable the Purchaser to carry out the erection, commissioning, operation and maintenance (including running repairs) of all parts of the Plant. Such information and drawings shall be the property of the Purchaser and the restrictions on their use set out in paragraph 2 hereof shall not apply thereto. Provided that if the Vendor so stipulates, they shall remain confidential.

4. PACKING

4. 1　Unless otherwise specified:

> (a) prices shown in price-lists and catalogues shall be deemed to apply to unpacked Plant;
>
> (b) prices quoted in tenders and in the contract shall include the cost of packing or protection required under normal transport conditions to prevent damage to or deterioration of the Plant before it reaches its destination as stated in the Contract.

5. INSPECTION AND TESTS

Inspection

5. 1　If expressly agreed in the Contract, the Purchaser shall be entitled to have the quality of the materials used and the parts of the Plant, both during manufacture and when completed, inspected and checked by his authorised representatives. Such inspection and checking shall be carried out at the place of manufacture during normal working hours after agreement with the Vendor as to date and time.

5. 2　If as a result of such inspection and checking the Purchaser shall be of the opinion that any materials or parts are defective or not in accordance with the Contract, he shall state in writing his objections and the reasons therefor.

Tests

5. 3　Acceptance tests will be carried out and, unless otherwise agreed, will be made at the Vendor's works and during normal working hours. If the technical requirements of the tests are not specified in the Contract, the tests will be carried out in accordance with the general practice obtaining in the appropriate branch of the industry in the country where the Plant is manufactured.

5. 4　The Vendor shall give to the Purchaser sufficient notice of the tests to permit the Purchaser's representatives to attend. If the Purchaser is not represented at the tests, the test report shall be communicated by the Vendor to the Purchaser and shall be accepted as accurate by the Purchaser.

5. 5　If on any test (other than a test on site, where tests on site are provided for in the Contract) the Plant shall be found to be defective or not in accordance with the Contract, the Vendor shall with all speed and at his own expense (including any transport expenses) make good the defect or ensure that the Plant complies with the Contract. Thereafter, if the Purchaser so requires, the test shall be repeated.

5. 6　Unless otherwise agreed, the Vendor shall bear all the expenses of tests carried out in his works, except the personal expenses of the Purchaser's representatives

5. 7　If the Contract provides for tests on site, the terms and conditions governing such tests shall be such as may be specially agreed between the parties.

6. PASSING OF RISK

6. 1　Where no indication is given in the Contract of the form of sale, the Plant shall be deemed to be sold "ex works".

6. 2　Save as provided in paragraph 7. 6., the moment when the risks pass shall, unless the parties shall have otherwise agreed, be determined as follows:

> (a) On a sale "ex works", the risk shall pass from the Vendor to the Purchaser when the Plant has been placed at the disposal of the Purchaser in accordance with the Contract, provided that the Vendor gives to the Purchaser notice in writing of the date on and after which the Purchaser may take delivery of the Plant. The notice of the Vendor must be given in sufficient time to allow the Purchaser to take such measures as are normally necessary for the purpose of taking delivery.
>
> (b) On a sale FOB or CIF, the risk shall pass from the Vendor to the Purchaser when the Plant has effectively passed the ship's rail at the agreed port of shipment.
>
> (c) On a sale "free at frontier", the risks shall pass from the Vendor to the Purchaser when the Customs formalities have been concluded at the frontier of the country from which the Plant is exported.
>
> (d) In any of the cases mentioned in paragraphs (b) and (c) hereof, the Vendor shall give to the Purchaser sufficiently early advice of the dispatch of the Plant to enable the Puchaser to take any neceaaary measures.

6. 3　On any other form of sale, the time when the risks pass shall be determined in accordance with the agreement of the parties.

7. DELIVERY

7. 1　Unless otherwise agreed, the delivery period shall run from the latest of the following dates:

> (a) the date of the formation of the Contract as defined in Clause 2;
>
> (b) the date in which the Vendor receives notice of the issue of a valid import licence where such is necessary for the execution of the Contract;
>
> (c) the date of the receipt by the Vendor of such payment in advance of manufacture as is stipulated in the Contract.

7. 2　Should delay in delivery be caused by any of the circumstances mentioned in Clause 10 or by an act or omission of the Purchaser and whether such cause occur before or after the time or extended time for delivery, there shall be granted subject to the provisions of paragraph 5 hereof such extension of the delivery period as is reasonable, having regard to all the circumstances of the case.

7. 3　If a fixed time for delivery is provided for in the Contract and the Vendor fails to deliver within such time or any extension thercof granted under paragraph 2 hereof, the Purchaser shall be entitled, on giving to the Vendor within a reasonable time notice in writing, to claim a reduction of the price payable under the Contract, unless it can be reasonably concluded from the circumstances of the particular case that the Purchaser has suffered no loss. Such reduction shall equal the percentage

named in paragraph A of the Appendix of that part of the price payable under the Contract which is prorerly attributable to such portion of the Plant as cannot in consequence of the said failure be put to the use intended for each complete week of delay commencing on the due date of delivery, but shall not exceed the maximum percentage named in paragraph B of the Appendix. Such reduction shall be allowed when a payment becomes due on or after delivery. Save as provided in paragraph 5 hereof, such reduction of price shall be to the exclusion of any other remedy of the Purchaser in respect of the Vendor's failure to deliver as aforesaid.

7. 4   If the time for delivery mentioned in the Contract is an estimate only, either party may after the expiration of two thirds of such estimated time require the other party in writing to agree a fixed time.

Where no time for delivery is mentioned in the Contract, this course shall be open to either party after the expiration of six months from the formation of the Contract.

If in either case the parties fail to agree, either party may have recourse to arbitration, in accordance with the provisions of Clause 13, to determine a reasonable time for delivery and the time so determined shall be deemed to be the fixed time for delivery provided for in the Contract and paragraph 3 hereof shall apply accordingly.

7. 5   If any portion of the Plant in respect of which the Purchaser has become entitled to the maximum reduction provided for by paragraph 3 hereof, or in respect of which he would have been so entitled had he given the notice referred to therein, remains undelivered, the Purchaser may by notice in writing to the Vendor require him to deliver and by such last mentioned notice fix a final time for delivery which shall be reasonable taking into account such delay as has already occured. If for any reason whatever the Vendor fails within such time to do everything that he must do to effect delivery, the Purchaser shall be entitled by notice in writing to the Vendor, and without requiring the consent of any Court, to terminate the Contract in respect of such portion of the Plant and thereupon to recover from the Vendor any loss suffered by the Purchaser by reason of the failure of the Vendor as aforesaid up to an amount not exceeding the sum named in paragraph C of the Appendix or, if no sum be named, that part of the price payable under the Contract which is properly attributable to such portion of the Plant as could not in consequence of the Vendor's failure be put to the use intended.

7. 6   If the Purchaser fails to accept delivery on due date, he shall nevertheless make any payment conditional on delivery as if the plant had been delivered. The Vendor shall arrange for the storage of the Plant at the risk and cost of the Purchaser. If required by the Purchaser, the Vendor shall insure the Plant at the cost of the Purchaser. Provided that if the delay in accepting delivery is due to one of the circumstances mentioned in Clause 10 and the Vendor is in a position to store it in his premises without prejudice to his business, the cost of storing the Plant shall not be borne by the Purchaser.

7. 7   Unless the failure of the Purchaser is due to any of the circumstances mentioned in Clause 10, the Vendor may require the Purchaser by notice in writing to accept delivery within a reasonable time.

If the Purchaser fails for any reason whatever to do so within such time, the Vendor shall be entitled by notice in writing to the Purchaser, and without requiring the consent of any Court, to terminate the Contract in respect of such portion of the Plant as is by reason of the failure of the Purchaser aforesaid not delivered and thereupon to recover from the Purchaser any loss, suffered by reason of such failure up to an amount not exceeding the sum named in paragraph D of the Appendix or, if no sum be named, that part of the price payable under the Contract which is properly attributable to such portion of the Plant.

8. PAYMENT

8. 1　Payment shall be made in the manner and at the time or times agreed by the parties.

8. 2　Any advance payments made by the Purchaser are payments on account and do not constitute a deposit, the abandonment of which would entitle either party to terminate the Contract.

8. 3 If delivery has been made before payment of the whole sum payable under the Contract, Plant delivered shall, to the extent permitted by the law of the country where the Plant is situated after delivery, remain the property of the Vendor until such payment has been effected. If such law does not permit the Vendor to retain the property in the Plant, the Vendor shall be entitled to the benefit of such other rights in respect thereof as such law permits him to retain. The Purchaser shall give the Vendor every assistance in taking any measures required to protect the Vendor's right of property or such other rights as aforesaid.

8. 4　A payment conditional on the fulfilment of an obligation by the Vendor shall not be due until such obligation has been fulfilled, unless the failure of the Vendor is due to an act or omission of the Purchaser.

8. 5　If the Purchaser delays in making any payment, the Vendor may postpone the fulfilment of his own obligations until such payment is made, unless the failure of the Purchaser is due to an act or omission of the Vendor.

8. 6　If delay by the Purchaser in making any payment is due to one of the circumstances mentioned in Clause 10, the Vendor shall not be entitled to any interest on the sum due.

8. 7　Save as aforesaid, if the Purchaser delays in making any payment, the Vendor shall on giving to the Purchaser within a reasonable time notice in writing be entitled to the payment of interest on the sum due at the rate fixed in paragraph E of the Appendix from the date on which such sum became due. If at the end of the period fixed in paragraph F of the Appendix, the Purchaser shall still have failed to pay the sum due, the Vendor shall be entitled by notice in writing to the Purchaser, and without requiring the consent of any Court, to terminate the Contract and thereupon to recover from the Purchaser the amount of his loss up to the sum mentioned in paragraph D of the Appendix.

9. GUARANTEE

9. 1　Subject as hereinafter set out, the Vendor undertakes to remedy any defect resulting from faulty design, materials or workmanship.

9. 2　This liability is limited to defects which appear during the period (hereinafter called "the Guarantee Period") specified in paragraph G of the Appendix.

9. 3　In fixing this period due account has been taken of the time normally required for transport as contemplated in the Contract.

9. 4　In respect of such parts (whether of the Vendor's own manufacture or not) of the Plant as are expressly mentioned in the Contract, the Guarantee Period shall

be such other period (if any) as is specified in respect of each of such parts.

9. 5　The Guarantee Period shall start from the date on which the Purchaser receives notification in writing from the Vendor that the Plant is ready for dispatch from the works. If dispatch is delayed, the Guarantee Period shall be extended by a period equivalent to the amount of the delay so as to permit the Purchaser the full benefit of the time given for trying out the Plant. Provided however that if such delay is due to a cause beyond the control of the Vendor such extension shall not exceed the number of months stated in paragraph H of the Appendix. And provided also that, if the parties so agree, the Guarantee Period shall start from the date of delivery.

9. 6　The parties, having taken into account the nature of the Plant, may provide in the Contract for a reduction of the Guarantee Period if the use of the Plant is abnormally intensive.

9. 7　A fresh Guarantee Period equal to that stated in paragraph G of the Appendix shall apply, under the same terms and conditions as those applicable to the original Plant, to parts supplied in replacement of defective parts or to parts renewed in pursuance of this Clause. This provision shall not apply to the remaining parts of the Plant, the Guarantee Period of which shall be extended only by a period equal to the period during which the Plant is out of action as a result of a defect covered by this Clause.

9. 8　In order to be able to avail himself of his rights under this Clause the Purchaser shall notify the Vendor in writing without delay of any defects that have appeared and shall give him every opportunity of inspecting and remedying them.

9. 9　On receipt of such notification the Vendor shall remedy the defect forthwith and, save as mentioned in paragraph 10 hereof, at his own expense. Save where the nature of the defect is such that it is appropriate to effect repairs on site, the Purchaser shall return to the Vendor any part in which a defect covered by this Clause has appeared, for repair or replacement by the Vendor, and in such case the delivery to the Purchaser of such part properly repaired or a part in replacement thereof shall be deemed to be a fulfilment by the Vendor of his obligations under this paragraph in respect of such defective part.

9. 10　Unless otherwise agreed, the Purchaser shall bear the cost and risk of transport of defective parts and of repaired parts or parts supplied in replacement of such defective parts between the place where the Plant is situated and one of the following points:

    (i) the Vendor's works if the Contract is "ex works" or F. O. R.;

    (ii) the port from which the Vendor dispatched the Plant if the Contract is F. O. B., F. A. S., C. I. F. or C. & F.;

    (iii) in all other cases the frontier of the country from which the Vendor dispatched the Plant.

9. 11　Where, in pursuance of paragraph 9 hereof, repairs are required to be effected on site, the conditions covering the attendance of the Vendor's representatives on site shall be such as may be specially agreed between the parties.

9. 12　Defective parts replaced in accordance with this Clause shall be placed at the disposal of the Vendor.

9. 13　If the Vendor refuses to fulfil his obligations under this Clause or fails to proceeed with due diligence after being required so to do, the Purchaser may proceed

to do the necessary work at the Vendor's risk and expense, provided that he does so in a reasonable manner.

9. 14　The Vendor's liability does not apply to defects arising out of materials provided, or out of a design stipulated, by the Purchaser.

9. 15　The Vendor's liability shall apply only to defects that appear under the conditions of operation provided for by the Contract and under proper use. It does not cover defects due to causes arising after the risk in the Plant has passed in accordance with Clause 6. In particular it does not cover defects arising from the Purchaser's faulty maintenance or erection, or from alterations carried out without the Vendor's consent in writing, or from repairs carried out improperly by the Purchaser, nor does it cover normal deterioration.

9. 16　Save as in this Clause expressed, the Vendor shall be under no liability in respect of defects after the risk in the Plant has passed in accordance with Clause 6, even if such defects are due to causes existing before the risk so passed. It is expressly agreed that the Purchaser shall have no claim in respect of personal injury or of damage to property not the subject matter of the Contract or of loss of profit unless it is shown from the circumstances of the case that the Vendor has been guilty of gross misconduct.

9. 17　"Gross misconduct" does not comprise any and every lack of proper care or skill, but means an act or omission on the part of the Vendor implying either a failure to pay due regard to serious consequences which a conscientious Contractor would normally foresee as likely to ensue, or a deliberate disregard of any consequences of such act or omission.

10 RELIEFS

10. 1　Any circumstances beyond the control of the parties intervening after the formation of the contract and impeding its reasonable performance shall be considered as cases of relief. For the purposes of this clause circumstances not due to the fault of the party invoking them shall be deemed to be beyond the control of the parties.

10. 2　The party wishing to claim relief by reason of any of the said circumstances shall notify the other party in writing without delay on the intervention and on the cessation thereof.

10. 3　The effects of the said circumstances, so far as they affect the timely perfor-mance of their obligations by the parties, are defined in Clauses 7and 8. Save as provided in paragaphs 7.5, 7.7 and 8.7, if, by reason of any of the said circumstances, the performance of the Contract within a reasonable time becomes impossible, either party shall be entitled to terminate the Contract by notice in writing to the other party without requiring the consent of any Court.

10. 4　If the Contract is terminated in accordance with paragraph 3 hereof, the division of the expenses incurred in respect of the Contract shall be determined by agreement between the parties.

10. 5　In default of agreement it shall be determined by the arbitrator which party has been prevented from performing his obligations and that party shall refund to the other the amount of the said expenses incurred by the other less any amount to be credited in accordance with paragraph 7 hereof, or, where the amount to be so credited exceeds the amount of such expenses, shall be entitled to recover the excess.

　　If the arbitrator determines that both parties have been prevented from performing their obligations, he shall apportion the said expenses between the parties in such manner as to him seems fair and reasonable, having regard to all the circumstances of the case.

10. 6   For the purposes of this clause "expenses" means actual out-of-pocket expenses reasonably incurred after both parties shall have mitigated their losses as far as possible. Provided that as respects Plant delivered to the Purchaser the Vendor's expenses shall be deemed to be that part of the price payable under the Contract which is properly attributable thereto.

10. 7   There shall be credited to the Purchaser against the Vendor's expenses all sums paid or payable under the Contract by the Purchaser to the Vendor.

There shall be credited to the Vendor against the Purchaser's expenses that part of the price payable under the Contract which is properly attributable to Plant delivered to the Purchaser or, in the case of an incomplete unit, the value of such Plant having regard to its incomplete state.

11. LIMITATION OF DAMAGES

11. 1   Where either party is liable in damages to the other, these shall not exceed the damage which the party in default could reasonably have foreseen at the time of the formation of the Contract.

11. 2   The party who sets up a breach of the Contract shall be under a duty to take all necessary measures to mitigate the loss which has occurred provided that he can do so without unreasonable inconvenience or cost. Should he fail to do so, the party guilty of the breach may claim a reduction in the damages.

12. RIGHTS AT TERMINATION

12. 1   Termination of the Contract, from whatever cause arising, shall be without prejudice to the rights of the parties accrued under the Contract up to the time of termination.

13. ARBITRATION AND LAW APPLICABLE

13. 1   Any dispute arising out of or in connexion with the Contract shall be finally settled by arbitration without recourse to the Courts. The procedure shall be such as may be agreed between the parties.

13. 2   Unless otherwise agreed, the Contract shall be governed by the law of the Vendor's country.

APPENDIX

(To be completed by parties to the Contract)

CLAUSE

A. Percentage to be deducted for each week's delay	7.3 .... per cent
B. Maximum percentage which the deductions above may not exceed	7.3 .... per cent
C. Maximum amount recoverable for non-delivery	7.5 .... (in the agreed currency)
D. Maximum amount recoverable on termination by Vendor for failure to take delivery or make payment	7.7 .... (in the agreed currency) and 8.7
E. Rate of interest on overdue payments	8.7 .... per cent per annum
F. Period of delay in payment authoriz-	

ing termination by Vendor	8.7 .... months	
G. Guarantee Period for original Plant and parts replaced or renewed	9.2 and .... months 9.7	
H. Maximum extension of Guarantee Period	9.5 .... months	

SUPPLEMENTARY CLAUSE
PRICE REVISION

Should any change occur in the cost of the relevant materials and/or wages during the period of execution of the contract, the agreed prices shall be subject to revision on the basis of the following formula:

$$P1 = \frac{P0}{100} (a + b\frac{M1}{M0} + c\frac{S1}{S0})$$

where:

$P1 =$ final price for invoicing

$P0 =$ initial price of goods, as stipulated in the contract and as prevailing at the date of .... (1)

$M1 =$ mean (2) of the prices (or price indices) for (type of materials concerned) ... . over the period .... (3)

$M0 =$ prices (or price indices) for the same materials at the date stipulated above for $P0$

$S1 =$ mean (2) of the wages (including social charges) or relevant indices (4) in respect of .... (specify categories of labour and social charges) over the period .... (3)

$S0 =$ wages (including social charges) or relevant indices (4) in respect of the same categories at the date stipulated above for $P0$

a, b, c, represent the contractually agreed percentage of the individual elements of the initial price, which add up to 100.

$(a+b+c=100)$

a = fixed proportion = ...

b = percentage proportion of materials = ...

c = percentage proportion of wages = ...
  (including social charges)

Where necessary, b (and if need be, c) can be broken down into as many partial percentages (b1, b2, b3 ....) as there are variables taken into account (b1+b2 .... +bn=b).

DOCUMENTATION For the purpose of determining the values of materials and wages, the parties agree to use the following documents as sources of reference:

1. Materials: prices.. (type of materials)
    (or price indices)
    published by ....
    under the headings ....

2. Wages: wages (including related social charges)
    (or relevant indices)
    published by..........................
    under the headings .... (5)

Rules for applying the Clause. In the case of partial deliveries which are invoiced separately, the final price shall be calculated separately for each such delivery.

Period of application of the Clause. The revision clause shall cover the delivery period fixed in the contract, together with any extension thereof granted under Clause 7.2., but shall in no case apply after the date on which manufacture is completed.

Tolerances. Prices shall not be revised unless the application of the formula produces a plus or minus variation of .... (6)

Saving Clause. If the parties wish the revision formula to be adjusted or replaced by a more accurate method of calculation when the plus or minus variation exceeds a certain percentage, they shall expressly so agree.

---

(1) It is recommended that the parties should, as far as possible, adopt as the initial price the price prevailing at the date of the contract and not at an earlier date. This is normally the contract price less cost of packing, transport and insurance.

(2) Arithmetical or weighted.

(3) Specify the datum period, which may be defined as part or the whole of the delivery period.

(4) If legal social charges are covered by the index, they need not be taken into account again.

(5) Indices relating specifically to the engineering and electrical industries should be used as far as possible.

(6) State the percentage plus or minus variation which must be exceeded before the formula is applied.

730

GENERAL CONDITIONS OF SALE FOR THE IMPORT AND EXPORT OF DURABLE CONSUMER GOODS AND OF OTHER ENGINEERING STOCK ARTICLES*

Prepared under the auspices of the
UNITED NATIONS ECONOMIC COMMISSION FOR EUROPE
Geneva, March 1961

1. PREAMBLE
1. 1　These General Conditions shall apply if both parties refer to them, save as varied by express agreement confirmed in writing by both parties.
2. FORMATION OF CONTRACT
2. 1　The contract shall be deemed to have been entered into, when, upon receipt of an order, the Vendor has sent an acceptance in writing within the time-limit (if any) fixed by the Purchaser.
2. 2　Where the Vendor, in drawing up his tender, has fixed a time-limit for acceptance, the contract shall be deemed to have been entered into when the Purchaser has sent an acceptance in writing before the expiration of such time-limit.
2. 3　Where an export or import licence, a foreign exchange control authorization or similar authorization is required for the performance of the contract, the party responsible for obtaining the licence or authorization shall act with due diligence to obtain it in good time. If on the expiration of the period specified in paragraph A of the appendix from the date of the formation of the contract, or where no such period is specified then on the expiration of three months, the requisite licence or authorization cannot be obtained, either party shall be entitled to regard the contract as never having been formed provided that such party informs the other party of his decision without delay.
3. DESCRIPTIVE DOCUMENTS AND INSTRUCTION LEAFLETS RELATING TO USE AND MAINTENANCE
3. 1　The weights, dimensions, capacities, prices, performance ratings and other data included in catalogues, prospectuses, circulars, advertisements, illustrated matter and price lists shall not be binding save to the extent that they are by reference expressly included in the contract.
3. 2　The Vendor shall furnish free of charge to the Purchaser, not later than the commencement of the Guarantee Period, his instruction leaflets relating to the use

---

*　The English, French and Russian texts are equally authentic.

The observations of the experts who drew up these General Conditions, together with a description of the procedure followed, are embodied in the "Commentary on the General Conditions of sale for the import and export of durable consumer goods and of other engineering stock articles, No. 730" (Document E/ECE/426) published by the Economic Commission for Europe. It can be obtained direct from the Sales Section of the European Office of the United Nations, Geneva, Switzerland, or through United Nations Sales Agents.

and maintenance of the goods.

4. PACKING

4. 1　Unless otherwise specified:

　(a) prices shown in price-lists and catalogues shall be deemed to apply to unpacked goods;

　(b) prices quoted in tenders and in the contract shall include the cost of packing or protection required under normal transport conditions to prevent damage to or deterioration of the goods before they reach their destination as stated in the contract.

5. PASSING OF THE RISK

5. 1　Where no indication is given in the contract of the form of sale, the goods shall be deemed to be sold "ex works".

5. 2　Save as provided in paragraph 6.5, and unless the parties have otherwise agreed, the moment when the risk passes shall be determined as follows:

　(a) On a sale "ex works", the risk shall pass from the Vendor to the Purchaser when the goods have been placed at the disposal of the Purchaser in accordance with the contract, provided that the Vendor gives to the Purchaser notice in writing of the date on and after which the Purchaser may take delivery of the goods. The notice of the Vendor must be given in sufficient time to allow the Purchaser to take such measures as are normally necessary for the purpose of taking delivery;

　(b) On a sale wagon, lorry, barge (agreed point of departure) or on a sale "carriage paid up to –", the risk shall pass from the Vendor to the Purchaser when the carrier takes over the loaded vehicle or craft;

　(c) On a sale FOB or CIF, the risk shall pass from the Vendor to the Purchaser when the goods have effectively passed the ship's rail at the agreed port of shipment;

　(d) On a sale "delivered at frontier" (without any other precision) or "delivered at frontier of exporting country", the risk shall pass from the Vendor to the Purchaser when the customs formalities have been concluded at the frontier of the country from which the goods are exported;

　(e) On a sale "delivered (agreed frontier post of importing country) or (agreed point in the interior of the importing country)" the risk shall pass from the Vendor to the Purchaser when the Purchaser is required to take delivery of the goods upon their arrival at the agreed destination point;

　(f) In any of the cases mentioned in paragraphs (b), (c), (d) and (e) hereof, the Vendor shall give to the Purchaser sufficiently early advice of the dispatch of the goods to enable the Purchaser to take any necessary measures.

5. 3　On any other form of sale, the time when the risk passes shall be determined in accordance with the agreement of the parties.

6. DELIVERY

6. 1　Unless otherwise agreed, the delivery period shall run from the latest of the following dates:

　(a) the date of the formation of the contract;

　(b) the date of the receipt by the Vendor of such payment in advance of delivery as is stipulated in the contract.

6. 2　On expiry of the delivery period provided for in the contract, the Vendor shall

be entitled to the period of grace specified in paragraph B of the Appendix, or where no such period is specified, to a period of grace of one month from the expiry of the delivery period provided for in the contract.

6. 3　Should delay in delivery be caused by any of the circumstances mentioned in Clause 10 or by an act or omission of the Purchaser, there shall be granted such extension of the delivery period as is reasonable, having regard to all the circumstances of the case. This provision shall not apply where the delay in delivery occurs after the expiry of the period of grace referred to in paragraph 6.2, unless such delay is due to an act or omission of the Purchaser.

6. 4　Should the Vendor fail to deliver the goods after the period of grace mentioned in paragraph 6.2, the Purchaser shall be entitled to terminate the contract by notice in writing to the Vendor, both in respect of all goods undelivered, and in respect of goods which though delivered cannot be properly used without the undelivered goods. Where the Purchaser so terminates the contract he shall be entitled, to the exclusion of any other remedy for delay in delivery, to recover any payment which he has made both in respect of all goods undelivered and in respect of goods which although delivered cannot be properly used without the undelivered goods, to reject the goods delivered which are unusable and to recover any expenses properly incurred in performing the contract.

6. 5　Where the Purchaser does not take the goods at the place and time provided for by the contract for any reason other than an act or omission of the Vendor, he shall nevertheless make any payments provided for in the contract as if the goods had been delivered. In such a case, once the goods have been appropriated to the contract, the Vendor shall arrange for their storage at the risk and cost of the Purchaser. The Vendor shall further be entitled, to the exclusion of any other remedy for the Purchaser's failure to take the goods, to recover any expenses properly incurred in performing the contract and not covered by payments received.

7. PAYMENT

7. 1　Payment shall be made in the manner and at the time or times agreed by the parites. In the absence of agreement to the contrary, express or implied, payment shall be due in the case of a sale "ex works" thirty days after notification from the Vendor to the Purchaser that the goods have been placed at his disposal, and in any other case thirty days after notification from the Vendor to [the Purchaser that the goods have been dispatched.

7. 2　Where the Purchaser delays in making any payment and the delay is not due to an act or omission of the Vendor, the Vendor may:

(a) postpone the fulfilment of his own obligations until snch payment is made; and

(b) recover after written notice sent in good time to the Purchaser, interest on the sum due, from the time fixed for payment, at the rate of 6% unless otherwise provided.

7. 3　Where at the end of the period specified in paragraph C of the Appendix, or where no such period is fixed, then after the expiry of one month from the date on which payment became due, the Purchaser shall still have failed to pay the sum due, the Vendor shall be entitled by notice in writing, and to the exclusion of any other remedy against the Purchaser by reason of the latter's delay, to terminate the contract, without prejudice to his right to recover any payment due in respect of delivered goods and all expenses properly incurred by the Vendor in performing the

contract.

8. THE PURCHASER'S RIGHT OF REJECTION

8. 1　During the period specified in paragraph D of the Appendix, or where no such period is specified, then within such reasonable period as will allow inspection, the Purchaser shall be entitled to reject goods which do not conform with the contract (excepting any defect caused after the passage of risk), provided that before the Purchaser can exercise his right of rejection the Vendor shall have an opportunity to make good any default at his expense within a reasonable period.

8. 2　The Purchaser's right of rejection shall also apply to goods which, although delivered and accepted, cannot be properly used without the goods mentioned in paragraph 8. 1.

8. 3　The Vendor shall be entitled to have rejected goods returned to him at his risk and expense.

9. GUARANTEE

9. 1　Subject as hereinafter set out, the Vendor undertakes to remedy any defect resulting from faulty design, materials or workmanship.

9. 2　This liability is limited to defects which appear during the period (called "the guarantee period") commencing on the passage of risk and continuing for the period specified in paragraph E or F of the Appendix whichever shall first expire. In the absence of express specification in the Appendix the periods shall be twelve months in the case of paragraph E, and six months in the case of pargraph F.

9. 3　In respect of such parts of the goods as are expressly mentioned in the contract, the guarantee period shall be such other period (if any) as is specified in respect of each of such parts.

9. 4　The parties may specify in the contract that the Vendor assumes no liability other than that for gross misconduct as defined in paragraph 9. 11.

9. 5　Where the Purchaser wishes to avail himself of the guarantee, he shall notify the Vendor in writing without delay of any defect that has appeared. On receipt of such notification the Vendor shall if the defect is one that is covered by this clause at his option:

(a) repair the defective goods in situ; or

(b) have the defective goods or parts returned to him for repair; or

(c) replace the defective goods; or

(d) replace the defective parts in order to enable the Purchaser to carry out the necessary repairs at the Vendor's expense.

9. 6　Where the Vendor has returned to him defective goods or parts for replacement or repair, unless otherwise agreed, the Purchaser shall bear the cost and risk of carriage. Unless otherwise agreed, the return to the Purchaser of goods or parts sent by way of replacement or of repaired goods or parts shall take place at the cost and risk of the Vendor.

9. 7　Defective goods or parts replaced in accordance with this clause shall be placed at the disposal of the Vendor.

9. 8　Where the Vendor fails to fulfil his obligations under this clause within a reasonable period after receipt of notification under paragraph 9. 5, the Purchaser may proceed to have the defect remedied at the Vendor's expense, provided that he does so in a reasonable manner.

9. 9　The Vendor's liability shall apply only to defects that appear under the con-

ditions of operation provided for by the contract and under proper use. In particular it does not cover defects arising from faulty installation, maintenance or repairs, carried out by a person other than the Vendor or his agent, or from alterations carried out without the Vendor's consent in writing, nor does it cover normal deterioration.

9. 10　Subject to the provisions of clause 8　and　save as in this　clause expressed, the Vendor shall be under no liability in respect of defects after the risk in the goods has passed even if such defects are due to causes existing before the risk passed. It is expressly agreed that the Purchaser shall have no claim in respect of personal injury or of damage to property not the subject matter of the contract or of loss of profit unless it is shown from the circumstances of the case that the Vendor has been guilty of gross misconduct.

9. 11　"Gross misconduct" does not comprise any and every lack of proper care or skill, but means an act or omission on the part of the Vendor implying either a failure to pay due regard to serious consequences which a conscientious contractor would normally foresee as likely to ensue, or a deliberate disregard of any conse- quences of such act or omission.

10. RELIEFS

10. 1　Any circumstances beyond the control of the parties intervening after the formation of the contract and impeding its reasonable performance shall be considered as cases of relief. For the purposes of this clause circumstances not due to the default of the party invoking them shall be deemed to be beyond the control of the parties.

10. 2　The party wishing to claim relief by reason of any of the said circumstances shall notify the other party in writing without delay on the intervention and on the cessation thereof.

10. 3　Where by reason of any of the circumstances referred to in paragraph 10. 1 the performance of the contract within a reasonable time becomes impossible, either party shall be entitled to terminate the contract by notice in writing to the other party and in that event there　shall be such restitution (if any) whether by way of repayment of money, return of goods, or otherwise as shall be just and as the circumstances referred to in paragraph 10. 1 may permit.

11. ARBITRATION AND APPLICABLE LAW

11. 1　Any dispute arising out of or in connexion with the contract, which the parties have been unable to settle by agreement shall be settled finally out of court by arbitration by the arbitral body specified in paragraph G of the Appendix.

11. 2　Unless otherwise agreed, the contract shall be governed by the law of the Vendor's country.

APPENDIX

(To be completed by parties to the contract)

Paragraphs of General Conditions

A.　Period after which the parties are entitled to consider the contract as never having been formed if the necessary licence or authorization cannot be obtained　　　　　2.3 ....

B. Length of the period of grace for delivery 6.2 ....

C. Period of delay in payment authorizing termination by the Vendor 7.3 ....

D. Period for exercise of the Purchaser's right of rejection 8.1 ....

E. Guarantee period starting on passing of the risk 9.2 ....

F. Guarantee period from sale of goods to first end user 9.2 ....

G. Designation of arbitral body specified by the parties for the purpose of settling disputes arising out of or in connexion with the contract 11.1................................
....
....

　　一般從事國際貿易之業者，在進行接洽業務時，往往祇談交易之主要條件，對產品之詳細說明及其他一般契約條款，則先行印就檢寄，或洽談時面交研議，于事後雙方簽約；或將契約之一般條款印在主要條件之後，俾易校核簽字。該附在契約後面之一般條款，爲契約之一部份，與主要條件具有同等之法律效力。

6-2　標準契約格式之廣泛採用

　　目前國際間之大宗農工產品業者，基於多年來之交易習慣成例，業已訂定一種同業間通用之標準契約格式 (Standard Contract Form)。英國爲貿易先進國家，其各業公會所訂標準契約格式，已爲世界各國所廣泛採用，例如英國羊毛業公會、倫敦可可協會、英國油脂聯合會、穀類飼料商業公會、倫敦蔗業公會、倫敦橡膠商業公會、倫敦精糖公會、英國木材商業聯合會、倫敦基本金屬交易所、國際毛織品組織及利物浦棉業公會等所訂標準契約格式是❹。其中頗多係與國際同業公會聯合會所共同訂定，並經普遍廣爲採用者。此項標準契約格式，多由公會邀請同業及專家學者共同研訂印發業者採用，正面印「主要條件」，供業者在與買方洽妥後塡入，背面則印標準之「一般條款」，供買賣雙方遵照履行。在此擬介紹較具參考性之國際生皮及皮革輸出業公會及國際製革業協會共同訂定之正式契約格式（Official Contract Form）如下，並予翻譯，以供讀者參考。

---

❹　Schmitthoff: *Export Trade*, ch. 3, pp. 51-53.

國際生皮及皮革第一號契約格式

本契約適用於各種生皮及皮革，包括下列各條款，並得使用所附適當之附錄條件：

（註：如係 CIF 契約，可取消第 6 及16. 3條；C&F 契約取消第6. 11及16. 3條與第12條之保險條款；FOB 契約取消第 7 及11條與12條之保險條款）

1. 契約內容	賣方與買方本日簽訂本買賣契約各條款如下：
1.1　賣方	
1.2　買方	
1.3　簽約日期	
1.4　條件(挿入 CIF, C&F, FOB 定期班輪或 FOB 不定期貨輪或到達交貨等條件)	
1.5　數量	
1.6　標嘜說明	
1.7　品質/選擇/化學分析	
1.8　重量/大小/本質	
1.9　價格	
1.10　重量及尺碼條件	
1.11　裝船期間	
1.12　裝貨港/收貨地點/在海上	
1.13　目的港/交貨地點	
1.14　保險	
1.15　付款	
1.16　過磅/檢驗地點	
1.17　仲裁/訴訟地點	
1.18　附屬條件C之尺碼校對機構	
1.19　其他條款	

2. 定義

2.1 多數包含單數。

2.2 本約所稱皮革，除非另有說明，包括生皮。

2.3 生皮係指牛、馬及其他大動物之皮，並包括小動物之皮。

2.4 日或月係指陽曆之日或月。

2.5 除非另有說明，第一日裝船係指訂約日之次日。

2.6 輪船係指 Lloyd's 100A1 級之任何船隻（或等級相等之其他註册船隻），能製發提單，並適于裝運皮革者。

2.7 第一條款所稱 delivered，僅涉及價格基礎有關者爲準，係指賣方負責運至交貨地點之所有成本及費用，但不包括進口稅捐及海關費用。所有其他有關部份，應仍以 CIF 契約爲限。

2.8 一公斤等于英制2.2046磅。

2.9 不可抗力 (force majeure) 應解釋爲天災(Acts of God)、罷工(strikes)、停工 (lock-outs)、勞工騷亂 (labour disturbances)、貿易糾紛 (trade disputes)、戰爭 (war)、政府行爲 (government actions)、暴亂 (riots)、內亂 (civil commotions)、火災 (fires)、水災 (floods) 及傳染病 (epidemics)。

2.10 通知係指以電話（除非立卽書面確認）、電報或電傳電報作適當之通知。

3. 品質

3.1 皮革必須具有標謬說明之公平的平均品質 (of fair average quality)，如有任何缺陷，可以酌量減價。

3.2 賣方不保證皮革適于特別需要之目的用途；對皮革在製作時顯現之任何隱藏或其他缺陷不予負責，對製造過程及使用中發生之任何毀損，亦不負責。

4. 數量

4.1 可容許之差誤，多少不得超過百分之五，但如遇不履行契約估計損失時，不考慮此項容差。

5. 標謬

5.1 所售皮革，將分等包裝運輸，每包並分別標誌清楚。

5.2 所售皮革，均每張分別標明產地，俾抵達目的地時易于識別；如相同尺寸之皮革合併包紮，必須在包紮上註明尺碼。

5.3 如各類皮革抵達目的地後發現尚未標誌，所有重新分類費用由賣方負擔。

6. 目的地及運費

(僅適于 FOB 定期班輪交貨契約)

6.1 買方應于接獲賣方要求後八天內通知交貨目的地，但並不強制在許可裝船第一天前八天通知。

6.2 如賣方以買方之代理身分為買方安排船位，必須盡力按最新近之運率洽租，但如遇洽定船位困難時，賣方並不負延遲交貨之責。賣方如在裝船期限內洽定船位發生困難時，應即通知買方同意裝運第一艘可能之船隻 (first available steamer) 逕運指定之目的港；否則，買方應自行在裝貨港或收貨地提貨。

6.3 如買方自行洽定船位，應在適當時間內通知賣方船名及開航日期。如開航日期較規定之裝船日期延遲，或該船不能或全部拒絕裝運或拒裝一部份，抑廣告裝貨期限前已截止收貨，買方不得因此延遲裝運而向賣方索賠。

7. 運費

(僅適于 CIF 及 C&F 契約)

7.1 運費係按銷售時當天之費率計算，裝船時運費費率如有變動，其增加之差額由買方負擔。

8. 裝船

8.1 依照輪船所發提單之條款裝運，輪船公司有權直接運往或轉運。

8.2 如無相反之確定性證明，提單日期即證明係裝船日期。

8.3 依照當地習慣提供「裝上船」(on board) 之提單。如係貨櫃運輸提單，應以皮革最後一批送達收貨地點或裝運港之日期為提單日期。所有各批送達發票，亦應以此最後日期為發票日期。

8.4 除不同等級及重量之說明外，如非另有指示，每批貨運應視為不同之契約，但每部份裝貨，均係同一契約，同一價格及同一品質者，不在此限。

8.5 在同一輪船裝運之各批貨物，視同一批。

8.6 凡以取得船位為交貨條件者，除非在裝運期限內適有船可裝運，否則，在取得船位之當月最後一天裝船，亦視同「依期交貨」。賣方為求保障，可將此情況立即通知買方，並附原預定船位證明及開航文件。

8.7 如因受不可抗力阻礙，不克在規定之裝船限期內交運，得延期六個星期裝運；如屆期仍無法裝船，除非雙方同意再延，否則該契約無效。

9. 裝運通知

9.1 裝運通知應告知皮革價值，並註明船名。如係貨櫃裝運，應通知擬裝船名、貨櫃數量；如可能，由賣方儘早通知代理名稱，倘須改裝其他船隻，亦應儘早告知船名。

10. 風險與物權

10.1 賣方之皮革運輸風險，直至在船上交貨為止。如係貨櫃運輸，其負擔之風險，至第一個指定之收貨地點為止。倘賣方已履行其他應盡之各項義務，則此後一切滅失或損害，應由買方負擔。

10.2 買方或其全權代理已依照第一條付款條款支付賣方貨款後，皮革之所有權（title to the skins）始轉移買方；如有變更，照書面協議辦理。不拘皮革已否在買方掌握中，在買方未付款前，該批皮革之所有權仍屬賣方。買方僅可以賣方信託人之方式，在未付款前控制該批貨物，但**無權處理**或使用該貨。

11. 保險

　　(僅適于 CIF 契約)

11.1 賣方必須提供海上貨運保單或保險證明單，按契約價格加10% 投保 Warehouse to Warehouse 之**協會**全險，另附加兵險及罷工暴亂險，並註明甲板貨保險費另議（任何增加之保費，由賣方負擔）。所有賠償，按契約貨幣計算。

11.2 兵險按習用條款投保，訂約後任何增加之差額兵險保費，由買方負擔。

12. 裝船文件

12.1 文件包括發票、全套提單（或保證遺失之副本）或船方提貨單（Delivery

order)（必要時，須由銀行、船公司代理、船長或大副附署）及保險單。如經常需要重量、尺碼單，亦應照辦，費用由賣方負擔。

12.2 如裝運國可以取得並需要衞生證明單、產地證明及其他證件，其費用由賣方負擔。領事發票（如買方在簽約後要求）及其簽證費，由買方負擔。買方所需文件，必須列具詳細清單，並給予賣方充份之時間準備。

12.3 如無須提供提單及保險單，買方應以同等地位視同已提供提單及保險單。

12.4 裝船文件在寄遞至買方前，風險由賣方負擔。

12.5 買方須接受包括戰爭變更航程及其他公認之兵險保單。

12.6 賣方須負擔延遲提送貨運文件之所有額外費用，除非延誤非賣方之責。

12.7 如轉船須提具新提單方可付款時，賣方應提供在契約規定期間裝運之證明。

12.8 如係 CIF 或 C&F 契約，賣方必須提供運費已付或到付之提單；如屬後者，發票不應開列運費，以免違反契約規定，引起買方任何支付上之不便。

13. 發票

13.1 發票係依據賣方之件數、重量或尺碼等說明開列。

13.2 每包須標明件數；如可能，並註明尺碼。

13.3 如遇全損（total loss），以賣方之發票爲準。

13.4 如係分批裝運，應每批個別付款。

14. 付款

14.1 開送銀行以買方爲付款人並由其負擔風險之滙票，該付款銀行應保證付款。

14.2 凡以船到後付款交單爲條件者，如航程正常，應不遲于輪船或貨櫃船抵達目的港或處所時付款，無論如何最遲應在提單日起計九十天內付清。

14.3 如買方簽約後不能如期付款係由於政府管制外滙，賣方在買方未付款前，得隨時于七日前通知取消契約。賣方之停止履約，可參照下列第二十二條之規定選擇處理，但不得提出其他要求。

14.4 如遇輪船已正式報告滅失，應照第一條款之規定在第一次提送文件時付款。

15. 檢重及扣重

15.1 凡以卸重或抵達時重量爲計算標準者，如屬材料，得由公定檢重師檢定之。必要時，得由賣方代表會同檢查，費用由買方負擔。

15.2 除非過磅處僅有地磅之設置，否則不接受地磅之過磅。

15.3 最後買者必須將正式過磅單於卸貨後四十五天內航寄中間商轉交賣方。

15.4 如皮革之銷售訂有重量容差特權者，任何不足數額超過容許限額時，依照實重計算，由賣方補償差額價款。

15.5 皮革必須于卸貨後立卽過磅，最遲不得超過最後卸完日起計八天。

15.6 生皮之過磅，從輪船卸貨最後一日起計（FOB 裝船者，按提單日起計六星期）超過八天者，其卸貨重量應照下列方式調整加重：

乾生皮	第一星期，每天加重	0.05%
	超過一星期，每天加重	0.025%
乾鹽生皮	第一星期，每天加重	0.10%
	超過一星期，每天加重	0.05%
濕鹽生皮	第一星期，每天加重	0.20%
	超過一星期，每天加重	0.10%

如貨物非在卸裝後二十九天內過磅者，以賣方發票重量爲最後重量。貨物之裝船、進艙、卸貨及過磅在正常之情況下進行，而航程又在正常期間抵達，應認爲合理。

15.7 倘生皮係由內陸地點送至裝船港或接收地點裝運者，在裝運期前，如遇不可抗力事故延期，其在不可抗力延誤期內之計重，照前條辦理。

15.8 （本條僅適于由買方預定船位之 FOB 契約）——如生皮之裝運延遲，係由於輪船遲到或輪船截止承載，其計重方式，如延遲超過八天者，應依上條辦理。

15.9 皮革（非生皮）係按件數計價而未訂重量容差者，應按卸貨淨重或到達重量計算，但應不低於契約最低淨重或調整之重量爲準。

15.10 如濕鹽皮之包裝皮重，過磅不低于百分之十，應放在格子桌面或其他清潔之平面，加予雙面打擊後再加過磅。除除去覆蓋外皮之鹽外，不得加予清掃。如係桶裝者，須將全部桶打開，使排水最多四十八小時後，照上條雙面打擊過磅淨重。過磅前，應合理除去覆蓋之鹽。該抵達後卸載之包皮，可在最後結帳時計算。

15.11 乾皮及乾鹽皮可用包皮包裝，並容許其他無關之雜質。

15.12 使用作包皮之材料（包括墊板及包裝材料），應按卸載或抵達毛重定一百分比爲原則。

15.13 賣方對發票價格所作任何調整，應於接獲過磅單三十天內付清。

16. 檢驗

16.1 如不可能在碼頭檢驗，買賣雙方應另行協議地點檢驗。

16.2 買方如因不可抗力事故不能檢驗，可仍保留該檢驗權。

16.3 （僅適于 FOB 契約）──除非雙方同意皮革必須先經買方認可後裝船，否則，適當之檢驗應在買方指定之目的港或交貨地點。

17. 索賠

17.1 除非在本約第一條特別指明，皮革一旦從公用碼頭或船塢移運，賣方卽不受理任何對品質、規格或條件之賠償要求；惟經買賣雙方代表先行安排在目的港或交貨地點取樣供仲裁者，不在此限。（如檢驗地點不在目的港，則必須有原包裝之百分之八十貨物在檢驗地。）無論如何，最後買者必須在九天前通知準備皮革檢驗（如經由中間商者，應增加四天）。

17.2 品質不良或低于所訂規格或條件之糾紛，不宜心存拒絕付款之動機。買方接受之貨運文件，必須完整而不損害其權益。

18. 拒絕

18.1 如劣質貨物已達或超過契約總價之百分之十，買方得減價承受或拒絕接受；但本條並不影響仲裁人之裁斷，認定該項不良之交貨應予拒絕。

18.2 如皮革已被拒絕，買方無義務再接受其更換貨物。

19. 違約

19.1 如一方不履行契約義務，該違約之一方應賠償對方之損失。

19.2 如賣方違約：──其損害賠償，應限於契約價格與違約後第七天之市場價格的差額（除非仲裁人有充分之理由不照此項規定）。

19.3　如買方違約：——賣方可絕對自由為其皮革權益設想，採取任何之適當措施。所有風險及費用，由買方負擔。賣方並得於買方違約第七天後廢止契約，並依照本條19.2款辦法要求買方賠償差價。

19.4　如無可能估計市價，可比照類似品質之皮革估價。

20.　出口稅

20.1　皮革之出口稅及訂約後之該項變更稅額，概由賣方負擔。

21.　不可抗力事故之通知

21.1　任何一方要求引用不可抗力條款時，須儘速通知對方。如有必要，應提具不可抗力事故發生之滿意證明。

22.　破產

22.1　在履約前，任何一方應依照破產法之規定，停止付款，並通知所有債務人業已無能付款、或已停止付款、抑準備停止應付債務，且將召集債權人會議，通過決議，交付清單，或要求延期償付、繼續營業，或認定業已違約、指定一人接收。

22.2　無論為破產或清算，被通知一方如認為對方業已違約，得結束該約，酌情逕行轉賣或再買。此項再賣或再買之價格，將視為清算價格。

22.3　如任何一方對此項再賣或再買價格不滿意，得交付仲裁。如無再賣或再買行為，該清算價格必須是上述情況發生之當天皮革市價。如無法協議，將由仲裁人決定市價。

23.　仲裁及上訴

23.1　本約任何糾紛，將儘可能私自商談解決，否則應依照貿易慣例及仲裁與上訴規定，在指定地交付仲裁。

23.2　糾紛交付仲裁而未裁定前，任何一方不得向法院採取訴訟行為，僅仲裁後之裁斷得交法院執行。

23.3　仲裁判決應付之款項，必須在十四天內立即照付，除非已提出上訴或經仲裁人或上訴法院延長其付款期限。

23.4　如原定仲裁地之國家尚無仲裁機構之設置，該糾紛得照本約第二十四條之規定辦理。

23.5　如任何一方對仲裁或上訴之裁斷加予輕視或拒絕履行，該代表上項裁判國家之賣方或買方的皮革業公會（如該國法律許可），將通知該公會之國際組織轉知各國皮革公會此項判決之執行失敗。該提報國之皮革輸出業公會及生皮皮革輸出業國際協會與國際製革協會得將此項消息公告或通知其會員國之公會週知。本約之雙方均同意如此做法。

24. 本約適用法律

24.1　為仲裁、上訴及其他法律程序與契約之構成效力，本約仲裁地及履約地所在國家之法律，即為本約之適用法律，縱使有關要約、承諾、付款之訴訟亦如此。

24.2　本約之任何一方，其現住地或營業處所不在仲裁地國家者，為法律程序之進行目的，其所屬國駐在該仲裁國或其鄰近國家之領事館，得視同其原居住地或營業處所。

24.3　如無其他法律規定，進行法律程序送達當事人之通知書，送由駐在該仲裁國或其鄰近國之各該當事人所屬國家之領事館轉交，並以副本一份掛號寄交當事人住址，應屬最佳服務。

25. 契約正文

25.1　本約以英文為確定之正文

賣方：（簽字）　　　　　　　　買方：（簽字）

簽約地點：　　　　　　　　　　地點：

日期：　　　　　　　　　　　　日期：

（註：附件 A.B.C. 請自行參閱，不再迻譯）

ICC Rules

EX WORKS

A. The seller must:

1 Supply the goods in conformity with the contract of sale, together with such evidence of conformity as may be required by the contract.

2 Place the goods at the disposal of the buyer at the time as provided in the contract, at the point of delivery named or which is usual for the delivery of such goods and for their loading on the conveyance to be provided by the buyer.

3 Provide at his own expense the packing, if any, that is necessary to enable the buyer to take delivery of the goods.

4 Give the buyer reasonable notice as to when the goods will be at his disposal.

5 Bear the cost of checking operations (such as checking quality, measuring, weighing, counting) which are necessary for the purpose of placing the goods at the disposal of the buyer.

6 Bear all risks and expense of the goods until they have been placed at the disposal of the buyer at the time as provided in the contract, provided that the goods have been duly appropriated to the contract, that is to say, clearly set aside or otherwise identified as the contract goods.

7 Render the buyer, at the latter's request, risk and expense, every assistance in obtaining any documents which are issued in the country of delivery and/or of origin and which the buyer may require for the purposes of exportation and/or importation (and, where necessary, for their passage in transit through another country).

B. The buyer must:

1 Take delivery of the goods as soon as they are placed at his disposal at the place and at the time, as provided in the contract, and pay the price as provided in the contract.

2 Bear all charges and risks of the goods from the time when they have been so placed at his disposal, provided that the goods have been duly appropriated to the contract, that is to say, clearly set aside or otherwise identified as the contract goods.

3 Bear any customs duties and taxes that may be levied by reason of exportation.

4 Where he shall have reserved to himself a period within which to take delivery of the goods and/or the right to choose the place of delivery, and should he fail to give instructions in time, bear the additional costs thereby incurred and all risks of the goods from the date of the expiration of the period fixed, provided that the goods shall have been duly appropriated to the contract, that is to say, clearly set aside or otherwise identified as the contract goods.

5 Pay all costs and charges incurred in obtaining the documents mentioned in article A.7, including the cost of certificates of origin, export licence and consular fees.

FREE CARRIER
...(NAMED POINT)

A. The seller must:

1 Supply the goods in conformity with the contract of sale, together with such evidence of conformity as may be required by the contract.

2 Deliver the goods into the charge of the carrier named by the buyer on the date or within the period agreed for delivery at the named point in the manner expressly agreed or customary at such point. If no specific point has been named, and if there are several points available, the seller may select the point at the place of delivery which best suits his purposes.

3 At his own risk and expense obtain any export licence or other official authorization necessary for the export of the goods.

4 Subject to the provisions of article B.5 below, pay any taxes, fees and charges levied in respect of the goods because of exportation.

5 Subject to the provisions of article B.5 below, bear all costs payable in respect of the goods until such time as they will have been delivered in accordance with the provisions of article A.2 above.

6 Subject to the provisions of article B.5 below, bear all risks of the goods until such time as they have been delivered in accordance with the provisions of article A.2 above.

7 Provide at his own expense the customary packing of the goods, unless it is the custom of the trade to dispatch the goods unpacked.

8 Pay the cost of any checking operations (such as checking quality, measuring, weighing, counting) which shall be necessary for the purpose of delivering the goods.

9 Give the buyer without delay notice by telecommunication channels of the delivery of the goods.

10 In the circumstances referred to in article B.5 below, give the buyer prompt notice by telecommunication channels of the occurrence of said circumstances.

11 At his own expense, provide the buyer, if customary, with the usual document or other evidence of the delivery of the goods in accordance with the provisions of article A.2 above.

12 Provide the buyer with the commercial invoice in proper form so as to facilitate compliance with applicable regulations and, at the buyer's request and expense, with the certificate of origin.

13 Render the buyer, at his request, risk and expense, every assistance in obtaining any document other than those mentioned in article A.12 above issued in the country of departure and/or of origin and which the buyer may require for the importation of the goods into the country of destination (and, where necessary, for their passage in transit through another country).

B. The buyer must:

1 At his own expense, contract for the carriage of the goods from the named point and give the seller due notice of the name of the carrier and of the time for delivering the goods to him.

2 Bear all costs payable in respect of the goods from the time when they have been delivered in accordance with the provisions of article A.2 above, except as provided in article A.4 above.

3 Pay the price as provided in the contract.

4 Bear all risks of the goods from the time when they have been delivered in accordance with the provisions of article A.2 above.

5 Bear any additional costs incurred because the buyer fails to name the carrier, or the carrier named by him fails to take the goods into his charge, at the time agreed, and bear all risks of the goods from the date of expiry of the period stipulated for delivery, provided, however, that the goods will have been duly appropriated to the contract, that is to say, clearly set aside or otherwise identified as the contract goods.

6 Bear all costs, fees and charges incurred in obtaining the documents mentioned in article 10 above, including the cost of consular documents, as well as the costs of certificates of origin.

FOR/FOT
FREE ON RAIL/FREE ON TRUCK

A. The seller must:

1 Supply the goods in conformity with the contract of sale, together with such evidence of conformity as may be required by the contract.

2 In the case of goods constituting either a wagon-load (carload, truckload) lot or a sufficient weight to obtain quantity rates for wagon loading, order in due time a wagon (car, truck) of suitable type and dimensions, equipped, where necessary, with tarpaulins, and load it at his own expense at the date or within the period fixed, the ordering of the wagon (car, truck) and the loading being carried out in accordance with the regulations of the dispatching station.

3 In the case of a load less than either a wagonload (carload, truckload) or a sufficient weight to obtain quantity rates for wagon loading, deliver the goods into the custody of the railway either at the dispatching station or, where such facilities are included in the rate of freight, into a vehicle provided by the railway, at the date or within the period fixed, unless the regulations of the dispatching station shall require the seller to load the goods on the wagon (car, truck).

Nevertheless, it shall be understood that if there are several stations at the point of departure, the seller may select the station which best suits his purpose, provided it customarily accepts goods for the destination nominated by the buyer, unless the buyer shall have reserved to himself the right to choose the dispatching station.

4 Subject to the provisions of article B.5 below, bear all costs and risks of the goods until such time as the wagon (car, truck) on which they are loaded shall have been delivered into the custody of the railway or, in the case provided for in article A.3, until such time as the goods shall have been delivered into the custody of the railway.

5 Provide at his own expense the customary packing of the goods, unless it is the custom of the trade to dispatch the goods unpacked.

6 Pay the costs of any checking operations (such as checking quality, measuring, weighing, counting) which shall be necessary for the purpose of loading the goods or of delivering them into the custody of the railway.

7 Give notice, without delay, to the buyer that the goods have been loaded or delivered into the custody of the railway.

8 At his own expense, provide the buyer, if customary, with the usual transport document.

9 Provide the buyer, at the latter's request and expense (see B.6), with the certificate of origin.

10 Render the buyer, at the latter's request, risk and expense, every assistance in obtaining the documents issued in the country of dispatch and/or of origin which the buyer may require for purposes of exportation and/or importation (and, where necessary, for their passage in transit through another country).

B. The buyer must:

1 Give the seller in time the necessary instructions for dispatch.

2 Take delivery of the goods from the time when they have been delivered into the custody of the railway and pay the price as provided in the contract.

3 Bear all costs and risks of the goods (including the cost, if any, of hiring tarpaulins) from the time when the wagon (car, truck) on which the goods are loaded shall have been delivered into the custody of the railway or, in the case provided for in article A.3, from the time when the goods shall have been delivered into the custody of the railway.

4 Bear any customs duties and taxes that may be levied by reason of exportation.

5 Where he shall have reserved to himself a period within which to give the seller instructions for dispatch and/or the right to choose the place of loading, and should he fail to give instructions in time, bear the additional costs thereby incurred and all risks of the goods from the time of expiration of the period fixed, provided, however, that the goods shall have been duly appropriated to the contract, that is to say, clearly set aside or otherwise identified as the contract goods.

6 Pay all costs and charges incurred in obtaining the documents mentioned in articles A.9 & 10 above, including the cost of certificates of origin and consular fees.

FOB AIRPORT

A. The seller must:

1 Supply the goods in conformity with the contract of sale, together with such evidence of conformity as may be required by the contract.

2 Deliver the goods into the charge of the air carrier or his agent or any other person named by the buyer, or, if no air carrier, agent or other person has been so named, of an air carrier or his agent chosen by the seller. Delivery shall be made on the date or within the period agreed for delivery, and at the named airport of departure in the manner customary at the airport or at such other place as may be designated by the buyer in the contract.

3 Contract at the buyer's expense for the carriage of the goods, unless the buyer or the seller gives prompt notice to the contrary to the other party. When contracting for the carriage as aforesaid, the seller shall do so, subject to the buyer's instructions as provided for under article B.1, on usual terms to the airport of destination named, to the nearest airport available for such carriage to the buyer's place of business, by a usual route in an aircraft of a type normally used for the transport of goods of the contract description.

4 At his own risk and expense obtain any export licence or other official authorization necessary for the export of the goods.

5 Subject to the provisions of articles B.6 and B.7 below, pay any taxes, fees and charges levied in respect of the goods because of exportation.

6 Subject to the provisions of articles B.6 and B.7 below, bear any further costs payable in respect of the goods until such time as they will have been delivered, in accordance with the povisions of article A.2 above.

7 Subject to the provisions of articles B.6 and B.7 below, bear all risks of the goods until such time as they will have been delivered, in accordance with the provisions of article A.2 above.

8 Provide at his own expense adequate protective packing suitable to dispatch of the goods by air unless it is the custom of the trade to dispatch the goods unpacked.

9 Pay the costs of any checking operations (such as checking quality, measuring, weighing, counting) which shall be necessary for the purpose of delivering the goods.

10 Give the buyer notice of the delivery of the goods without delay by telecommunication channels at his own expense.

11 In the circumstances referred to in articles B.6 and B.7 below, give the buyer prompt notice by telecommunication channels of the occurrence of said circumstances.

12 Provide the buyer with the commercial invoice in proper form so as to facilitate compliance with applicable regulations and, at the buyer's request and expense, with the certificate of origin.

13 Render the buyer, at his request, risk and expense, every assistance in obtaining any document other than those mentioned in article A.12 above issued in the country of departure and/or of origin and which the buyer may require for the importation of the goods into the country of destination (and, where necessary, for their passage in transit through another country).

14 Render the buyer, at his request, risk and expense and subject to the provisions of article B.9 below, every assistance in bringing any claim against the air carrier or his agent in respect of the carriage of the goods.

B. The buyer must:

1 Give the seller due notice of the airport of destination and give him proper instructions (where required) for the carriage of the goods by air from the named airport of departure.

2 If the seller will not contract for the carriage of the goods, arrange at his own expense for said carriage from the named airport of departure and give the seller due notice of said arrangements, stating the name of the air carrier or his agent or of any other person into whose charge delivery is to be made.

3 Bear all costs payable in respect of the goods from the time when they have been delivered in accordance with the provisions of article A.2 above, except as provided in article A.5 above.

4 Pay the price invoiced as provided in the contract as well as the cost of air freight if paid by or on behalf of the seller.

5 Bear all risks of the goods from the time when they have been delivered, in accordance with the provisions of article A.2 above.

6 Bear any additional costs incurred because the air carrier, his agent or any other person named by the buyer fails to take the goods into his charge when tendered by the seller, and bear all risks of the goods from the time of such tender, provided, however, that the goods will have been duly appropriated to the contract, that is to say, clearly set aside or otherwise identified as the contract goods.

7 Should he fail to provide proper instructions (where required) to the seller for the carriage of the goods, bear any additional costs incurred because of said failure and all risks of the goods from the date agreed for delivery or from the end of the period agreed for delivery, provided, however, that the goods will have been duly appropriated to the contract, that is to say, clearly set aside or otherwise identified as the contract goods.

8 Bear all costs, fees and charges incurred in obtaining the documents mentioned in article A.13 above, including the costs of consular documents, as well as the costs of certificates of origin.

9 Bear all costs, fees and charges incurred by the seller in bringing and pursuing any claim against the air carrier or his agent in respect of the carriage of the goods.

FAS
FREE ALONGSIDE SHIP

A. The seller must:

1 Supply the goods in conformity with the contract of sale, together with such evidence of conformity as may be required by the contract.

2 Deliver the goods alongside the vessel at the loading berth named by the buyer, at the named port of shipment, in the manner customary at the port, at the date or within the period stipulated, and notify the buyer, without delay, that the goods have been delivered alongside the vessel.

3 Render the buyer at the latter's request, risk and expense, every assistance in obtaining any export licence or other governmental authorization necessary for the export of the goods.

4 Subject to the provisions of articles B.3 and B.4 below, bear all costs and risks of the goods until such time as they shall have been effectively delivered alongside the vessel at the named port of shipment, Including the costs of any formalities which he shall have to fulfil in order to deliver the goods alongside the vessel.

5 Provide at his own expense the customary packing of the goods, unless it is the custom of the trade to ship the goods unpacked.

6 Pay the costs of any checking operations (such as checking quality, measuring, weighing, counting) which shall be necessary for the purpose of delivering the goods alongside the vessel.

7 Provide at his own expense the customary clean document in proof of delivery of the goods alongside the named vessel.

8 Provide the buyer, at the latter's request and expense (see B.5), with the certificate of origin.

9 Render the buyer, at the latter's request, risk and expense, every assistance in obtaining any documents other than that mentioned in article A.8, issued in the country of shipment and/or of origin (excluding a bill of lading and/or consular documents) and which the buyer may require for the importation of the goods into the country of destination (and, where necessary, for their passage in transit through another country).

B. The buyer must:

1 Give the seller due notice of the name, loading berth of and delivery dates to the vessel.

2 Bear all the charges and risks of the goods from the time when they shall have been effectively delivered alongside the vessel at the named port of shipment, at the date or within the period stipulated, and pay the price as provided in the contract.

3 Bear any additional costs incurred because the vessel named by him shall have failed to arrive on time, or shall be unable to take the goods, or shall close for cargo earlier than the stipulated date, and all the risks of the goods from the time when the seller shall place them at the buyer's disposal provided, however, that the goods shall have been duly appropriated to the contract, that is to say, clearly set aside or otherwise identified as the contract goods.

4 Should he fail to name the vessel in time or, if he shall have reserved to himself a period within which to take delivery of the goods and/or the right to choose the port of shipment, should he fail to give detailed instructions in time, bear any additional costs incurred because of such failure and all the risks of the goods from the date of expiration of the period stipulated for delivery, provided, however, that the goods shall have been duly appropriated to the contract, that is to say, clearly set aside or otherwise identified as the contract goods.

5 Pay all costs and charges incurred in obtaining the documents mentioned in articles A.3, A.8 and A.9 above.

FOB

A. The seller must:

1 Supply the goods in conformity with the contract of sale, together with such evidence of conformity as may be required by the contract.

2 Deliver the goods on board the vessel named by the buyer, at the named port of shipment, in the manner customary at the port, at the date or within the period stipulated, and notify the buyer, without delay, that the goods have been delivered on board.

3 At his own risk and expense obtain any export licence or other governmental authorisation necessary for the export of the goods.

4 Subject to the provisions of articles B.3 and B.4 below, bear all costs and risks of the goods until such time as they shall have effectively passed the ship's rail at the named port of shipment, including any taxes, fees or charges levied because of exportation, as well as the costs of any formalities which he shall have to fulfil in order to load the goods on board.

5 Provide at his own expense the customary packing of the goods, unless it is the custom of the trade to ship the goods unpacked.

6 Pay the costs of any checking operations (such as checking quality, measuring, weighing, counting) which shall be necessary for the purpose of delivering the goods.

7 Provide at his own expense the customary clean document in proof of delivery of the goods alongside the named vessel.

8 Provide the buyer, at the latter's request and expense (see B.6), with the certificate of origin.

9 Render the buyer, at the latter's request, risk and expense, every assistance in obtaining a bill of lading and any documents, other than that mentioned in the previous article, issued in the country of shipment and/or of origin and which the buyer may require for the importation of the goods into the country of destination (and, where necessary, for their passage in transit through another country).

B. The buyer must:

1 At his own expense, charter a vessel or reserve the necessary space on board a vessel and give the seller due notice of the name, loading berth of and delivery dates to the vessel.

2 Bear all costs and risks of the goods from the time when they shall have effectively passed the ship's rail at the named port of shipment, and pay the price as provided in the contract.

3 Bear any additional costs incurred because the vessel named by him shall have failed to arrive on the stipulated date or by the end of the period specified, or shall be unable to take the goods or shall close for cargo earlier than the stipulated date or the end of the period specified and all the risks of the goods from the date of expiration of the period stipulated, provided, however, that the goods shall have been duly appropriated to the contract, that is to say, clearly set aside or otherwise identified as the contract goods.

4 Should he fail to name the vessel in time or, if he shall have reserved to himself a period within which to take delivery of the goods and/or the right to choose the port of shipment, should he fail to give detailed instructions in time, bear any additional costs incurred because of such failure, and all the risks of the goods from the date of expiration of the period stipulated for delivery, provided, however, that the goods shall have been duly appropriated to the contract, that is to say, clearly set aside or otherwise identified as contract goods.

5 Pay any costs and charges for obtaining a bill of lading if incurred under article A.9 above.

6 Pay all costs and charges incurred in obtaining the documents mentioned in articles A.8 and A.9 above, including the costs of certificates of origin and consular documents.

C&F
COST AND FREIGHT

A. The seller must:

1 Supply the goods in conformity with the contract of sale, together with such evidence of conformity as may be required by the contract.

2 Contract on usual terms at his own expense for the carriage of the goods to the agreed port of destination by the usual route, in a seagoing vessel (not being a sailing vessel) of the type normally used for transport of goods of the contract description, and pay freight charges and any charges for unloading at the port of discharge which may be levied by regular shipping lines at the time and port of shipment.

3 At his own risk and expense obtain any export licence or other governmental authorization necessary for the export of the goods.

4 Load the goods at his own expense on board the vessel at the port of shipment and at the date or within the period fixed or, if neither date nor time has been stipulated, within a reasonable time, and notify the buyer, without delay, that the goods have been loaded on board the vessel.

5 Subject to the provisions of article B.4 below, bear all risks of the goods until such time as they shall have effectively passed the ship's rail at the port of shipment.

6 At his own expense furnish to the buyer without delay a clean negotiable bill of lading for the agreed port of destination, as well as the invoice of the goods shipped. The bill of lading must cover the contract goods, be dated within the period agreed for shipment, and provide by endorsement or otherwise for delivery to the order of the buyer or buyer's agreed representative. Such bill of lading must be a full set of "on board" or "shipped" bills of lading, or a "received for shipment" bill of lading duly endorsed by the shipping company to the effect that the goods are on board, such endorsement to be dated within the period agreed for shipment. If the bill of lading contains a reference to the charter-party, the seller must also provide a copy of this latter document.

Note: A clean bill of lading is one which bears no superimposed clauses expressly declaring a defective condition of the goods or packaging.
The following clauses do not convert a clean into an unclean bill of lading:

a) clauses which do not expressly state that the goods or packaging are unsatisfactory, e.g. "second-hand cases", "used drum", etc; b) clauses which emphasize carrier's non-liability for risks arising through the nature of the goods or the packaging; c) clauses which disclaim on the part of the carrier knowledge of contents, weight, measurement, quality, or technical specification of the goods.

7 Provide at his own expense the customary packaging of the goods, unless it is the custom of the trade to ship the goods unpacked.

8 Pay the costs of any checking operations (such as checking quality, measuring, weighing, counting) which shall be necessary for the purpose of loading the goods.

9 Pay any dues and taxes incurred in respect of the goods, up to the time of their loading, including any taxes, fees or charges levied because of exportation, as well as the costs of any formalities which he shall have to fulfil in order to load the goods on board.

10 Provide the buyer, at the latter's request and expense (see B.5), with the certificate of origin and the consular invoice.

11 Render the buyer, at the latter's request, risk and expense, every assistance in obtaining any documents, other than those mentioned in the previous article, issued in the country of shipment and/or of origin and which the buyer may require for the importation of the goods into the country of destination (and, where necessary, for their passage in transit through another country).

B. The buyer must:

1 Accept the documents when tendered by the seller, if they are in conformity with the contract of sale, and pay the price as provided in the contract.

2 Receive the goods at the agreed port of destination and bear, with the exception of the freight, all costs and charges incurred in respect of the goods in the course of their transit by sea until their arrival at the port of destination, as well as unloading costs, including lighterage and wharfage charges, unless such costs and charges shall have been included in the freight or collected by the steamship company at the time freight was paid.

Note: If the goods are sold "C & F landed", unloading costs, including lighterage and wharfage charges, are borne by the seller.

3 Bear all risks of the goods from the time when they shall have effectively passed the ship's rail at the port of shipment.

4 In case he may have reserved to himself a period within which to have the goods shipped and/or the right to choose the port of destination, and he fails to give instructions in time, bear the additional costs thereby incurred and all risks of the goods from the date of the expiration of the period fixed for shipment, provided always that the goods shall have been duly appropriated to the contract, that is to say, clearly set aside or otherwise identified as the contract goods.

5 Pay the costs and charges incurred in obtaining the certificate of origin and consular documents.

6 Pay all costs and charges incurred in obtaining the documents mentioned in article A.11 above.

7 Pay all customs duties as well as any other duties and taxes payable at the time of or by reason of the importation.

8 Procure and provide at his own risk and expense any import licence or permit or the like which he may require for the importation of the goods at destination.

CIF
COST, INSURANCE AND FREIGHT

A. The seller must:

1 Supply the goods in conformity with the contract of sale, together with such evidence of conformity as may be required by the contract.

2 Contract on usual terms at his own expense for the carriage of the goods to the agreed port of destination by the usual route, in a seagoing vessel (not being a sailing vessel) of the type normally used for the transport of goods of the contract description, and pay freight charges and any charges for unloading at the port of discharge which may be levied by regular shipping lines at the time and port of shipment.

3 At his own risk and expense obtain any export licence or other governmental authorization necessary for the export of the goods.

4 Load the goods at his own expense on board the vessel at the port of shipment and at the date or within the period fixed or, if neither date nor time has been stipulated, within a reasonable time, and notify the buyer, without delay, that the goods have been loaded on board the vessel.

5 Procure, at his own cost and in a transferable form, a policy of marine insurance against the risks of carriage involved in the contract. The insurance shall be contracted with underwriters or insurance companies of good repute on FPA terms, and shall cover the CIF price plus ten per cent. The insurance shall be provided in the currency of the contract, if procurable (1).

Unless otherwise agreed, the risks of carriage shall not include special risks that are covered in specific trades or against which the buyer may wish individual protection. Among the special risks that should be considered and agreed upon between seller and buyer are theft, pilferage, leakage, breakage, chipping, sweat, contact with other cargoes and others peculiar to any particular trade.

When required by the buyer, the seller shall provide, at the buyer's expense, war risk insurance in the currency of the contract, if procurable.

(1) CIF A.5 provides for the minimum terms (FPA) and period of insurance (warehouse to warehouse). Whenever the buyer wishes more than the minimum liability to be included in the contract, then he should take care to specify that the basis of the contract is to be "Incoterms" with whatever addition he requires.

6 Subject to the provisions of article B.4 below, bear all risks of the goods until such time as they shall have effectively passed the ship's rail at the port of shipment.

7 At his own expense furnish to the buyer without delay a clean negotiable bill of lading for the agreed port of destination, as well as the invoice of the goods shipped and the insurance policy or, should the insurance policy not be available at the time the documents are tendered, a certificate of insurance issued under the authority of the underwriters and conveying to the bearer the same rignts as if he were in possession of the policy and reproducing the essential provisions thereof. The bill of lading must cover the contract goods, be dated within the period agreed for shipment, and provide by endorsement or otherwise for delivery to the order of the buyer or buyer's agreed representative. Such bill of lading must be a full set of "on board" or "shipped" bills of lading, or a "received for shipment" bill of lading duly endorsed by the shipping company to the effect that the goods are on board, such endorsement to be dated within the period agreed for shipment. If the bill of lading contains a reference to the charter-party, the seller must also provide a copy of this latter document.

Note : A clean bill of lading is one which bears no superimposed clauses expressly declaring a defective condition of the goods or packaging.

The following clauses do not convert a clean into an unclean bill of lading :

a) clauses which do not expressly state that the goods or packaging are unsatisfactory, e.g. "second-hand cases", "used drums", etc. **b)** clauses which emphasize the carrier's non-liability for risks arising through the nature of the goods or the packaging; **c)** clauses which disclaim on the part of the carrier knowledge of contents, weight, measurement, quality, or technical specification of the goods.

8 Provide at his own expense the customary packing of the goods, unless it is the custom of the trade to ship the goods unpacked.

9 Pay the costs of any checking operations (such as checking quality, measuring, weighing, counting) which shall be necessary for the purpose of loading the goods.

10 Pay any dues and taxes incurred in respect of the goods up to the time of their loading, including any taxes, fees or charges levied because of exportation, as well as the costs of any formalities which he shall have to fulfil in order to load the goods on board.

11 Provide the buyer, at the latter's request and expense (see B.5), with the certificate of origin and the consular invoice.

12 Render the buyer, at the latter's request, risk and expense, every assistance in obtaining any documents, other than those mentioned in the previous article, issued in the country of shipment and/or of origin and which the buyer may require for the importation of the goods into the country of destination (and, where necessary, for their passage in transit through another country).

3 Bear all risks of the goods from the time when they shall have effectively passed the ship's rail at the port of shipment.

4 In case he may have reserved to himself a period within which to have the goods shipped and/or the right to choose the port of destination, and he fails to give instructions in time, bear the additional costs thereby incurred and all risks of the goods from the date of the expiration of the period fixed for shipment, provided always that the goods shall have been duly appropriated to the contract, that is to say, clearly set aside or otherwise identified as the contract goods.

5 Pay the costs and charges incurred in obtaining the certificate of origin and consular documents.

6 Pay all costs and charges incurred in obtaining the documents mentioned in article A.12 above.

7 Pay all customs duties as well as any other duties and taxes payable at the time of or by reason of the importation.

8 Procure and provide at his own risk and expense any import licence or permit or the like which he may require for the importation of the goods at destination.

B. The buyer must:

1 Accept the documents when tendered by the seller, if they are in conformity with the contract o sale, and pay the price as provided in the contract.

2 Receive the goods at the agreed port of destination and bear, with the exception of the freight and marine insurance, all costs and charges incurred in respec of the goods in the course of their transit by sea until thei arrival at the port of destination, as well as unloading costs, including lighterage and wharfage charges, unless such costs and charges shall have been included ii the freight or collected by the steamship company at th time freight was paid.

If war insurance is provided, it shall be at the expens of the buyer (see A.5).

Note: If the goods are sold "CIF landed", unloading cost including lighterage and wharfage charges, are borne by the seller

FREIGHT CARRIAGE } PAID TO

A. The seller must:

1 Supply the goods in conformity with the contract of sale, together with such evidence of conformity as may be required by the contract.

2 Contract at his own expense for the carriage of the goods by a usual route and in a customary manner to the agreed point at the place of destination. If the point is not agreed or is not determined by custom, the seller may select the point at the place of destination which best suits his purpose.

3 Subject to the provisions of article B.3 below, bear all risks of the goods until they shall have been delivered into the custody of the first carrier, at the time as provided in the contract.

4 Give the buyer without delay notice by telecommunication channels that the goods have been delivered into the custody of the first carrier.

5 Provide at his own expense the customary packing of the goods, unless it is the custom of the trade to dispatch the goods unpacked.

6 Pay the costs of any checking operations (such as checking quality, measuring, weighing, counting) which shall be necessary for the purpose of loading the goods or of delivering them into the custody of the first carrier.

7 At his own expense, provide the buyer, if customary, with the usual transport document.

8 At his own risk and expense obtain any export licence or other governmental authorization necessary for the export of the goods, and pay any dues and taxes incurred in respect of the goods in the country of dispatch, including any export duties, as well as the costs of any formalities he shall have to fulfil in order to load the goods.

9 Provide the buyer with the commercial invoice in proper form so as to facilitate compliance with applicable regulations and, at the buyer's request and expense, with the certificate of origin.

10 Render the buyer, at the latter's request, risk and expense, every assistance in obtaining any documents, other than those mentioned in the previous article, issued in the country of loading and/or of origin and which the buyer may require for the importation of the goods into the country of destination (and, where necessary, for their passage in transit through another country).

B. The buyer must:

1 Receive the goods at the agreed point at the place of destination and pay the price as provided in the contract, and bear, with the exception of the freight, all costs and charges incurred in respect of the goods in the course of their transit until their arrival at the point of destination, as well as unloading costs unless such costs and charges shall have been included in the freight or collected by the carrier at the time freight was paid.

2 Bear all risks of the goods from the time when they shall have been delivered into the custody of the first carrier in accordance with article A.3.

3 Where he shall have reserved to himself a period within which to have the goods forwarded to him and/or the right to choose the point of destination, and should he fail to give instructions in time, bear the additional costs thereby incurred and all risks of the goods from the date of expiry of the period fixed, provided always that the goods shall have been duly appropriated to the contract, that is to say, clearly set aside or otherwise identified as the contract goods.

4 Bear all costs and charges incurred in obtaining the documents mentioned in article A.10 above, including the cost of consular documents, as well as the costs of certificates of origin.

5 Pay all customs duties as well as any other duties and taxes payable at the time of or by reason of the importation.

2 Bear all risks of the goods from the time when they shall have been delivered into the custody of the first carrier in accordance with article A.3.

3 Where he shall have reserved to himself a period within which to have the goods forwarded to him and/or the right to choose the point of destination, and should he fail to give instructions in time, bear the additional costs thereby incurred and all risks of the goods from the date of expiry of the period fixed, provided always that the goods shall have been duly appropriated to the contract, that is to say, clearly set aside or otherwise identified as the contract goods.

4 Bear all costs, fees and charges incurred in obtaining the documents mentioned in article A.10 above, including the cost of consular documents, as well as the costs of certificates of origin.

5 Pay all customs duties as well as any other duties and taxes payable at the time of or by reason of the importation.

FREIGHT CARRIAGE | AND INSURANCE PAID TO

A. The seller must:

1 Supply the goods in conformity with the contract of sale, together with such evidence of conformity as may be required by the contract.

2 Contract at his own expense for the carriage of the goods by a usual route and in a customary manner to the agreed point at the place of destination. If the point is not agreed or is not determined by custom, the seller may select the point at the place of destination which best suits his purpose.

3 Subject to the provisions of article B.3 below, bear all risks of the goods until they shall have been delivered into the custody of the first carrier, at the time as provided in the contract.

4 Give the buyer without delay notice by telecommunication channels that the goods have been delivered into the custody of the first carrier.

5 Provide at his own expense the customary packing of the goods, unless it is the custom of the trade to dispatch the goods unpacked.

6 Pay the costs of any checking operations (such as checking quality, measuring, weighing, counting) which shall be necessary for the purpose of loading the goods or of delivering them into the custody of the first carrier.

7 At his own expense, provide the buyer, if customary, with the usual transport document.

8 At his own risk and expense obtain any export licence or other governmental authorization necessary for the export of the goods, and pay any dues and taxes incurred in respect of the goods in the country of dispatch, including any export duties, as well as the costs of any formalities he shall have to fulfil in order to load the goods.

9 Provide the buyer with the commercial invoice in proper form so as to facilitate compliance with applicable regulations and, at the buyer's request and expense, with the certificate of origin.

10 Render the buyer, at the latter's request, risk and expense, every assistance in obtaining any documents, other than those mentioned in the previous article, issued in the country of loading and/or of origin and which the buyer may require for the importation of the goods into the country of destination (and, where necessary, for their passage in transit through another country).

11 Procure, at his own cost, transport insurance as agreed in the contract and upon such terms that the buyer, or any other person having an insurable interest in the goods, shall be entitled to claim directly from the insurer, and provide the buyer with the insurance policy or other evidence of insurance cover. The insurance shall be contracted with parties of good repute and, failing express agreement, on such terms as are in the seller's view appropriate having regard to the custom of the trade, the nature of the goods and other circumstances affecting the risk. In this latter case, the seller shall inform the buyer of the extent of the insurance cover so as to enable him to take out any additional insurance that he may consider necessary before the risks of the goods are borne by him in accordance with article B.2.

The insurance shall cover the price provided in the contract plus ten per cent and shall be provided in the currency of the contract, if procurable. When required by the buyer, the seller shall provide, at the buyer's expense, war risk insurance in the currency of the contract, if procurable. (1).

(1) It should be observed that the insurance provision under A.11 of the present term differs from that under A.5 of the C.I.F. term.

B. The buyer must:

1 Receive the goods at the agreed point at the place of destination and pay the price as provided in the contract, and bear, with the exception of the freight and the cost of transport insurance, all costs and charges incurred in respect of the goods in the course of their transit until their arrival at the point of destination, as well as unloading costs, unless such costs and charges shall have been included in the freight or collected by the carrier at the time freight was paid.

EX SHIP

A. The seller must:

1 Supply the goods in conformity with the contract of sale, together with such evidence of conformity as may be required by the contract.

2 Place the goods effectively at the disposal of the buyer, at the time as provided in the contract, on board the vessel at the usual unloading point in the named port, in such a way as to enable them to be removed from the vessel by unloading equipment appropriate to the nature of the goods.

3 Bear all risks and expense of the goods until such time as they shall have been effectively placed at the disposal of the buyer in accordance with article A.2, provided, however, that they have been duly appropriated to the contract, that is to say, clearly set aside or otherwise identified as the contract goods.

4 Provide at his own expense the customary packing of the goods, unless it is the custom of the trade to ship the goods unpacked.

5 Pay the costs of any checking operations (such as checking quality, measuring, weighing, counting) which shall be necessary for the purpose of placing the goods at the disposal of the buyer in accordance with article A.2.

6 At his own expense, notify the buyer, without delay, of the expected date of arrival of the named vessel, and provide him in due time with the bill of lading or delivery order and/or any other documents which may be necessary to enable the buyer to take delivery of the goods.

7 Provide the buyer, at the latter's request and expense (see B.3), with the certificate of origin and the consular invoice.

8 Render the buyer, at the latter's request, risk and expense, every assistance in obtaining any documents, other than those mentioned in the previous articles, issued in the country of shipment and/or of origin and which the buyer may require for the importation of the goods into the country of destination (and where necessary, for their passage in transit through another country).

B. The buyer must:

1 Take delivery of the goods as soon as they have been placed at his disposal in accordance with the provisions of article A.2, and pay the price as provided in the contract.

2 Bear all risks and expense of the goods from the time when they shall have been effectively placed at his disposal in accordance with article A.2, provided always that they have been duly appropriated to the contract, that is to say, clearly set aside or otherwise identified as the contract goods.

3 Bear all expenses and charges incurred by the seller in obtaining any of the documents referred to in articles A.7 & 8.

4 At his own risk and expense, procure all licences or similar documents which may be required for the purpose of unloading and/or importing the goods.

5 Bear all expenses and charges of customs duties and clearance, and all other duties and taxes payable at the time or by reason of the unloading and/or importing of the goods.

EX QUAY

A. The seller must:

1 Supply the goods in conformity with the contract of sale, together with such evidence of conformity as may be required by the contract.

2 Place the goods at the disposal of the buyer on the wharf or quay at the agreed port and at the time, as provided in the contract.

3 At his own risk and expense, provide the import licence and bear the cost of any import duties or taxes, including the costs of customs clearance, as well as any other taxes, fees or charges payable at the time or by reason of importation of the goods and their delivery to the buyer.

4 At his own expense, provide for customary conditioning and packing of the goods, regard being had to their nature and to their delivery from the quay.

5 Pay the costs of any checking operations (such as checking quality, measuring, weighing, counting) which shall be necessary for the purpose of placing the goods at the disposal of the buyer in accordance with article A.2.

6 Bear all risks and expense of the goods until such time as they shall have been effectively placed at the disposal of the buyer in accordance with article A.2, provided, however, that they have been duly appropriated to the contract, that is to say, clearly set aside or otherwise identified as the contract goods.

7 At his own expense, provide the delivery order and/or any other documents which the buyer may require in order to take delivery of the goods and to remove them from the quay.

B. The buyer must:

1 Take delivery of the goods as soon as they have been placed at his disposal in accordance with article A.2, and pay the price as provided in the contract.

2 Bear all expense and risks of the goods from the time when they have been effectively placed at his disposal in accordance with article A.2, provided always that they have been duly appropriated to the contract, that is to say, clearly set aside or otherwise identified as the contract goods.

Ex Quay (duties on buyer's account).
There are two "Ex Quay" contracts in use, namely Ex Quay (duty paid) which has been defined above and Ex Quay (duties on buyer's account) in which the liabilities specified in A.3 above are to be met by the buyer instead of by the seller.
Parties are recommended always to use the full descriptions of these terms, namely Ex Quay (duty paid) or Ex Quay (duties on buyer's account), or else there may be uncertainty as to who is to be responsible for the liabilities in A.3. above.

DELIVERED AT FRONTIER

A. The seller must:

1 Supply the goods in conformity with the contract of sale, together with such evidence of conformity as may be stipulated in the contract of sale.

2 At his own risk and expense :

a) Put the contract goods at the disposal of the buyer at the named place of delivery at the frontier on the date or within the period stipulated in the contract of sale, and at the same time supply the buyer with a customary document of transport, warehouse warrant, dock warrant, delivery order, or the like, as the case may be, providing by endorsement or otherwise for the delivery of the goods to the buyer or to his order at the frontier, and also with an export licence and such other documents, if any, as may be strictly required at that time and place for the purpose of enabling the buyer to take delivery of the goods for their subsequent movement, as provided in articles B.1 and 2.

The goods so put at the disposal of the buyer must be clearly set aside or otherwise identified as the contract goods.

b) Comply with all formalities he may have to fulfil for these purposes, and pay any Customs fees and charges, internal taxes, excise duties, statistical taxes, and so on, levied in the country of dispatch or elsewhere, which he may have to incur in discharge of his duties up to the time when he puts the goods at the disposal of the buyer in accordance with article A.2 a).

3 Bear all the risks of the goods up to the time when he has fulfilled his obligations under article A.2a).

4 Procure, at his own risk and expense, in addition to the documents contemplated in article A.2 a), any exchange control authorization or other similar administrative document required for the purpose of clearing the goods for exportation at the named place of delivery at the frontier and any other documents he may require for the purpose of dispatching the goods to that place, passing them in transit through one or more third countries (if need be), and putting them at the disposal of the buyer in accordance with these Rules.

5 Contract on usual terms, at his own risk and expense, for the transport of the goods (including their passage in transit through one or more third countries, if necessary) to the named place of delivery at the frontier, bear and pay the freight or other costs of transport to that place and also, subject to the provisions of articles A.6 and 7, any other expenses of or incidental to any movement whatsoever of the goods up to the time when they are duly put at the disposal of the buyer at that place.

Nevertheless, the seller shall, subject to the provisions of articles A.6 and 7 at his own risk and expense, be at liberty to use his own means of transport, provided that in the exercise of such liberty he shall perform all his other duties under these Rules.

If no particular point (station, pier, quay, wharf, warehouse, or as the case may be) at the named place of delivery at the frontier is stipulated in the contract of sale or prescribed by the regulations of the Customs or other competent authority concerned, or by the regulations of the public carrier, the seller may, if there are several points to choose from, select the point which suits him best, provided it offers such Customs and other proper facilities as may be necessary to enable the parties to perform their respective duties under these Rules (1). The point so chosen by the seller must be notified to the buyer (2), and thereupon that point shall be deemed for the purposes of these Rules to be the point at the named place of delivery at which the goods shall be put at the disposal of the buyer and the risk of the goods shall pass.

6 Provide the buyer, at the buyer's request and risk, with a through document of transport normally procurable in the country of dispatch covering on usual terms the transport of the goods from the point of departure in that country to the point of final destination in the country of importation named by the buyer, provided that in so doing the seller shall not be deemed to assume any duty or to incur any risks or expenses other than those he would normally be called upon to incur, perform, bear and pay under these Rules.

7 If it is necessary or customary for the goods to be unloaded, discharged or landed on their arrival at the named place of delivery at the frontier, bear and pay the expenses of such operations (including lightering and handling charges).

If the seller elects to use his own means of transport for sending the goods to the named place of delivery then, in such case, he shall bear and pay all the expenses of or incidental to the necessary or customary operations contemplated in the last preceding paragraph.

8 Notify the buyer at seller's expense that the goods have been dispatched to the named place of delivery at the frontier. Such notice must be given in sufficient time to allow the buyer to take such measures as are normally necessary to enable him to take delivery of the goods (3).

(1) If at the named place of delivery at the frontier there are two customs-posts of different nationalities, it is recommended that the parties should either stipulate which one has been agreed upon, or leave the choice to the seller.
(2) See article A.8 footnote.
(3) Such notice may be served by the seller upon the buyer by sending it through the post by air mail and addressed to the buyer at his place of business given in the contract of sale. But if the goods have been dispatched by air, or if the distance between the point of departure of the country of dispatch and the named place of delivery at the frontier is short, or if the business addresses of the seller and the buyer are so far apart as to be likely to cause undue delay in the delivery of notice sent through the post then, in any such case, the seller shall be bound to give such notice to the buyer by sending the same by cable, telegram or telex.

9 Provide, at his own expense, packaging customary for the transport of goods of the contract description to the named place of delivery, unless it is the usage of the particular trade to dispatch goods of the contract description unpacked.

10 Bear and pay the expenses of or incidental to any checking operations, such as measuring, weighing, counting or analysing of quality, which may be necessary to enable him to transport the goods to the named place of delivery at the frontier and to put them at the disposal of the buyer at that place.

11 Bear and pay in addition to any expenses to be borne and paid by the seller in accordance with the preceding articles, any other expenses of or incidental to the performance of the seller's duty to put the goods at the disposal of the buyer at the named place of delivery at the frontier.

12 Render to the buyer, at buyer's request, risk and expense, a reasonable amount of assistance in obtaining any documents other than those already mentioned, which may be obtainable in the country of dispatch or of origin, or in both countries and which the buyer may require for the purposes contemplated in articles B.2 and 6.

B. The buyer must:

1 Take delivery of the goods as soon as the seller has duly put them at his disposal at the named place of delivery at the frontier, and be responsible for handling all subsequent movements of the goods.

2 Comply at his own expense with any Customs and other formalities that may have to be fulfilled at the named place of delivery at the frontier, or elsewhere, and pay any duties that may be payable at the time or by reason of the entry of the goods into the adjoining country or of any other movement of the goods subsequent to the time when they have been duly put at his disposal.

3 Bear and pay the expenses of or incidental to unloading, discharging or landing the goods on their arrival at the named place of delivery at the frontier, in so far as such expenses are not payable by the seller in accordance with the provisions of article A.7.

4 Bear all risks of the goods and pay any expenses whatsoever incurred in respect thereof including Customs duties, fees and charges from the time when they have been duly put at his disposal at the named place of delivery at the frontier.

5 If he fails to take delivery of the goods as soon as they have been duly put at his disposal, bear all the risks of the goods and pay any additional expenses incurred, whether by the seller or by the buyer, because of such failure, provided that the goods shall have been clearly set aside or otherwise identified as the contract goods.

6 Procure, at his own risk and expense, any import licence, exchange control authorization, permits or other documents issued in the country of importation, or elsewhere, that he may require in connection with any movement of the goods subsequent to the time when they have been duly put at his disposal at the named place of delivery at the frontier.

7 Bear and pay any additional expenses which the seller may have to incur for the purpose of obtaining a through document of transport in accordance with article A.6.

8 At seller's request and at buyer's expense, place such import licence, exchange control authorization, permits and other documents, or certified copies thereof, at the disposal of the seller for the limited purpose of obtaining the through document of transport contemplated in article A.6.

9 Supply the seller, at his request, with the address of the final destination of the goods in the country of importation, if the seller requires such information for the purpose of applying for such licences and other documents as are contemplated in articles A.4 and A.6.

10 Bear and pay the expenses incurred by the seller in providing the buyer with any expert third-party certificate of conformity of the goods stipulated in the contract of sale.

11 Bear and pay any expenses the seller may incur in or about his endeavours to assist the buyer in obtaining any of the documents contemplated in article A.12

DELIVERED DUTY PAID

A. The seller must:

1 Supply the goods in conformity with the contract of sale, together with such evidence of conformity as may be stipulated in the contract of sale.

2 At his own risk and expense :

a) Put the contract goods at the disposal of the buyer, duty paid, at the named place of destination in the country of importation on the date or within the period stipulated in the contract of sale, and at the same time supply the buyer with a customary document of transport, warehouse warrant, dock warrant, delivery order, or the like, as the case may be, providing by endorsement or otherwise for the delivery of the goods to the buyer or to his order at the named place of destination in the country of importation and also with such other documents, if any, as may be strictly required at that time and place for the purpose of enabling the buyer to take delivery of the goods, as provided in article B.1.

The goods so put at the disposal of the buyer must be clearly set aside or otherwise identified as the contract goods.

b) Provide the import licence or permit and bear the cost of any import duties or taxes, including the cost of Customs clearance, as well as any other taxes, fees or charges payable at the named place of destination at the time of the importation of the goods, so far as such payments are necessary for the purpose of enabling the seller to put the goods duty paid at the disposal of the buyer at that place.

c) Comply with all formalities he may have to fulfil for these purposes.

3 Bear all the risks of the goods up to the time when he has fulfilled his obligations under article A.2 a).

4 Procure at his own risk and expense, in addition to the documents contemplated in article A.2 a), any export licence or permit, exchange control authorization, certificates, consular invoice and other documents issued by the public authorities concerned, which he may require for the purposes of dispatching the goods, exporting them from the country of dispatch, passing them in transit through one or more third countries (if necessary), importing them into the country of the named place of destination, and putting them at the disposal of the buyer at the place.

5 Contract on usual terms, at his own risk and expense, for the transport of the goods from the point of departure in the country of dispatch to the named place of destination, bear and pay the freight or other costs of transport to that place, and also, subject to the provisions of article A.6, any other expenses of or incidental to any movement whatsoever of the goods up to the time when they are duly put at the disposal of the buyer at the named place of destination.

Nevertheless, the seller shall, at his own risk and expense, be at liberty to use his own means of transport, provided that in the exercise of such liberty he shall perform all his other duties under these Rules.

If no particular point (station, pier, quay, wharf, warehouse, or as the case may be) at the named place of destination in the country of importation is stipulated in the contract of sale or prescribed by the regulations of the Customs or other competent authority concerned, or by the regulations of the public carrier, the seller may, if there are several points to choose from, select the point which suits him best, provided it offers such Customs and other proper facilities as may be necessary to enable the parties to perform their respective duties under these Rules. The point so chosen by the seller must be notified to the buyer (1), and thereupon that point shall be deemed for the purposes of these Rules to be the point at the named place of destination at which the goods shall be put at the disposal of the buyer and the risks of the goods shall pass.

6 If it is necessary or customary for the goods to be unloaded, discharged or landed on their arrival at the named place of destination for the purpose of putting them duty paid at the disposal of the buyer at that place, bear and pay the expenses of such operations, including any lightering, wharfing, warehousing and handling charges.

7 Notify the buyer, at seller's expense, that the goods have been placed in the custody of the first carrier for dispatch to the named place of destination, or that they have been dispatched to that destination by the seller's own means of transport, as the case may be. Any such notice must be given in sufficient time to allow the buyer to take such measures as are normally necessary for the purpose of enabling him to take delivery of the goods (2).

8 Provide, at his own expense, packaging customary for transport of goods of the contract description to the named place of destination, unless it is the usage of the particular trade to dispatch goods of the contract description unpacked.

9 Bear and pay the expenses of or incidental to any checking operations, such as measuring, weighing, counting or analysing of quality, which may be necessary to enable him to transport the goods to the named place of destination and to put them at the disposal of the buyer at that place.

(1) See article A.7 footnote.
(2) Such notice may be served by the seller upon the buyer by sending it through the post by air mail, and addressed to the buyer at his place of business given in the contract of sale. But if the goods have been dispatched by air, or if the business addresses of the seller and the buyer are so far apart as to be likely to cause undue delay in the delivery of notice sent through the post then, in any such case, the seller shall be bound to give such notice to the buyer by sending the same by cable, telegram or telex.

10 Bear and pay, in addition to any expenses to be borne and paid by the seller in accordance with articles A.1 to 9 inclusive, any other expenses of or incidental to the performance of the seller's duty to put the goods at the disposal of the buyer at the named place of destination in accordance with these Rules.

B. The buyer must:

1 Take delivery of the goods as soon as the seller has duly put them at his disposal at the named place of destination, and be responsible for handling all subsequent movement of the goods.

2 Bear and pay the expenses of or incidental to unloading, discharging or landing the goods on their arrival at the named place of destination, in so far as such expenses are not payable by the seller in accordance with the provisions of article A.6.

3 Bear all the risks of the goods and pay any expenses whatsoever incurred in respect thereof from the time when they have been put at his disposal at the named place of destination in accordance with article A.2 a).

4 If he fails to take delivery of the goods as soon as they have been duly put at his disposal, bear all the risks of the goods and pay any additional expenses incurred, whether by the seller or by the buyer, because of such failure, provided that the goods shall have been clearly set aside or otherwise identified as the contract goods.

5 Supply the seller, at his request, with the address of the final destination of the goods in the country of importation, if the seller requires such information for the purpose of applying for such documents as are contemplated in article A.2 b).

6 Bear and pay the expenses incurred by the seller in providing the buyer with any expert third-party certificate of conformity of the goods stipulated in the contract of sale.

7 Render to the seller, at seller's request, risk and expense, a reasonable amount of assistance in obtaining any documents which may be issued in the country of importation and which the seller may require for the purpose of putting the goods at the disposal of the buyer in accordance with these Rules.

UNITED NATIONS CONVENTION ON CONTRACTS FOR THE
INTERNATIONAL SALE OF GOODS

THE STATES PARTIES TO THIS CONVENTION,

BEARING IN MIND the broad objectives in the resolutions adopted by the sixth special
session of the General Assembly of the United Nations on the establishment of a New
International Economic Order,

CONSIDERING that the development of international trade on the basis of equality and
mutual benefit is an important element in promoting friendly relations among States,

BEING OF THE OPINION that the adoption of uniform rules which govern contracts for the
international sale of goods and take into account the different social, economic and legal
systems would contribute to the removal of legal barriers in international trade and promote
the development of international trade,

HAVE AGREED as follows:

PART I

SPHERE OF APPLICATION AND GENERAL PROVISIONS

Chapter I

SPHERE OF APPLICATION

Article 1

(1) This Convention applies to contracts of sale of goods between parties whose places
of business are in different States:

(a) when the States are Contracting States; or

(b) when the rules of private international law lead to the application of the law of a
Contracting State.

(2) The fact that the parties have their places of business in different States is to be
disregarded whenever this fact does not appear either from the contract or from any dealings
between, or from information disclosed by, the parties at any time before or at the conclusion
of the contract.

(3) Neither the nationality of the parties nor the civil or commercial character of the parties or of the contract is to be taken into consideration in determining the application of this Convention.

Article 2

This Convention does not apply to sales:

(a) of goods bought for personal, family or household use, unless the seller, at any time before or at the conclusion of the contract, neither knew nor ought to have known that the goods were bought for any such use;

(b) by auction;

(c) on execution or otherwise by authority of law;

(d) of stocks, shares, investment securities, negotiable instruments or money;

(e) of ships, vessels, hovercraft or aircraft;

(f) of electricity.

Article 3

(1) Contracts for the supply of goods to be manufactured or produced are to be considered sales unless the party who orders the goods undertakes to supply a substantial part of the materials necessary for such manufacture or production.

(2) This Convention does not apply to contracts in which the preponderant part of the obligations of the party who furnishes the goods consists in the supply of labour or other services.

Article 4

This Convention governs only the formation of the contract of sale and the rights and obligations of the seller and the buyer arising from such a contract. In particular, except as otherwise expressly provided in this Convention, it is not concerned with:

(a) the validity of the contract or of any of its provisions or of any usage;

(b) the effect which the contract may have on the property in the goods sold.

2

Article 5

This Convention does not apply to the liability of the seller for death or personal injury caused by the goods to any person.

Article 6

The parties may exclude the application of this Convention or, subject to article 12, derogate from or vary the effect of any of its provisions.

Chapter II

GENERAL PROVISIONS

Article 7

(1) In the interpretation of this Convention, regard is to be had to its international character and to the need to promote uniformity in its application and the observance of good faith in international trade.

(2) Questions concerning matters governed by this Convention which are not expressly settled in it are to be settled in conformity with the general principles on which it is based or, in the absence of such principles, in conformity with the law applicable by virtue of the rules of private international law.

Article 8

(1) For the purposes of this Convention statements made by and other conduct of a party are to be interpreted according to his intent where the other party knew or could not have been unaware what that intent was.

(2) If the preceding paragraph is not applicable, statements made by and other conduct of a party are to be interpreted according to the understanding that a reasonable person of the same kind as the other party would have had in the same circumstances.

(3) In determining the intent of a party or the understanding a reasonable person would have had, due consideration is to be given to all relevant circumstances of the case including the negotiations, any practices which the parties have established between themselves, usages and any subsequent conduct of the parties.

3

Article 9

(1) The parties are bound by any usage to which they have agreed and by any practices which they have established between themselves.

(2) The parties are considered, unless otherwise agreed, to have impliedly made applicable to their contract or its formation a usage of which the parties knew or ought to have known and which in international trade is widely known to, and regularly observed by, parties to contracts of the type involved in the particular trade concerned.

Article 10

For the purposes of this Convention:

(a) if a party has more than one place of business, the place of business is that which has the closest relationship to the contract and its performance, having regard to the circumstances known to or contemplated by the parties at any time before or at the conclusion of the contract;

(b) if a party does not have a place of business, reference is to be made to his habitual residence.

Article 11

A contract of sale need not be concluded in or evidenced by writing and is not subject to any other requirement as to form. It may be proved by any means, including witnesses.

Article 12

Any provision of article 11, article 29 or Part II of this Convention that allows a contract of sale or its modification or termination by agreement or any offer, acceptance or other indication of intention to be made in any form other than in writing does not apply where any party has his place of business in a Contracting State which has made a declaration under article 96 of this Convention. The parties may not derogate from or vary the effect of this article.

Article 13

For the purposes of this Convention "writing" includes telegram and telex.

4

PART II

FORMATION OF THE CONTRACT

Article 14

(1) A proposal for concluding a contract addressed to one or more specific persons constitutes an offer if it is sufficiently definite and indicates the intention of the offeror to be bound in case of acceptance. A proposal is sufficiently definite if it indicates the goods and expressly or implicitly fixes or makes provision for determining the quantity and the price.

(2) A proposal other .than one addressed to one or more specific persons is to be considered merely as an invitation to make offers, unless the contrary is clearly indicated by the person making the proposal.

Article 15

(1) An offer becomes effective when it reaches the offeree.

(2) An offer, even if it is irrevocable, may be withdrawn if the withdrawal reaches the offeree before or at the same time as the offer.

Article 16

(1) Until a contract is concluded an offer may be revoked if the revocation reaches the offeree before he has dispatched an acceptance.

(2) However, an offer cannot be revoked:

(a) if it indicates, whether by stating a fixed time for acceptance or otherwise, that it is irrevocable; or

(b) if it was reasonable for the offeree to rely on the offer as being irrevocable and the offeree has acted in reliance on the offer.

5

Article 17

An offer, even if it is irrevocable, is terminated when a rejection reaches the offeror.

Article 18

(1) A statement made by or other conduct of the offeree indicating assent to an offer is an acceptance. Silence or inactivity does not in itself amount to acceptance.

(2) An acceptance of an offer becomes effective at the moment the indication of assent reaches the offeror. An acceptance is not effective if the indication of assent does not reach the offeror within the time he has fixed or, if no time is fixed, within a reasonable time, due account being taken of the circumstances of the transaction, including the rapidity of the means of communication employed by the offeror. An oral offer must be accepted immediately unless the circumstances indicate otherwise.

(3) However, if, by virtue of the offer or as a result of practices which the parties have established between themselves or of usage, the offeree may indicate assent by performing an act, such as one relating to the dispatch of the goods or payment of the price, without notice to the offeror, the acceptance is effective at the moment the act is performed, provided that the act is performed within the period of time laid down in the preceding paragraph.

Article 19

(1) A reply to an offer which purports to be an acceptance but contains additions, limitations or other modifications is a rejection of the offer and constitutes a counter-offer.

(2) However, a reply to an offer which purports to be an acceptance but contains additional or different terms which do not materially alter the terms of the offer constitutes an acceptance, unless the offeror, without undue delay, objects orally to the discrepancy or dispatches a notice to that effect. If he does not so object, the terms of the contract are the terms of the offer with the modifications contained in the acceptance.

(3) Additional or different terms relating, among other things, to the price, payment, quality and quantity of the goods, place and time of delivery, extent of one party's liability to the other or the settlement of disputes are considered to alter the terms of the offer materially.

Article 20

(1) A period of time for acceptance fixed by the offeror in a telegram or a letter begins to run from the moment the telegram is handed in for dispatch or from the date shown on the letter or, if no such date is shown, from the date shown on the envelope. A period of time for acceptance fixed by the offeror by telephone, telex or other means of instantaneous communication, begins to run from the moment that the offer reaches the offeree.

(2) Official holidays or non-business days occurring during the period for acceptance are included in calculating the period. However, if a notice of acceptance cannot be delivered at the address of the offeror on the last day of the period because that day falls on an official holiday or a non-business day at the place of business of the offeror, the period is extended until the first business day which follows.

Article 21

(1) A late acceptance is nevertheless effective as an acceptance if without delay the offeror orally so informs the offeree or dispatches a notice to that effect.

(2) If a letter or other writing containing a late acceptance shows that it has been sent in such circumstances that if its transmission had been normal it would have reached the offeror in due time, the late acceptance is effective as an acceptance unless, without delay, the offeror orally informs the offeree that he considers his offer as having lapsed or dispatches a notice to that effect.

Article 22

An acceptance may be withdrawn if the withdrawal reaches the offeror before or at the same time as the acceptance would have become effective.

Article 23

A contract is concluded at the moment when an acceptance of an offer becomes effective in accordance with the provisions of this Convention.

Article 24

For the purposes of this Part of the Convention, an offer, declaration of acceptance or any other indication of intention "reaches" the addressee when it is made orally to him or delivered by any other means to him personally, to his place of business or mailing address or, if he does not have a place of business or mailing address, to his habitual residence.

PART III

SALE OF GOODS

Chapter I

GENERAL PROVISIONS

Article 25

A breach of contract committed by one of the parties is fundamental if it results in such detriment to the other party as substantially to deprive him of what he is entitled to expect under the contract, unless the party in breach did not foresee and a reasonable person of the same kind in the same circumstances would not have foreseen such a result.

Article 26

A declaration of avoidance of the contract is effective only if made by notice to the other party.

Article 27

Unless otherwise expressly provided in this Part of the Convention, if any notice, request or other communication is given or made by a party in accordance with this Part and by means appropriate in the circumstances, a delay or error in the transmission of the communication or its failure to arrive does not deprive that party of the right to rely on the communication.

Article 28

If, in accordance with the provisions of this Convention, one party is entitled to require performance of any obligation by the other party, a court is not bound to enter a judgement for specific performance unless the court would do so under its own law in respect of similar contracts of sale not governed by this Convention.

Article 29

(1) A contract may be modified or terminated by the mere agreement of the parties.

(2) A contract in writing which contains a provision requiring any modification or termination by agreement to be in writing may not be otherwise modified or terminated by agreement. However, a party may be precluded by his conduct from asserting such a provision to the extent that the other party has relied on that conduct.

Chapter II

OBLIGATIONS OF THE SELLER

Article 30

The seller must deliver the goods, hand over any documents relating to them and transfer the property in the goods, as required by the contract and this Convention.

Section I. Delivery of the goods and handing over of documents

Article 31

If the seller is not bound to deliver the goods at any other particular place, his obligation to deliver consists:

(a) if the contract of sale involves carriage of the goods - in handing the goods over to the first carrier for transmission to the buyer;

(b) if, in cases not within the preceding subparagraph, the contract relates to specific goods, or unidentified goods to be drawn from a specific stock or to be manufactured or produced, and at the time of the conclusion of the contract the parties knew that the goods were at, or were to be manufactured or produced at, a particular place - in placing the goods at the buyer's disposal at that place;

9

(c) in other cases - in placing the goods at the buyer's disposal at the place where the seller had his place of business at the time of the conclusion of the contract.

Article 32

(1) If the seller, in accordance with the contract or this Convention, hands the goods over to a carrier and if the goods are not clearly identified to the contract by markings on the goods, by shipping documents or otherwise, the seller must give the buyer notice of the consignment specifying.the goods.

(2) If the seller is bound to arrange for carriage of the goods, he must make such contracts as are necessary for carriage to the place fixed by means of transportation appropriate in the circumstances and according to the usual terms for such transportation.

(3) If the seller is not bound to effect insurance in respect of the carriage of the goods, he must, at the buyer's request, provide him with all available information necessary to enable him to effect such insurance.

Article 33

The seller must deliver the goods:

(a) if a date is fixed by or determinable from the contract, on that date;

(b) if a period of time is fixed by or determinable from the contract, at any time within that period unless circumstances indicate that the buyer is to choose a date; or

(c) in any other case, within a reasonable time after the conclusion of the contract.

Article 34

If the seller is bound to hand over documents relating to the goods, he must hand them over at the time and place and in the form required by the contract. If the seller has handed over documents before that time, he may, up to that time, cure any lack of conformity in the documents, if the exercise of this right does not cause the buyer unreasonable inconvenience or unreasonable expense. However, the buyer retains any right to claim damages as provided for in this Convention.

10

Section II. Conformity of the goods and third party claims

Article 35

(1) The seller must deliver goods which are of the quantity, quality and description required by the contract and which are contained or packaged in the manner required by the contract.

(2) Except where the parties have agreed otherwise, the goods do not conform with the contract unless they:

(a) are fit for the purposes for which goods of the same description would ordinarily be used;

(b) are fit for any particular purpose expressly or impliedly made known to the seller at the time of the conclusion of the contract, except where the circumstances show that the buyer did not rely, or that it was unreasonable for him to rely, on the seller's skill and judgement;

(c) possess the qualities of goods which the seller has held out to the buyer as a sample or model;

(d) are contained or packaged in the manner usual for such goods or, where there is no such manner, in a manner adequate to preserve and protect the goods.

(3) The seller is not liable under subparagraphs (a) to (d) of the preceding paragraph for any lack of conformity of the goods if at the time of the conclusion of the contract the buyer knew or could not have been unaware of such lack of conformity.

Article 36

(1) The seller is liable in accordance with the contract and this Convention for any lack of conformity which exists at the time when the risk passes to the buyer, even though the lack of conformity becomes apparent only after that time.

(2) The seller is also liable for any lack of conformity which occurs after the time indicated in the preceding paragraph and which is due to a breach of any of his obligations, including a breach of any guarantee that for a period of time the goods will remain fit for their ordinary purpose or for some particular purpose or will retain specified qualities or characteristics.

Article 37

If the seller has delivered goods before the date for delivery, he may, up to that date, deliver any missing part or make up any deficiency in the quantity of the goods delivered, or deliver goods in replacement of any non-conforming goods delivered or remedy any lack of conformity in the goods delivered, provided that the exercise of this right does not cause the buyer unreasonable inconvenience or unreasonable expense. However, the buyer retains any right to claim damages as provided for in this Convention.

Article 38

(1) The buyer must examine the goods, or cause them to be examined, within as short a period as is practicable in the circumstances.

(2) If the contract involves carriage of the goods, examination may be deferred until after the goods have arrived at their destination.

(3) If the goods are redirected in transit or redispatched by the buyer without a reasonable opportunity for examination by him and at the time of the conclusion of the contract the seller knew or ought to have known of the possibility of such redirection or redispatch, examination may be deferred until after the goods have arrived at the new destination.

Article 39

(1) The buyer loses the right to rely on a lack of conformity of the goods if he does not give notice to the seller specifying the nature of the lack of conformity within a reasonable time after he has discovered it or ought to have discovered it.

(2) In any event, the buyer loses the right to rely on a lack of conformity of the goods if he does not give the seller notice thereof at the latest within a period of two years from the date on which the goods were actually handed over to the buyer, unless this time-limit is inconsistent with a contractual period of guarantee.

Article 40

The seller is not entitled to rely on the provisions of articles 38 and 39 if the lack of conformity relates to facts of which he knew or could not have been unaware and which he did not disclose to the buyer.

12

Article 41

The seller must deliver goods which are free from any right or claim of a third party, unless the buyer agreed to take the goods subject to that right or claim. However, if such right or claim is based on industrial property or other intellectual property, the seller's obligation is governed by article 42.

Article 42

(1) The seller must deliver goods which are free from any right or claim of a third party based on industrial property or other intellectual property, of which at the time of the conclusion of the contract the seller knew or could not have been unaware, provided that the right or claim is based on industrial property or other intellectual property:

(a) under the law of the State where the goods will be resold or otherwise used, if it was contemplated by the parties at the time of the conclusion of the contract that the goods would be resold or otherwise used in that State; or

(b) in any other case, under the law of the State where the buyer has his place of business.

(2) The obligation of the seller under the preceding paragraph does not extend to cases where:

(a) at the time of the conclusion of the contract the buyer knew or could not have been unaware of the right or claim; or

(b) the right or claim results from the seller's compliance with technical drawings, designs, formulae or other such specifications furnished by the buyer.

Article 43

(1) The buyer loses the right to rely on the provisions of article 41 or article 42 if he does not give notice to the seller specifying the nature of the right or claim of the third party within a reasonable time after he has become aware or ought to have become aware of the right or claim.

(2) The seller is not entitled to rely on the provisions of the preceding paragraph if he knew of the right or claim of the third party and the nature of it.

13

Article 44

Notwithstanding the provisions of paragraph (1) of article 39 and paragraph (1) of article 43, the buyer may reduce the price in accordance with article 50 or claim damages, except for loss of profit, if he has a reasonable excuse for his failure to give the required notice.

Section III. Remedies for breach of contract by the seller

Article 45

(1) If the seller fails to perform any of his obligations under the contract or this Convention, the buyer may:

(a) exercise the rights provided in articles 46 to 52;

(b) claim damages as provided in articles 74 to 77.

(2) The buyer is not deprived of any right he may have to claim damages by exercising his right to other remedies.

(3) No period of grace may be granted to the seller by a court or arbitral tribunal when the buyer resorts to a remedy for breach of contract.

Article 46

(1) The buyer may require performance by the seller of his obligations unless the buyer has resorted to a remedy which is inconsistent with this requirement.

(2) If the goods do not conform with the contract, the buyer may require delivery of substitute goods only if the lack of conformity constitutes a fundamental breach of contract and a request for substitute goods is made either in conjunction with notice given under article 39 or within a reasonable time thereafter.

(3) If the goods do not conform with the contract, the buyer may require the seller to remedy the lack of conformity by repair, unless this is unreasonable having regard to all the circumstances. A request for repair must be made either in conjunction with notice given under article 39 or within a reasonable time thereafter.

Article 47

(1) The buyer may fix an additional period of time of reasonable length for performance by the seller of his obligations.

(2) Unless the buyer has received notice from the seller that he will not perform within the period so fixed, the buyer may not, during that period, resort to any remedy for breach of contract. However, the buyer is not deprived thereby of any right he may have to claim damages for delay in performance.

Article 48

(1) Subject to article 49, the seller may, even after the date for delivery, remedy at his own expense any failure to perform his obligations, if he can do so without unreasonable delay and without causing the buyer unreasonable inconvenience or uncertainty of reimbursement by the seller of expenses advanced by the buyer. However, the buyer retains any right to claim damages as provided for in this Convention.

(2) If the seller requests the buyer to make known whether he will accept performance and the buyer does not comply with the request within a reasonable time, the seller may perform within the time indicated in his request. The buyer may not, during that period of time, resort to any remedy which is inconsistent with performance by the seller.

(3) A notice by the seller that he will perform within a specified period of time is assumed to include a request, under the preceding paragraph, that the buyer make known his decision.

(4) A request or notice by the seller under paragraph (2) or (3) of this article is not effective unless received by the buyer.

Article 49

(1) The buyer may declare the contract avoided:

(a) if the failure by the seller to perform any of his obligations under the contract or this Convention amounts to a fundamental breach of contract; or

(b) in case of non-delivery, if the seller does not deliver the goods within the additional period of time fixed by the buyer in accordance with paragraph (1) of article 47 or declares that he will not deliver within the period so fixed.

(2) However, in cases where the seller has delivered the goods, the buyer loses the right to declare the contract avoided unless he does so:

(a) in respect of late delivery, within a reasonable time after he has become aware that delivery has been made;

(b) in respect of any breach other than late delivery, within a reasonable time:

(i) after he knew or ought to have known of the breach;

(ii) after the expiration of any additional period of time fixed by the buyer in accordance with paragraph (1) of article 47, or after the seller has declared that he will not perform his obligations within such an additional period; or

(iii) after the expiration of any additional period of time indicated by the seller in accordance with paragraph (2) of article 48, or after the buyer has declared that he will not accept performance.

Article 50

If the goods do not conform with the contract and whether or not the price has already been paid, the buyer may reduce the price in the same proportion as the value that the goods actually delivered had at the time of the delivery bears to the value that conforming goods would have had at that time. However, if the seller remedies any failure to perform his obligations in accordance with article 37 or article 48 or if the buyer refuses to accept performance by the seller in accordance with those articles, the buyer may not reduce the price.

Article 51

(1) If the seller delivers only a part of the goods or if only a part of the goods delivered is in conformity with the contract, articles 46 to 50 apply in respect of the part which is missing or which does not conform.

(2) The buyer may declare the contract avoided in its entirety only if the failure to make delivery completely or in conformity with the contract amounts to a fundamental breach of the contract.

16

Article 52

(1) If the seller delivers the goods before the date fixed, the buyer may take delivery or refuse to take delivery.

(2) If the seller delivers a quantity of goods greater than that provided for in the contract, the buyer may take delivery or refuse to take delivery of the excess quantity. If the buyer takes delivery of all or part of the excess quantity, he must pay for it at the contract rate.

Chapter III

OBLIGATIONS OF THE BUYER

Article 53

The buyer must pay the price for the goods and take delivery of them as required by the contract and this Convention.

Section I. Payment of the price

Article 54

The buyer's obligation to pay the price includes taking such steps and complying with such formalities as may be required under the contract or any laws and regulations to enable payment to be made.

Article 55

Where a contract has been validly concluded but does not expressly or implicitly fix or make provision for determining the price, the parties are considered, in the absence of any indication to the contrary, to have impliedly made reference to the price generally charged at the time of the conclusion of the contract for such goods sold under comparable circumstances in the trade concerned.

Article 56

If the price is fixed according to the weight of the goods, in case of doubt it is to be determined by the net weight.

Article 57

(1) If the buyer is not bound to pay the price at any other particular place, he must pay it to the seller:

(a)　at the seller's place of business;　or

(b)　if the payment is to be made against the handing over of the goods or of documents, at the place where the handing over takes place.

(2) The seller must bear any increase in the expenses incidental to payment which is caused by a change in his place of business subsequent to the conclusion of the contract.

Article 58

(1) If the buyer is not bound to pay the price at any other specific time, he must pay it when the seller places either the goods or documents controlling their disposition at the buyer's disposal in accordance with the contract and this Convention. The seller may make such payment a condition for handing over the goods or documents.

(2) If the contract involves carriage of the goods, the seller may dispatch the goods on terms whereby the goods, or documents controlling their disposition, will not be handed over to the buyer except against payment of the price.

(3) The buyer is not bound to pay the price until he has had an opportunity to examine the goods, unless the procedures for delivery or payment agreed upon by the parties are inconsistent with his having such an opportunity.

Article 59

The buyer must pay the price on the date fixed by or determinable from the contract and this Convention without the need for any request or compliance with any formality on the part of the seller.

Section II. Taking delivery

Article 60

The buyer's obligation to take delivery consists:

(a) in doing all the acts which could reasonably be expected of him in order to enable the seller to make delivery; and

(b) in taking over the goods.

Section III. Remedies for breach of contract by the buyer

Article 61

(1) If the buyer fails to perform any of his obligations under the contract or this Convention, the seller may:

(a) exercise the rights provided in articles 62 to 65;

(b) claim damages as provided in articles 74 to 77.

(2) The seller is not deprived of any right he may have to claim damages by exercising his right to other remedies.

(3) No period of grace may be granted to the buyer by a court or arbitral tribunal when the seller resorts to a remedy for breach of contract.

Article 62

The seller may require the buyer to pay the price, take delivery or perform his other obligations, unless the seller has resorted to a remedy which is inconsistent with this requirement.

Article 63

(1) The seller may fix an additional period of time of reasonable length for performance by the buyer of his obligations.

(2) Unless the seller has received notice from the buyer that he will not perform within the period so fixed, the seller may not, during that period, resort to any remedy for breach of contract. However, the seller is not deprived thereby of any right he may have to claim damages for delay in performance.

19

Article 64

(1) The seller may declare the contract avoided:

(a) if the failure by the buyer to perform any of his obligations under the contract or this Convention amounts to a fundamental breach of contract; or

(b) if the buyer does not, within the additional period of time fixed by the seller in accordance with paragraph (1) of article 63, perform his obligation to pay the price or take delivery of the goods, or if he declares that he will not do so within the period so fixed.

(2) However, in cases where the buyer has paid the price, the seller loses the right to declare the contract avoided unless he does so:

(a) in respect of late performance by the buyer, before the seller has become aware that performance has been rendered; or

(b) in respect of any breach other than late performance by the buyer, within a reasonable time:

   (i) after the seller knew or ought to have known of the breach; or

   (ii) after the expiration of any additional period of time fixed by the seller in accordance with paragraph (1) of article 63, or after the buyer has declared that he will not perform his obligations within such an additional period.

Article 65

(1) If under the contract the buyer is to specify the form, measurement or other features of the goods and he fails to make such specification either on the date agreed upon or within a reasonable time after receipt of a request from the seller, the seller may, without prejudice to any other rights he may have, make the specification himself in accordance with the requirements of the buyer that may be known to him.

(2) If the seller makes the specification himself, he must inform the buyer of the details thereof and must fix a reasonable time within which the buyer may make a different specification. If, after receipt of such a communication, the buyer fails to do so within the time so fixed, the specification made by the seller is binding.

20

Chapter IV

PASSING OF RISK

Article 66

Loss of or damage to the goods after the risk has passed to the buyer does not discharge him from his obligation to pay the price, unless the loss or damage is due to an act or omission of the seller.

Article 67

(1) If the contract of sale involves carriage of the goods and the seller is not bound to hand them over at a particular place, the risk passes to the buyer when the goods are handed over to the first carrier for transmission to the buyer in accordance with the contract of sale. If the seller is bound to hand the goods over to a carrier at a particular place, the risk does not pass to the buyer until the goods are handed over to the carrier at that place. The fact that the seller is authorized to retain documents controlling the disposition of the goods does not affect the passage of the risk.

(2) Nevertheless, the risk does not pass to the buyer until the goods are clearly identified to the contract, whether by markings on the goods, by shipping documents, by notice given to the buyer or otherwise.

Article 68

The risk in respect of goods sold in transit passes to the buyer from the time of the conclusion of the contract. However, if the circumstances so indicate, the risk is assumed by the buyer from the time the goods were handed over to the carrier who issued the documents embodying the contract of carriage. Nevertheless, if at the time of the conclusion of the contract of sale the seller knew or ought to have known that the goods had been lost or damaged and did not disclose this to the buyer, the loss or damage is at the risk of the seller.

Article 69

(1) In cases not within articles 67 and 68, the risk passes to the buyer when he takes over the goods or, if he does not do so in due time, from the time when the goods are placed at his disposal and he commits a breach of contract by failing to take delivery.

(2) However, if the buyer is bound to take over the goods at a place other than a place of business of the seller, the risk passes when delivery is due and the buyer is aware of the fact that the goods are placed at his disposal at that place.

(3) If the contract relates to goods not then identified, the goods are considered not to be placed at the disposal of the buyer until they are clearly identified to the contract.

Article 70

If the seller has committed a fundamental breach of contract, articles 67, 68 and 69 do not impair the remedies available to the buyer on account of the breach.

Chapter V

PROVISIONS COMMON TO THE OBLIGATIONS OF THE SELLER AND OF THE BUYER

Section I. Anticipatory breach and instalment contracts

Article 71

(1) A party may suspend the performance of his obligations if, after the conclusion of the contract, it becomes apparent that the other party will not perform a substantial part of his obligations as a result of:

(a) a serious deficiency in his ability to perform or in his creditworthiness; or

(b) his conduct in preparing to perform or in performing the contract.

(2) If the seller has already dispatched the goods before the grounds described in the preceding paragraph become evident, he may prevent the handing over of the goods to the buyer even though the buyer holds a document which entitles him to obtain them. The present paragraph relates only to the rights in the goods as between the buyer and the seller.

(3) A party suspending performance, whether before or after dispatch of the goods, must immediately give notice of the suspension to the other party and must continue with performance if the other party provides adequate assurance of his performance.

Article 72

(1) If prior to the date for performance of the contract it is clear that one of the parties will commit a fundamental breach of contract, the other party may declare the contract avoided.

(2) If time allows, the party intending to declare the contract avoided must give reasonable notice to the other party in order to permit him to provide adequate assurance of his performance.

(3) The requirements of the preceding paragraph do not apply if the other party has declared that he will not perform his obligations.

Article 73

(1) In the case of a contract for delivery of goods by instalments, if the failure of one party to perform any of his obligations in respect of any instalment constitutes a fundamental breach of contract with respect to that instalment, the other party may declare the contract avoided with respect to that instalment.

(2) If one party's failure to perform any of his obligations in respect of any instalment gives the other party good grounds to conclude that a fundamental breach of contract will occur with respect to future instalments, he may declare the contract avoided for the future, provided that he does so within a reasonable time.

(3) A buyer who declares the contract avoided in respect of any delivery may, at the same time, declare it avoided in respect of deliveries already made or of future deliveries if, by reason of their interdependence, those deliveries could not be used for the purpose contemplated by the parties at the time of the conclusion of the contract.

Section II. Damages

Article 74

Damages for breach of contract by one party consist of a sum equal to the loss, including loss of profit, suffered by the other party as a consequence of the breach. Such damages may not exceed the loss which the party in breach foresaw or ought to have foreseen at the time of the conclusion of the contract, in the light of the facts and matters of which he then knew or ought to have known, as a possible consequence of the breach of contract.

Article 75

If the contract is avoided and if, in a reasonable manner and within a reasonable time after avoidance, the buyer has bought goods in replacement or the seller has resold the goods, the party claiming damages may recover the difference between the contract price and the price in the substitute transaction as well as any further damages recoverable under article 74.

Article 76

(1) If the contract is avoided and there is a current price for the goods, the party claiming damages may, if he has not made a purchase or resale under article 75, recover the difference between the price fixed by the contract and the current price at the time of avoidance as well as any further damages recoverable under article 74. If, however, the party claiming damages has avoided the contract after taking over the goods, the current price at the time of such taking over shall be applied instead of the current price at the time of avoidance.

(2) For the purposes of the preceding paragraph, the current price is the price prevailing at the place where delivery of the goods should have been made or, if there is no current price at that place, the price at such other place as serves as a reasonable substitute, making due allowance for differences in the cost of transporting the goods.

Article 77

A party who relies on a breach of contract must take such measures as are reasonable in the circumstances to mitigate the loss, including loss of profit, resulting from the breach. If he fails to take such measures, the party in breach may claim a reduction in the damages in the amount by which the loss should have been mitigated.

Section III. Interest

Article 78

If a party fails to pay the price or any other sum that is in arrears, the other party is entitled to interest on it, without prejudice to any claim for damages recoverable under article 74.

24

Section IV. Exemptions

Article 79

(1) A party is not liable for a failure to perform any of his obligations if he proves that the failure was due to an impediment beyond his control and that he could not reasonably be expected to have taken the impediment into account at the time of the conclusion of the contract or to have avoided or overcome it, or its consequences.

(2) If the party's failure is due to the failure by a third person whom he has engaged to perform the whole or a part of the contract, that party is exempt from liability only if:

(a) he is exempt under the preceding paragraph; and

(b) the person whom he has so engaged would be so exempt if the provisions of that paragraph were applied to him.

(3) The exemption provided by this article has effect for the period during which the impediment exists.

(4) The party who fails to perform must give notice to the other party of the impediment and its effect on his ability to perform. If the notice is not received by the other party within a reasonable time after the party who fails to perform knew or ought to have known of the impediment, he is liable for damages resulting from such non-receipt.

(5) Nothing in this article prevents either party from exercising any right other than to claim damages under this Convention.

Article 80

A party may not rely on a failure of the other party to perform, to the extent that such failure was caused by the first party's act or omission.

Section V. Effects of avoidance

Article 81

(1) Avoidance of the contract releases both parties from their obligations under it, subject to any damages which may be due. Avoidance does not affect any provision of the contract for the settlement of disputes or any other provision of the contract governing the rights and obligations of the parties consequent upon the avoidance of the contract.

(2) A party who has performed the contract either wholly or in part may claim restitution from the other party of whatever the first party has supplied or paid under the contract. If both parties are bound to make restitution, they must do so concurrently.

Article 82

(1) The buyer loses the right to declare the contract avoided or to require the seller to deliver substitute goods if it is impossible for him to make restitution of the goods substantially in the condition in which he received them.

(2) The preceding paragraph does not apply:

(a) if the impossibility of making restitution of the goods or of making restitution of the goods substantially in the condition in which the buyer received them is not due to his act or omission;

(b) if the goods or part of the goods have perished or deteriorated as a result of the examination provided for in article 38; or

(c) if the goods or part of the goods have been sold in the normal course of business or have been consumed or transformed by the buyer in the course of normal use before he discovered or ought to have discovered the lack of conformity.

Article 83

A buyer who has lost the right to declare the contract avoided or to require the seller to deliver substitute goods in accordance with article 82 retains all other remedies under the contract and this Convention.

Article 84

(1) If the seller is bound to refund the price, he must also pay interest on it, from the date on which the price was paid.

(2) The buyer must account to the seller for all benefits which he has derived from the goods or part of them:

(a) if he must make restitution of the goods or part of them; or

(b) if it is impossible for him to make restitution of all or part of the goods or to make restitution of all or part of the goods substantially in the condition in which he received them, but he has nevertheless declared the contract avoided or required the seller to deliver substitute goods.

26

Section VI. Preservation of the goods

Article 85

If the buyer is in delay in taking delivery of the goods or, where payment of the price and delivery of the goods are to be made concurrently, if he fails to pay the price, and the seller is either in possession of the goods or otherwise able to control their disposition, the seller must take such steps as are reasonable in the circumstances to preserve them. He is entitled to retain them until he has been reimbursed his reasonable expenses by the buyer.

Article 86

(1) If the buyer has received the goods and intends to exercise any right under the contract or this Convention to reject them, he must take such steps to preserve them as are reasonable in the circumstances. He is entitled to retain them until he has been reimbursed his reasonable expenses by the seller.

(2) If goods dispatched to the buyer have been placed at his disposal at their destination and he exercises the right to reject them, he must take possession of them on behalf of the seller, provided that this can be done without payment of the price and without unreasonable inconvenience or unreasonable expense. This provision does not apply if the seller or a person authorized to take charge of the goods on his behalf is present at the destination. If the buyer takes possession of the goods under this paragraph, his rights and obligations are governed by the preceding paragraph.

Article 87

A party who is bound to take steps to preserve the goods may deposit them in a warehouse of a third person at the expense of the other party provided that the expense incurred is not unreasonable.

Article 88

(1) A party who is bound to preserve the goods in accordance with article 85 or 86 may sell them by any appropriate means if there has been an unreasonable delay by the other party in taking possession of the goods or in taking them back or in paying the price or the cost of preservation, provided that reasonable notice of the intention to sell has been given to the other party.

(2)　If the goods are subject to rapid deterioration or their preservation would involve unreasonable expense, a party who is bound to preserve the goods in accordance with article 85 or 86 must take reasonable measures to sell them.　To the extent possible he must give notice to the other party of his intention to sell.

(3)　A party selling the goods has the right to retain out of the proceeds of sale an amount equal to the reasonable expenses of preserving the goods and of selling them.　He must account to the other party for the balance.

PART IV

FINAL PROVISIONS·

Article 89

The Secretary-General of the United Nations is hereby designated as the depositary for this Convention.

Article 90

This Convention does not prevail over any international agreement which has already been or may be entered into and which contains provisions concerning the matters governed by this Convention, provided that the parties have their places of business in States parties to such agreement.

Article 91

(1)　This Convention is open for signature at the concluding meeting of the United Nations Conference on Contracts for the International Sale of Goods and will remain open for signature by all States at the Headquarters of the United Nations, New York until 30 September 1981.

(2)　This Convention is subject to ratification, acceptance or approval by the signatory States.

(3)　This Convention is open for accession by all States which are not signatory States as from the date it is open for signature.

(4)　Instruments of ratification, acceptance, approval and accession are to be deposited with the Secretary-General of the United Nations.

28

Article 92

(1) A Contracting State may declare at the time of signature, ratification, acceptance, approval or accession that it will not be bound by Part II of this Convention or that it will not be bound by Part III of this Convention.

(2) A Contracting State which makes a declaration in accordance with the preceding paragraph in respect of Part II or Part III of this Convention is not to be considered a Contracting State within paragraph (1) of article 1 of this Convention in respect of matters governed by the Part to which the declaration applies.

Article 93

(1) If a Contracting State has two or more territorial units in which, according to its constitution, different systems of law are applicable in relation to the matters dealt with in this Convention, it may, at the time of signature, ratification, acceptance, approval or accession, declare that this Convention is to extend to all its territorial units or only to one or more of them, and may amend its declaration by submitting another declaration at any time.

(2) These declarations are to be notified to the depositary and are to state expressly the territorial units to which the Convention extends.

(3) If, by virtue of a declaration under this article, this Convention extends to one or more but not all of the territorial units of a Contracting State, and if the place of business of a party is located in that State, this place of business, for the purposes of this Convention, is considered not to be in a Contracting State, unless it is in a territorial unit to which the Convention extends.

(4) If a Contracting State makes no declaration under paragraph (1) of this article, the Convention is to extend to all territorial units of that State.

Article 94

(1) Two or more Contracting States which have the same or closely related legal rules on matters governed by this Convention may at any time declare that the Convention is not to apply to contracts of sale or to their formation where the parties have their places of business in those States. Such declarations may be made jointly or by reciprocal unilateral declarations.

(2) A Contracting State which has the same or closely related legal rules on matters governed by this Convention as one or more non-Contracting States may at any time declare that the Convention is not to apply to contracts of sale or to their formation where the parties have their places of business in those States.

(3) If a State which is the object of a declaration under the preceding paragraph subsequently becomes a Contracting State, the declaration made will, as from the date on which the Convention enters into force in respect of the new Contracting State, have the effect of a declaration made under paragraph (1), provided that the new Contracting State joins in such declaration or makes a reciprocal unilateral declaration.

Article 95

Any State may declare at the time of the deposit of its instrument of ratification, acceptance, approval or accession that it will not be bound by subparagraph (1)(b) of article 1 of this Convention.

Article 96

A Contracting State whose legislation requires contracts of sale to be concluded in or evidenced by writing may at any time make a declaration in accordance with article 12 that any provision of article 11, article 29, or Part II of this Convention, that allows a contract of sale or its modification or termination by agreement or any offer, acceptance, or other indication of intention to be made in any form other than in writing, does not apply where any party has his place of business in that State.

Article 97

(1) Declarations made under this Convention at the time of signature are subject to confirmation upon ratification, acceptance or approval.

(2) Declarations and confirmations of declarations are to be in writing and be formally notified to the depositary.

(3) A declaration takes effect simultaneously with the entry into force of this Convention in respect of the State concerned. However, a declaration of which the depositary receives formal notification after such entry into force takes effect on the first day of the month following the expiration of six months after the date of its receipt by the depositary. Reciprocal unilateral declarations under article 94 take effect on the first day of the month following the expiration of six months after the receipt of the latest declaration by the depositary.

30

(4) Any State which makes a declaration under this Convention may withdraw it at any time by a formal notification in writing addressed to the depositary. Such withdrawal is to take effect on the first day of the month following the expiration of six months after the date of the receipt of the notification by the depositary.

(5) A withdrawal of a declaration made under article 94 renders inoperative, as from the date on which the withdrawal takes effect, any reciprocal declaration made by another State under that article.

Article 98

No reservations are permitted except those expressly authorized in this Convention.

Article 99

(1) This Convention enters into force, subject to the provisions of paragraph (6) of this article, on the first day of the month following the expiration of twelve months after the date of deposit of the tenth instrument of ratification, acceptance, approval or accession, including an instrument which contains a declaration made under article 92.

(2) When a State ratifies, accepts, approves or accedes to this Convention after the deposit of the tenth instrument of ratification, acceptance, approval or accession, this Convention, with the exception of the Part excluded, enters into force in respect of that State, subject to the provisions of paragraph (6) of this article, on the first day of the month following the expiration of twelve months after the date of the deposit of its instrument of ratification, acceptance, approval or accession.

(3) A State which ratifies, accepts, approves or accedes to this Convention and is a party to either or both the Convention relating to a Uniform Law on the Formation of Contracts for the International Sale of Goods done at The Hague on 1 July 1964 (1964 Hague Formation Convention) and the Convention relating to a Uniform Law on the International Sale of Goods done at The Hague on 1 July 1964 (1964 Hague Sales Convention) shall at the same time denounce, as the case may be, either or both the 1964 Hague Sales Convention and the 1964 Hague Formation Convention by notifying the Government of the Netherlands to that effect.

(4) A State party to the 1964 Hague Sales Convention which ratifies, accepts, approves or accedes to the present Convention and declares or has declared under article 92 that it will not be bound by Part II of this Convention shall at the time of ratification, acceptance, approval or accession denounce the 1964 Hague Sales Convention by notifying the Government of the Netherlands to that effect.

(5) A State party to the 1964 Hague Formation Convention which ratifies, accepts, approves or accedes to the present Convention and declares or has declared under article 92 that it will not be bound by Part III of this Convention shall at the time of ratification, acceptance, approval or accession denounce the 1964 Hague Formation Convention by notifying the Government of the Netherlands to that effect.

(6) For the purpose of this article, ratifications, acceptances, approvals and accessions in respect of this Convention by States parties to the 1964 Hague Formation Convention or to the 1964 Hague Sales Convention shall not be effective until such denunciations as may be required on the part of those States in respect of the latter two Conventions have themselves become effective. The depositary of this Convention shall consult with the Government of the Netherlands, as the depositary of the 1964 Conventions, so as to ensure necessary co-ordination in this respect.

Article 100

(1) This Convention applies to the formation of a contract only when the proposal for concluding the contract is made on or after the date when the Convention enters into force in respect of the Contracting States referred to in subparagraph (1)(a) or the Contracting State referred to in subparagraph (1)(b) of article 1.

(2) This Convention applies only to contracts concluded on or after the date when the Convention enters into force in respect of the Contracting States referred to in subparagraph (1)(a) or the Contracting State referred to in subparagraph (1)(b) of article 1.

Article 101

(1) A Contracting State may denounce this Convention, or Part II or Part III of the Convention, by a formal notification in writing addressed to the depositary.

(2) The denunciation takes effect on the first day of the month following the expiration of twelve months after the notification is received by the depositary. Where a longer period for the denunciation to take effect is specified in the notification, the denunciation takes effect upon the expiration of such longer period after the notification is received by the depositary.

DONE at Vienna, this day of eleventh day of April, one thousand nine hundred and **eighty,** in a single original, of which the Arabic, Chinese, English, French, Russian and Spanish texts are equally authentic.

IN WITNESS WHEREOF the undersigned plenipotentiaries, being duly authorized by their respective Governments, have signed this Convention.

INSTITUTE CARGO CLAUSES (A)

RISKS COVERED

1 This insurance covers all risks of loss of or damage to the subject-matter insured except as provided in Clauses 4, 5, 6 and 7 below. *Risks Clause*

2 This insurance covers general average and salvage charges, adjusted or determined according to the contract of affreightment and/or the governing law and practice, incurred to avoid or in connection with the avoidance of loss from any cause except those excluded in Clauses 4, 5, 6 and 7 or elsewhere in this insurance. *General Average Clause*

3 This insurance is extended to indemnify the Assured against such proportion of liability under the contract of affreightment "Both to Blame Collision" Clause as is in respect of a loss recoverable hereunder. In the event of any claim by shipowners under the said Clause the Assured agree to notify the Underwriters who shall have the right, at their own cost and expense, to defend the Assured against such claim. *"Both to Blame Collision" Clause*

EXCLUSIONS

4 In no case shall this insurance cover *General Exclusions Clause*

  4.1 loss damage or expense attributable to wilful misconduct of the Assured

  4.2 ordinary leakage, ordinary loss in weight or volume, or ordinary wear and tear of the subject-matter insured

  4.3 loss damage or expense caused by insufficiency or unsuitability of packing or preparation of the subject-matter insured (for the purpose of this Clause 4.3 "packing" shall be deemed to include stowage in a container or liftvan but only when such stowage is carried out prior to attachment of this insurance or by the Assured or their servants)

  4.4 loss damage or expense caused by inherent vice or nature of the subject-matter insured

  4.5 loss damage or expense proximately caused by delay, even though the delay be caused by a risk insured against (except expenses payable under Clause 2 above)

  4.6 loss damage or expense arising from insolvency or financial default of the owners managers charterers or operators of the vessel

  4.7 loss damage or expense arising from the use of any weapon of war employing atomic or nuclear fission and/or fusion or other like reaction or radioactive force or matter.

5 5.1 In no case shall this insurance cover loss damage or expense arising from *Unseaworthiness and Unfitness Exclusion Clause*

      unseaworthiness of vessel or craft,

      unfitness of vessel craft conveyance container or liftvan for the safe carriage of the subject-matter insured,

    where the Assured or their servants are privy to such unseaworthiness or unfitness, at the time the subject-matter insured is loaded therein.

  5.2 The Underwriters waive any breach of the implied warranties of seaworthiness of the ship and fitness of the ship to carry the subject-matter insured to destination, unless the Assured or their servants are privy to such unseaworthiness or unfitness.

6 In no case shall this insurance cover loss damage or expense caused by *War Exclusion Clause*

  6.1 war civil war revolution rebellion insurrection, or civil strife arising therefrom, or any hostile act by or against a belligerent power

  6.2 capture seizure arrest restraint or detainment (piracy excepted), and the consequences thereof or any attempt thereat

  6.3 derelict mines torpedoes bombs or other derelict weapons of war.

7 In no case shall this insurance cover loss damage or expense *Strikes Exclusion Clause*

  7.1 caused by strikers, locked-out workmen, or persons taking part in labour disturbances, riots or civil commotions

  7.2 resulting from strikes, lock-outs, labour disturbances, riots or civil commotions.

  7.3 caused by any terrorist or any person acting from a political motive.

DURATION

8 8.1 This insurance attaches from the time the goods leave the warehouse or place of storage at the place named herein for the commencement of the transit, continues during the ordinary course of transit and terminates either *Transit Clause*

  8.1.1 on delivery to the Consignees' or other final warehouse or place of storage at the destination named herein,

  8.1.2 on delivery to any other warehouse or place of storage, whether prior to or at the destination named herein, which the Assured elect to use either

  8.1.2.1 for storage other than in the ordinary course of transit or

  8.1.2.2 for allocation or distribution,

      or

  8.1.3 on the expiry of 60 days after completion of discharge overside of the goods hereby insured from the oversea vessel at the final port of discharge,

  whichever shall first occur.

  8.2 If, after discharge overside from the oversea vessel at the final port of discharge, but prior to termination of this insurance, the goods are to be forwarded to a destination other than that to which they are insured hereunder, this insurance, whilst remaining subject to termination as provided for above, shall not extend beyond the commencement of transit to such other destination.

  8.3 This insurance shall remain in force (subject to termination as provided for above and to the provisions of Clause 9 below) during delay beyond the control of the Assured, any deviation, forced discharge, reshipment or transhipment and during any variation of the adventure arising from the exercise of a liberty granted to shipowners or charterers under the contract of affreightment.

9 If owing to circumstances beyond the control of the Assured either the contract of carriage is terminated at a port or place other than the destination named therein or the transit is otherwise terminated before delivery of the goods as provided for in Clause 8 above, then this insurance shall also terminate *unless prompt notice is given to the Underwriters and continuation of cover is requested when the insurance shall remain in force, subject to an additional premium if required by the Underwriters*, either

    9.1 until the goods are sold and delivered at such port or place, or, unless otherwise specially agreed, until the expiry of 60 days after arrival of the goods hereby insured at such port or place, whichever shall first occur,

        or

    9.2 if the goods are forwarded within the said period of 60 days (or any agreed extension thereof) to the destination named herein or to any other destination, until terminated in accordance with the provisions of Clause 8 above.

Termination of Contract of Carriage Clause

10 Where, after attachment of this insurance, the destination is changed by the Assured, *held covered at a premium and on conditions to be arranged subject to prompt notice being given to the Underwriters.*

Change of Voyage Clause

CLAIMS

11   **11.1** In order to recover under this insurance the Assured must have an insurable interest in the subject-matter insured at the time of the loss.

11.2 Subject to 11.1 above, the Assured shall be entitled to recover for insured loss occurring during the period covered by this insurance, notwithstanding that the loss occurred before the contract of insurance was concluded, unless the Assured were aware of the loss and the Underwriters were not.

Insurable Interest Clause

12 Where, as a result of the operation of a risk covered by this insurance, the insured transit is terminated at a port or place other than that to which the subject-matter is covered under this insurance, the Underwriters will reimburse the Assured for any extra charges properly and reasonably incurred in unloading storing and forwarding the subject-matter to the destination to which it is insured hereunder.

This Clause 12, which does not apply to general average or salvage charges, shall be subject to the exclusions contained in Clauses 4, 5, 6 and 7 above, and shall not include charges arising from the fault negligence insolvency or financial default of the Assured or their servants.

Forwarding Charges Clause

13 No claim for Constructive Total Loss shall be recoverable hereunder unless the subject-matter insured is reasonably abandoned either on account of its actual total loss appearing to be unavoidable or because the cost of recovering, reconditioning and forwarding the subject-matter to the destination to which it is insured would exceed its value on arrival.

Constructive Total Loss Clause

14   **14.1** If any Increased Value insurance is effected by the Assured on the cargo insured herein the agreed value of the cargo shall be deemed to be increased to the total amount insured under this insurance and all Increased Value insurances covering the loss, and liability under this insurance shall be in such proportion as the sum insured herein bears to such total amount insured.

In the event of claim the Assured shall provide the Underwriters with evidence of the amounts insured under all other insurances.

14.2 **Where this insurance is on Increased Value the following clause shall apply:**
The agreed value of the cargo shall be deemed to be equal to the total amount insured under the primary insurance and all Increased Value insurances covering the loss and effected on the cargo by the Assured, and liability under this insurance shall be in such proportion as the sum insured herein bears to such total amount insured.

In the event of claim the Assured shall provide the Underwriters with evidence of the amounts insured under all other insurances.

Increased Value Clause

BENEFIT OF INSURANCE

15 This insurance shall not inure to the benefit of the carrier or other bailee.

Not to Inure Clause

MINIMISING LOSSES

16 It is the duty of the Assured and their servants and agents in respect of loss recoverable hereunder

    16.1 to take such measures as may be reasonable for the purpose of averting or minimising such loss, and

    16.2 to ensure that all rights against carriers, bailees or other third parties are properly preserved and exercised

and the Underwriters will, in addition to any loss recoverable hereunder, reimburse the Assured for any charges properly and reasonably incurred in pursuance of these duties.

Duty of Assured Clause

17 Measures taken by the Assured or the Underwriters with the object of saving, protecting or recovering the subject-matter insured shall not be considered as a waiver or acceptance of abandonment or otherwise prejudice the rights of either party.

Waiver Clause

AVOIDANCE OF DELAY

18 It is a condition of this insurance that the Assured shall act with reasonable despatch in all circumstances within their control.

Reasonable Despatch Clause

LAW AND PRACTICE

19 This insurance is subject to English law and practice.

English Law and Practice Clause

NOTE:— *It is necessary for the Assured when they become aware of an event which is "held covered" under this insurance to give prompt notice to the Underwriters and the right to such cover is dependent upon compliance with this obligation.*

INSTITUTE CARGO CLAUSES (B)

RISKS COVERED

1.   This insurance covers, except as provided in Clauses 4, 5, 6 and 7 below,   *Risks Clause*

  1.1   loss of or damage to the subject-matter insured reasonably attributable to

  1.1.1   fire or explosion

  1.1.2   vessel or craft being stranded grounded sunk or capsized

  1.1.3   overturning or derailment of land conveyance

  1.1.4   collision or contact of vessel craft or conveyance with any external object other than water

  1.1.5   discharge of cargo at a port of distress

  1.1.6   earthquake volcanic eruption or lightning,

  1.2   loss of or damage to the subject-matter insured caused by

  1.2.1   general average sacrifice

  1.2.2   jettison or washing overboard

  1.2.3   entry of sea lake or river water into vessel craft hold conveyance container liftvan or place of storage,

  1.3   total loss of any package lost overboard or dropped whilst loading on to, or unloading from, vessel or craft.

2.   This insurance covers general average and salvage charges, adjusted or determined according to the contract of affreightment and/or the governing law and practice, incurred to avoid or in connection with the avoidance of loss from any cause except those excluded in Clauses 4, 5, 6 and 7 or elsewhere in this insurance.   *General Average Clause*

3.   This insurance is extended to indemnify the Assured against such proportion of liability under the contract of affreightment "Both to Blame Collision" Clause as is in respect of a loss recoverable hereunder. In the event of any claim by shipowners under the said Clause the Assured agree to notify the Underwriters who shall have the right, at their own cost and expense, to defend the Assured against such claim.   *"Both to Blame Collision" Clause*

EXCLUSIONS

4.   In no case shall this insurance cover   *General Exclusions Clause*

  4.1   loss damage or expense attributable to wilful misconduct of the Assured

  4.2   ordinary leakage, ordinary loss in weight or volume, or ordinary wear and tear of the subject-matter insured

  4.3   loss damage or expense caused by insufficiency or unsuitability of packing or preparation of the subject-matter insured (for the purpose of this Clause 4.3 "packing" shall be deemed to include stowage in a container or liftvan but only when such stowage is carried out prior to attachment of this insurance or by the Assured or their servants)

  4.4   loss damage or expense caused by inherent vice or nature of the subject-matter insured

  4.5   loss damage or expense proximately caused by delay, even though the delay be caused by a risk insured against (except expenses payable under Clause 2 above)

  4.6   loss damage or expense arising from insolvency or financial default of the owners managers charterers or operators of the vessel

  4.7   deliberate damage to or deliberate destruction of the subject-matter insured or any part thereof by the wrongful act of any person or persons

  4.8   loss damage or expense arising from the use of any weapon of war employing atomic or nuclear fission and/or fusion or other like reaction or radioactive force or matter.

5. 5.1   In no case shall this insurance cover loss damage or expense arising from   *Unseaworthiness, and Unfitness Exclusion Clause*

        unseaworthiness of vessel or craft,

        unfitness of vessel craft conveyance container or liftvan for the safe carriage of the subject-matter insured,

        where the Assured or their servants are privy to such unseaworthiness or unfitness, at the time the subject-matter insured is loaded therein.

  5.2   The Underwriters waive any breach of the implied warranties of seaworthiness of the ship and fitness of the ship to carry the subject-matter insured to destination, unless the Assured or their servants are privy to such unseaworthiness or unfitness.

6.   In no case shall this insurance cover loss damage or expense caused by   *War Exclusion Clause*

  6.1   war civil war revolution rebellion insurrection, or civil strife arising therefrom, or any hostile act by or against a belligerent power

  6.2   capture seizure arrest restraint or detainment, and the consequences thereof or any attempt thereat

  6.3   derelict mines torpedoes bombs or other derelict weapons of war.

7.   In no case shall this insurance cover loss damage or expense   *Strikes Exclusion Clause*

  7.1   caused by strikers, locked-out workmen, or persons taking part in labour disturbances, riots or civil commotions

  7.2   resulting from strikes, lock-outs, labour disturbances, riots or civil commotions

  7.3   caused by any terrorist or any person acting from a political motive.

DURATION

8. 8.1   This insurance attaches from the time the goods leave the warehouse or place of storage at the place named herein for the commencement of the transit, continues during the ordinary course of transit and terminates either   *Transit Clause*

  8.1.1   on delivery to the Consignees' or other final warehouse or place of storage at the destination named herein,

  8.1.2   on delivery to any other warehouse or place of storage, whether prior to or at the destination named herein, which the Assured elect to use either

  8.1.2.1   for storage other than in the ordinary course of transit or

  8.1.2.2   for allocation or distribution,

        or

  8.1.3   on the expiry of 60 days after completion of discharge overside of the goods hereby insured from the oversea vessel at the final port of discharge,

        whichever shall first occur.

8.2   If, after discharge overside from the oversea vessel at the final port of discharge, but prior to termination of this insurance, the goods are to be forwarded to a destination other than that to which they are insured hereunder, this insurance, whilst remaining subject to termination as provided for above, shall not extend beyond the commencement of transit to such other destination.

8.3   This insurance shall remain in force (subject to termination as provided for above and to the provisions of Clause 9 below) during delay beyond the control of the Assured, any deviation, forced discharge, reshipment or transhipment and during any variation of the adventure arising from the exercise of a liberty granted to shipowners or charterers under the contract of affreightment.

9   If owing to circumstances beyond the control of the Assured either the contract of carriage is terminated at a port or place other than the destination named therein or the transit is otherwise terminated before delivery of the goods as provided for in Clause 8 above, then this insurance shall also terminate *unless prompt notice is given to the Underwriters and continuation of cover is requested when the insurance shall remain in force, subject to an additional premium if required by the Underwriters,* either
                                               Termination of Contract of Carriage Clause

9.1   until the goods are sold and delivered at such port or place, or, unless otherwise specially agreed, until the expiry of 60 days after arrival of the goods hereby insured at such port or place, whichever shall first occur,

        or

9.2   if the goods are forwarded within the said period of 60 days (or any agreed extension thereof) to the destination named herein or to any other destination, until terminated in accordance with the provisions of Clause 8 above.

10   Where, after attachment of this insurance, the destination is changed by the Assured, *held covered at a premium and on conditions to be arranged subject to prompt notice being given to the Underwriters.*   *Change of Voyage Clause*

CLAIMS

11   11.1   In order to recover under this insurance the Assured must have an insurable interest in the subject-matter insured at the time of the loss.   *Insurable Interest Clause*

    11.2   Subject to 11.1 above, the Assured shall be entitled to recover for insured loss occurring during the period covered by this insurance, notwithstanding that the loss occurred before the contract of insurance was concluded, unless the Assured were aware of the loss and the Underwriters were not.

12   Where, as a result of the operation of a risk covered by this insurance, the insured transit is terminated at a port or place other than that to which the subject-matter is covered under this insurance, the Underwriters will reimburse the Assured for any extra charges properly and reasonably incurred in unloading storing and forwarding the subject-matter to the destination to which it is insured hereunder.   *Forwarding Charges Clause*

     This Clause 12, which does not apply to general average or salvage charges, shall be subject to the exclusions contained in Clauses 4, 5, 6 and 7 above, and shall not include charges arising from the fault negligence insolvency or financial default of the Assured or their servants.

13   No claim for Constructive Total Loss shall be recoverable hereunder unless the subject-matter insured is reasonably abandoned either on account of its actual total loss appearing to be unavoidable or because the cost of recovering, reconditioning and forwarding the subject-matter to the destination to which it is insured would exceed its value on arrival.   *Constructive Total Loss Clause*

14   14.1   If any Increased Value insurance is effected by the Assured on the cargo insured herein the agreed value of the cargo shall be deemed to be increased to the total amount insured under this insurance and all Increased Value insurances covering the loss, and liability under this insurance shall be in such proportion as the sum insured herein bears to such total amount insured.   *Increased Value Clause*

           In the event of claim the Assured shall provide the Underwriters with evidence of the amounts insured under all other insurances.

    14.2   **Where this insurance is on Increased Value the following clause shall apply:**
           The agreed value of the cargo shall be deemed to be equal to the total amount insured under the primary insurance and all Increased Value insurances covering the loss and effected on the cargo by the Assured, and liability under this insurance shall be in such proportion as the sum insured herein bears to such total amount insured.

           In the event of claim the Assured shall provide the Underwriters with evidence of the amounts insured under all other insurances.

BENEFIT OF INSURANCE

15   This insurance shall not inure to the benefit of the carrier or other bailee.   *Not to Inure Clause*

MINIMISING LOSSES

16   It is the duty of the Assured and their servants and agents in respect of loss recoverable hereunder   *Duty of Assured Clause*

    16.1   to take such measures as may be reasonable for the purpose of averting or minimising such loss, and

    16.2   to ensure that all rights against carriers, bailees or other third parties are properly preserved and exercised

     and the Underwriters will, in addition to any loss recoverable hereunder, reimburse the Assured for any charges properly and reasonably incurred in pursuance of these duties.

17   Measures taken by the Assured or the Underwriters with the object of saving, protecting or recovering the subject-matter insured shall not be considered as a waiver or acceptance of abandonment or otherwise prejudice the rights of either party.   *Waiver Clause*

AVOIDANCE OF DELAY

18   It is a condition of this insurance that the Assured shall act with reasonable despatch in all circumstances within their control.   *Reasonable Despatch Clause*

LAW AND PRACTICE

19   This insurance is subject to English law and practice.   *English Law and Practice Clause*

NOTE:— It is necessary for the Assured when they become aware of an event which is "held covered" under this insurance to give prompt notice to the Underwriters and the right to such cover is dependent upon compliance with this obligation.

INSTITUTE CARGO CLAUSES (C)

RISKS COVERED

1   This insurance covers, except as provided in Clauses 4, 5, 6 and 7 below,   *Risks Clause*

   1.1   loss of or damage to the subject-matter insured reasonably attributable to

     1.1.1   fire or explosion

     1.1.2   vessel or craft being stranded grounded sunk or capsized

     1.1.3   overturning or derailment of land conveyance

     1.1.4   collision or contact of vessel craft or conveyance with any external object other than water

     1.1.5   discharge of cargo at a port of distress,

   1.2   loss of or damage to the subject-matter insured caused by

     1.2.1   general average sacrifice

     1.2.2   jettison.

2   This insurance covers general average and salvage charges, adjusted or determined according to the contract of affreightment and/or the governing law and practice, incurred to avoid or in connection with the avoidance of loss from any cause except those excluded in Clauses 4, 5, 6 and 7 or elsewhere in this insurance.   *General Average Clause*

3   This insurance is extended to indemnify the Assured against such proportion of liability under the contract of affreightment "Both to Blame Collision" Clause as is in respect of a loss recoverable hereunder. In the event of any claim by shipowners under the said Clause the Assured agree to notify the Underwriters who shall have the right, at their own cost and expense, to defend the Assured against such claim.   *"Both to Blame Collision" Clause*

EXCLUSIONS

4   In no case shall this insurance cover   *General Exclusions Clause*

   4.1   loss damage or expense attributable to wilful misconduct of the Assured

   4.2   ordinary leakage, ordinary loss in weight or volume, or ordinary wear and tear of the subject-matter insured

   4.3   loss damage or expense caused by insufficiency or unsuitability of packing or preparation of the subject-matter insured (for the purpose of this Clause 4.3 "packing" shall be deemed to include stowage in a container or liftvan but only when such stowage is carried out prior to attachment of this insurance or by the Assured or their servants)

   4.4   loss damage or expense caused by inherent vice or nature of the subject-matter insured

   4.5   loss damage or expense proximately caused by delay, even though the delay be caused by a risk insured against (except expenses payable under Clause 2 above)

   4.6   loss damage or expense arising from insolvency or financial default of the owners managers charterers or operators of the vessel

   4.7   deliberate damage to or deliberate destruction of the subject-matter insured or any part thereof by the wrongful act of any person or persons

   4.8   loss damage or expense arising from the use of any weapon of war employing atomic or nuclear fission and/or fusion or other like reaction or radioactive force or matter.

5   5.1   In no case shall this insurance cover loss damage or expense arising from   *Unseaworthiness and Unfitness Exclusion Clause*

         unseaworthiness of vessel or craft,

         unfitness of vessel craft conveyance container or liftvan for the safe carriage of the subject-matter insured,

         where the Assured or their servants are privy to such unseaworthiness or unfitness, at the time the subject-matter insured is loaded therein.

   5.2   The Underwriters waive any breach of the implied warranties of seaworthiness of the ship and fitness of the ship to carry the subject-matter insured to destination, unless the Assured or their servants are privy to such unseaworthiness or unfitness.

6   In no case shall this insurance cover loss damage or expense caused by   *War Exclusion Clause*

   6.1   war civil war revolution rebellion insurrection, or civil strife arising therefrom, or any hostile act by or against a belligerent power

   6.2   capture seizure arrest restraint or detainment, and the consequences thereof or any attempt thereat

   6.3   derelict mines torpedoes bombs or other derelict weapons of war.

7   In no case shall this insurance cover loss damage or expense   *Strikes Exclusion Clause*

   7.1   caused by strikers, locked-out workmen, or persons taking part in labour disturbances, riots or civil commotions

   7.2   resulting from strikes, lock-outs, labour disturbances, riots or civil commotions

   7.3   caused by any terrorist or any person acting from a political motive.

DURATION

8   8.1   This insurance attaches from the time the goods leave the warehouse or place of storage at the place named herein for the commencement of the transit, continues during the ordinary course of transit and terminates either   *Transit Clause*

     8.1.1   on delivery to the Consignees' or other final warehouse or place of storage at the destination named herein,

     8.1.2   on delivery to any other warehouse or place of storage, whether prior to or at the destination named herein, which the Assured elect to use either

     8.1.2.1   for storage other than in the ordinary course of transit or

     8.1.2.2   for allocation or distribution,

             or

     8.1.3   on the expiry of 60 days after completion of discharge overside of the goods hereby insured from the oversea vessel at the final port of discharge,

         whichever shall first occur.

8.2 If, after discharge overside from the oversea vessel at the final port of discharge, but prior to termination of this insurance, the goods are to be forwarded to a destination other than that to which they are insured hereunder, this insurance, whilst remaining subject to termination as provided for above, shall not extend beyond the commencement of transit to such other destination.

8.3 This insurance shall remain in force (subject to termination as provided for above and to the provisions of Clause 9 below) during delay beyond the control of the Assured, any deviation, forced discharge, reshipment or transhipment and during any variation of the adventure arising from the exercise of a liberty granted to shipowners or charterers under the contract of affreightment.

9 If owing to circumstances beyond the control of the Assured either the contract of carriage is terminated at a port or place other than the destination named therein or the transit is otherwise terminated before delivery of the goods as provided for in Clause 8 above, then this insurance shall also terminate *unless prompt notice is given to the Underwriters and continuation of cover is requested when the insurance shall remain in force, subject to an additional premium if required by the Underwriters,* either

   9.1 until the goods are sold and delivered at such port or place, or, unless otherwise specially agreed, until the expiry of 60 days after arrival of the goods hereby insured at such port or place, whichever shall first occur,

   or

   9.2 if the goods are forwarded within the said period of 60 days (or any agreed extension thereof) to the destination named herein or to any other destination, until terminated in accordance with the provisions of Clause 8 above.

10 Where, after attachment of this insurance, the destination is changed by the Assured, *held covered at a premium and on conditions to be arranged subject to prompt notice being given to the Underwriters.*

CLAIMS

11 11.1 In order to recover under this insurance the Assured must have an insurable interest in the subject-matter insured at the time of the loss.

   11.2 Subject to 11.1 above, the Assured shall be entitled to recover for insured loss occurring during the period covered by this insurance, notwithstanding that the loss occurred before the contract of insurance was concluded, unless the Assured were aware of the loss and the Underwriters were not.

12 Where, as a result of the operation of a risk covered by this insurance, the insured transit is terminated at a port or place other than that to which the subject-matter is covered under this insurance, the Underwriters will reimburse the Assured for any extra charges properly and reasonably incurred in unloading storing and forwarding the subject-matter to the destination to which it is insured hereunder.

   This Clause 12, which does not apply to general average or salvage charges, shall be subject to the exclusions contained in Clauses 4, 5, 6 and 7 above, and shall not include charges arising from the fault negligence insolvency or financial default of the Assured or their servants.

13 No claim for Constructive Total Loss shall be recoverable hereunder unless the subject-matter insured is reasonably abandoned either on account of its actual total loss appearing to be unavoidable or because the cost of recovering, reconditioning and forwarding the subject-matter to the destination to which it is insured would exceed its value on arrival.

14 14.1 If any Increased Value insurance is effected by the Assured on the cargo insured herein the agreed value of the cargo shall be deemed to be increased to the total amount insured under this insurance and all Increased Value insurances covering the loss, and liability under this insurance shall be in such proportion as the sum insured herein bears to such total amount insured.

   In the event of claim the Assured shall provide the Underwriters with evidence of the amounts insured under all other insurances.

   14.2 **Where this insurance is on Increased Value the following clause shall apply:**
   The agreed value of the cargo shall be deemed to be equal to the total amount insured under the primary insurance and all Increased Value insurances covering the loss and effected on the cargo by the Assured, and liability under this insurance shall be in such proportion as the sum insured herein bears to such total amount insured.

   In the event of claim the Assured shall provide the Underwriters with evidence of the amounts insured under all other insurances.

BENEFIT OF INSURANCE

15 This insurance shall not inure to the benefit of the carrier or other bailee.

MINIMISING LOSSES

16 It is the duty of the Assured and their servants and agents in respect of loss recoverable hereunder

   16.1 to take such measures as may be reasonable for the purpose of averting or minimising such loss, and

   16.2 to ensure that all rights against carriers, bailees or other third parties are properly preserved and exercised

   and the Underwriters will, in addition to any loss recoverable hereunder, reimburse the Assured for any charges properly and reasonably incurred in pursuance of these duties.

17 Measures taken by the Assured or the Underwriters with the object of saving, protecting or recovering the subject-matter insured shall not be considered as a waiver or acceptance of abandonment or otherwise prejudice the rights of either party.

AVOIDANCE OF DELAY

18 It is a condition of this insurance that the Assured shall act with reasonable despatch in all circumstances within their control.

LAW AND PRACTICE

19 This insurance is subject to English law and practice.

NOTE:— It is necessary for the Assured when they become aware of an event which is "held covered" under this insurance to give prompt notice to the Underwriters and the right to such cover is dependent upon compliance with this obligation.

INSTITUTE CARGO CLAUSES (AIR)
(excluding sendings by Post)

RISKS COVERED

1　This insurance covers all risks of loss of or damage to the subject-matter insured except as provided in Clauses 2, 3 and 4 below. Risks Clause

EXCLUSIONS

2　In no case shall this insurance cover General Exclusions Clause

2.1　loss damage or expense attributable to wilful misconduct of the Assured

2.2　ordinary leakage, ordinary loss in weight or volume, or ordinary wear and tear of the subject-matter insured

2.3　loss damage or expense caused by insufficiency or unsuitability of packing or preparation of the subject-matter insured (for the purpose of this Clause 2.3 "packing" shall be deemed to include stowage in a container or liftvan but only when such stowage is carried out prior to attachment of this insurance or by the Assured or their servants)

2.4　loss damage or expense caused by inherent vice or nature of the subject-matter insured

2.5　loss damage or expense arising from unfitness of aircraft conveyance container or liftvan for the safe carriage of the subject-matter insured, where the Assured or their servants are privy to such unfitness at the time the subject-matter insured is loaded therein

2.6　loss damage or expense proximately caused by delay, even though the delay be caused by a risk insured against

2.7　loss damage or expense arising from insolvency or financial default of the owners managers charterers or operators of the aircraft

2.8　loss damage or expense arising from the use of any weapon of war employing atomic or nuclear fission and/or fusion or other like reaction or radioactive force or matter.

3　In no case shall this insurance cover loss damage or expense caused by War Exclusion Clause

3.1　war civil war revolution rebellion insurrection, or civil strife arising therefrom, or any hostile act by or against a belligerent power

3.2　capture seizure arrest restraint or detainment (piracy excepted), and the consequences thereof or any attempt thereat

3.3　derelict mines torpedoes bombs or other derelict weapons of war.

4　In no case shall this insurance cover loss damage or expense Strikes Exclusion Clause *

4.1　caused by strikers, locked-out workmen, or persons taking part in labour disturbances, riots or civil commotions

4.2　resulting from strikes, lock-outs, labour disturbances, riots or civil commotions

4.3　caused by any terrorist or any person acting from a political motive.

DURATION

5　5.1　This insurance attaches from the time the subject-matter insured leaves the warehouse, premises or place of storage at the place named herein for the commencement of the transit, continues during the ordinary course of transit and terminates either Transit Clause

5.1.1　on delivery to the Consignees' or other final warehouse, premises or place of storage at the destination named herein,

5.1.2　on delivery to any other warehouse, premises or place of storage, whether prior to or at the destination named herein, which the Assured elect to use either

5.1.2.1　for storage other than in the ordinary course of transit or

5.1.2.2　for allocation or distribution

or

5.1.3　on the expiry of 30 days after unloading the subject-matter insured from the aircraft at the final place of discharge,

whichever shall first occur.

5.2　If, after unloading from the aircraft at the final place of discharge, but prior to termination of this insurance, the subject-matter insured is forwarded to a destination other than that to which it is insured hereunder, this insurance, whilst remaining subject to termination as provided for above, shall not extend beyond the commencement of transit to such other destination.

5.3　This insurance shall remain in force (subject to termination as provided for above and to the provisions of Clause 6 below) during delay beyond the control of the Assured, any deviation, forced discharge, reshipment or transhipment and during any variation of the adventure arising from the exercise of a liberty granted to the air carriers under the contract of carriage.

6　If owing to circumstances beyond the control of the Assured either the contract of carriage is terminated at a place other than the destination named therein or the transit is otherwise terminated before delivery of the subject-matter insured as provided for in Clause 5 above, then this insurance shall also terminate *unless prompt notice is given to the Underwriters and continuation of cover is requested when the insurance shall remain in force, subject to an additional premium if required by the Underwriters,* either Termination of Contract of Carriage Clause

6.1　until the subject-matter is sold and delivered at such place or, unless otherwise specially agreed, until the expiry of 30 days after arrival of the subject-matter hereby insured at such place, whichever shall first occur,

or

6.2　if the subject-matter is forwarded within the said period of 30 days (or any agreed extension thereof) to the destination named herein or to any other destination, until terminated in accordance with the provisions of Clause 5 above.

7　Where, after attachment of this insurance, the destination is changed by the Assured, *held covered at a premium and on conditions to be arranged subject to prompt notice being given to the Underwriters.* Change of Transit Clause

CLAIMS

8   **8.1**   In order to recover under this insurance the Assured must have an insurable interest in the subject-matter insured at the time of the loss *Insurable Interest Clause*

        8.2   Subject to 8.1 above, the Assured shall be entitled to recover for insured loss occurring during the period covered by this insurance, notwithstanding that the loss occurred before the contract of insurance was concluded, unless the Assured were aware of the loss and the Underwriters were not.

9   Where, as a result of the operation of a risk covered by this insurance, the insured transit is terminated at a place other than that to which the subject-matter is covered under this insurance, the Underwriters will reimburse the Assured for any extra charges properly and reasonably incurred in unloading storing and forwarding the subject-matter to the destination to which it is insured hereunder. *Forwarding Charges Clause*

    This Clause 9, which does not apply to general average or salvage charges, shall be subject to the exclusions contained in Clauses 2, 3 and 4 above, and shall not include charges arising from the fault negligence insolvency or financial default of the Assured or their servants.

10   No claim for Constructive Total Loss shall be recoverable hereunder unless the subject-matter insured is reasonably abandoned either on account of its actual total loss appearing to be unavoidable or because the cost of recovering, reconditioning and forwarding the subject-matter to the destination to which it is insured would exceed its value on arrival. *Constructive Total Loss Clause*

11   **11.1**   If any Increased Value insurance is effected by the Assured on the cargo insured herein the agreed value of the cargo shall be deemed to be increased to the total amount insured under this insurance and all Increased Value insurances covering the loss, and liability under this insurance shall be in such proportion as the sum insured herein bears to such total amount insured. *Increased Value Clause*

        In the event of claim the Assured shall provide the Underwriters with evidence of the amounts insured under all other insurances.

        11.2   Where this insurance is on Increased Value the following clause shall apply:

        The agreed value of the cargo shall be deemed to be equal to the total amount insured under the primary insurance and all Increased Value insurances covering the loss and effected on the cargo by the Assured, and liability under this insurance shall be in such proportion as the sum insured herein bears to such total amount insured.

        In the event of claim the Assured shall provide the Underwriters with evidence of the amounts insured under all other insurances.

BENEFIT OF INSURANCE

12   This insurance shall not inure to the benefit of the carrier or other bailee. *Not to Inure Clause*

MINIMISING LOSSES

13   It is the duty of the Assured and their servants and agents in respect of loss recoverable hereunder *Duty of Assured Clause*

        13.1   to take such measures as may be reasonable for the purpose of averting or minimising such loss, and

        13.2   to ensure that all rights against carriers, bailees or other third parties are properly preserved and exercised

    and the Underwriters will, in addition to any loss recoverable hereunder, reimburse the Assured for any charges properly and reasonably incurred in pursuance of these duties.

14   Measures taken by the Assured or the Underwriters with the object of saving, protecting or recovering the subject-matter insured shall not be considered as a waiver or acceptance of abandonment or otherwise prejudice the rights of either party. *Waiver Clause*

AVOIDANCE OF DELAY

15   It is a condition of this insurance that the Assured shall act with reasonable despatch in all circumstances within their control. *Reasonable Despatch Clause*

LAW AND PRACTICE

16   This insurance is subject to English law and practice. *English Law and Practice Clause*

NOTE:— It is necessary for the Assured when they become aware of an event which is "held covered" under this insurance to give prompt notice to the Underwriters and the right to such cover is dependent upon compliance with this obligation.

INSTITUTE WAR CLAUSES
(sendings by Post)

RISKS COVERED

1 This insurance covers, except as provided in Clause 3 below, loss of or damage to the subject-matter insured caused by   _{Risks Clause}

   1.1 war civil war revolution rebellion insurrection, or civil strife arising therefrom, or any hostile act by or against a belligerent power

   .1.2 capture seizure arrest restraint or detainment, arising from risks covered under 1.1 above, and the consequences thereof or any attempt thereat

   1.3 derelict mines torpedoes bombs or other derelict weapons of war.

2 This insurance covers general average and salvage charges, adjusted or determined ¬according to the contract of affreightment and/or the governing law and practice, incurred to avoid or in connection with the avoidance of loss from a risk covered under these clauses.   General Average Clause

EXCLUSIONS

3 In no case shall this insurance cover   General Exclusions Clause

   3.1 loss damage or expense attributable to wilful misconduct of the Assured

   3.2 ordinary leakage, ordinary loss in weight or volume, or ordinary wear and tear of the subject-matter insured

   3.3 loss damage or expense caused by insufficiency or unsuitability of packing or preparation of the subject-matter insured (for the purpose of this Clause 3.3 "packing" shall be deemed to include stowage in a container or liftvan but only when such stowage is carried out prior to attachment of this insurance or by the Assured or their servants)

   3.4 loss damage or expense caused by inherent vice or nature of the subject-matter insured

   3.5 loss damage or expense proximately caused by delay, even though the delay be caused by a risk insured against (except expenses payable under Clause 2 above)

   3.6 any claim based upon loss of or frustration of the voyage or adventure

   3.7 loss damage or expense arising from any hostile use of any weapon of war employing atomic or nuclear fission and/or fusion or other like reaction or radioactive force or matter.

DURATION

4 This insurance attaches only as the subject-matter insured and as to any part as that part leaves the premises of the senders at the place named in the insurance for the commencement of the transit and continues, but with the exclusion of any period during which the subject-matter is in packers' premises, until the subject-matter insured and as to any part as that part is delivered to the address on the postal package(s) when this insurance shall terminate.   Transit Clause

5 Anything contained in this contract which is inconsistent with Clauses 3.6, 3.7 or 4 shall, to the extent of such inconsistency, be null and void.

CLAIMS

6 6.1 In order to recover under this insurance the Assured must have an insurable interest in the subject-matter insured at the time of the loss.   Insurable Interest Clause

   6.2 Subject to 6.1 above, the Assured shall be entitled to recover for insured loss occurring during the period covered by this insurance, notwithstanding that the loss occurred before the contract of insurance was concluded, unless the Assured were aware of the loss and the Underwriters were not.

MINIMISING LOSSES

7 It is the duty of the Assured and their servants and agents in respect of loss recoverable hereunder   Duty of Assured Clause

   7.1 to take such measures as may be reasonable for the purpose of averting or minimising such loss, and

   7.2 to ensure that all rights against carriers, bailees or other third parties are properly preserved and exercised

and the Underwriters will, in addition to any loss recoverable hereunder, reimburse the Assured for any charges properly and reasonably incurred in pursuance of these duties.

8 Measures taken by the Assured or the Underwriters with the object of saving, protecting or recovering the subject-matter insured shall not be considered as a waiver or acceptance of abandonment or otherwise prejudice the rights of either party.   Waiver Clause

AVOIDANCE OF DELAY

9 It is a condition of this insurance that the Assured shall act with reasonable despatch in all circumstances within their control.   Reasonable Despatch Clause

LAW AND PRACTICE

10 This insurance is subject to English law and practice.   English Law and Practice Clause

三民大專用書書目——經濟・財政